Praise for *The Road to Reinvention*

"*The Road to Reinvention* is a must-read if you want you and your team to reach the next level. Full of practical advice and engaging, illuminating anecdotes, Linkner's message is powerful, relevant, and inspiring."

    —**Keith Ferrazzi**, author, *Never Eat Alone* and *Who's Got Your Back*

"In *The Road to Reinvention*, Josh Linkner creates a clear path for how to achieve transformative change—the key to all future growth and success."

    —**Bill Emerson**, CEO, Quicken Loans

"Through clear principles and examples, Josh Linkner makes it easier for anyone to reinvent their brand, company, or even career. *The Road to Reinvention* creates a template to understand the critical leadership challenge of the decade: disrupt or be disrupted."

    —**David Butler**, VP, innovation and entrepreneurship, the Coca-Cola Company

"Don't let your competition read this book before you do. *The Road to Reinvention* offers powerful insights and navigable paths forward for both personal and business reinvention. Josh Linkner is a singularly thoughtful entrepreneur who understands how to illuminate a vision of the possible."

    —**Don Katz**, CEO and founder, Audible

"Protecting your existing model is no longer an option. *The Road to Reinvention* provides the tools you need in order to be the disruptor instead of becoming disrupted. A must-read."

    —**Steve Blank**, professor, Graduate School of Business, Stanford University, and author, *The Startup Owner's Manual*

"As someone who has had to reinvent many times to stay on top, I highly recommend Josh Linkner's book. *The Road to Reinvention* will help you come out ahead, even when facing the roughest circumstances."

    —**Les Gold**, star, *Hardcore Pawn*, and author, *For What It's Worth*

"With stories of people and companies that have succeeded (and failed) to reinvent, Josh Linkner shows you how to harness disruptive creativity so you end up on the side of success. I wish I had this book years ago!"
— **David Meerman Scott**, author, *The New Rules of Marketing and PR*

"With the pace of innovation and resulting changes in consumer behavior, no company can afford to sit still. Growing a successful company requires creative assessment and disruption. In *The Road to Reinvention*, Josh Linkner illustrates how to lead your employees not only to accept but embrace the need for continuous reinvention."
— **Carol Kruse**, global CMO, Tough Mudder, and former CMO, ESPN

"*The Road to Reinvention* is a powerful wake-up call for any organization, whether already thriving or looking for inspiration. It's also a toolkit for entrepreneurs seeking to build the next big thing."
— **Andrew Yang**, founder and CEO, Venture for America, and author, *Smart People Should Build Things*

"*The Road to Reinvention* is a valuable guide for renewing your organization in this age of disruption. Josh Linker, having created a wide array of successful businesses, shares his proven methods for leading innovation. *The Road to Reinvention* is a must-read for anyone who needs transformational tools to remake their organization."
— **Jeff DeGraff**, professor, Ross School of Business, University of Michigan, and author, *Innovation You*

"Josh Linkner is one of the most creative thinkers on the planet. *The Road to Reinvention* contains his prescriptions for changing your product mix, your approach to the marketplace, and even your customers. Read this book if you want your company to thrive in today's crazy competitive marketplace."
— **Nick Morgan**, president, PublicWords, and author, *Power Cues* and *Trust Me*

"Already in a creative field, I found the tools and exercises in *The Road to Reinvention* encouraged me to think about things differently, from songwriting to expanding my business and brand. Thank you for a great follow-up to *Disciplined Dreaming*!"

    —**Earl Klugh**, GRAMMY® Award–winning guitarist, songwriter, and producer

"Innovative approaches are the drivers of all human progress. In *The Road to Reinvention*, Josh Linkner shows you exactly how to reinvent your business and career with stunning precision."

    —**Brad Feld**, cofounder, Tech Stars and Foundry Group, and author, *Do More Faster* and *Venture Deals*

"*The Road to Reinvention* reflects true insight from a successful entrepreneur who has spent a career in the trenches of creative disruption. Josh Linkner has taken the concept of reinvention and broken it down into actionable, specific insights that can be put into practice on a daily basis."

    —**Al Callier**, VP, strategic innovation, Universal Studios

"*The Road to Reinvention* gives readers a clear path for renewal and resilience that is compelling, insightful, and practical. Josh Linkner presents a blueprint for leaders to follow so they are able not just to stay in the game but to stay ahead of it."

    —**Brian Owens**, head, global brand strategy, eBay Inc.

"Josh Linkner is among a rare breed of entrepreneurs. Driven and successful, yet reflective, cognizant that personal growth and professional success are intricately linked. In *The Road to Reinvention* he provides the most compelling case I've encountered for approaching today's increasingly complex business environment in a disruptive manner, all while inspiring us to truly begin living the life we've imagined for ourselves."

    —**Dave Zilko**, president and vice chairman, Garden Fresh Gourmet

"*The Road to Reinvention* is a thought-provoking work that offers a clear process for ongoing creative disruption. Josh Linkner has lived the process of leading a hyper-growth organization. *The Road to Reinvention* provides insight and inspiration through engaging stories, powerful examples, and easy-to-follow processes. Highly recommended."

—**Scott Dorsey**, CEO and cofounder, Exact Target

"Josh Linkner is an expert on reinvention, and this book is a must-read. *The Road to Reinvention* is a fascinating new roadmap to help you envision the future and control your own destiny."

—**Michael Abrashoff**, US Navy Commander, and author, *It's Your Ship*

THE ROAD TO REINVENTION

How to Drive Disruption and Accelerate Transformation

JOSH LINKNER

JB JOSSEY-BASS™

A Wiley Brand

Cover design by C. Wallace
Cover image: Evolution © iStockphoto/jgroup

Published by Jossey-Bass
A Wiley Brand
One Montgomery Street, Suite 1200, San Francisco, CA 94104-4594
www.josseybass.com

In Chapter Six, material from *Power Cues: The Subtle Science of Leading Groups, Persuading Others, and Maximizing Your Personal Impact,* by Nick Morgan, Harvard Business Review Press, 2014, is used by permission.

Jossey-Bass books and products are available through most bookstores. To contact Jossey-Bass directly call our Customer Care Department within the U.S. at 800-956-7739, outside the U.S. at 317-572-3986, or fax 317-572-4002.

Wiley publishes in a variety of print and electronic formats and by print-on-demand. Some material included with standard print versions of this book may not be included in e-books or in print-on-demand. If this book refers to media such as a CD or DVD that is not included in the version you purchased, you may download this material at http://booksupport.wiley.com. For more information about Wiley products, visit www.wiley.com.

Library of Congress Cataloging-in-Publication Data

Linkner, Josh, 1970-
    The road to reinvention : how to drive disruption and accelerate transformation / Josh
  Linkner. —First edition.
        pages   cm
    Includes bibliographical references and index.
      ISBN 978-0-470-92343-6 (hardback); ISBN 978-1-118-91032-0 (pdf);
    ISBN 978-1-118-91037-5 (epub)
        1.   Organizational change. 2.   Diffusion of innovations. 3.   New products. 4.   Strategic
  planning.   I. Title.
    HD58.8.L565   2014
    658.4'063 —dc23
                                                                      2014006753

Printed in the United States of America
FIRST EDITION
HB Printing 10 9 8 7 6 5 4 3 2 1

To my inspiring wife, Tia, who radiates love, laughter, and warmth . . . and some. I love you.

CONTENTS

THE ROAD TO
REINVENTION

Introduction

Monotony is the awful reward of the careful.
—A. G. BUCKHAM

We live in a time of brutal competition. Fickle consumer trends, friction-free markets, and political unrest threaten the existence of many organizations. Nearly every industry is in the midst of massive upheaval, with the old stalwarts falling quickly to the new breed of innovators. Dizzying speed, exponential complexity, and mind-numbing technology advances exacerbate the challenges we face as leaders.

With economic threats like these racing toward you, how do you react? Do you stand frozen in place with fear and anxiety? Or do you leap into action, finding a new and better way forward? Whether you have been knocked down by brutal market conditions or are planting a flag on the peak of achievement, now is the time to reinvent—to begin forging a new pathway toward your next success. Renegade leaders choose to upset the status quo long before there's a need to do so. Instead of losing ground, these innovators are accomplishing dramatic growth and spurring tremendous economic gain.

Companies, communities, and individuals fall for many reasons, but one of the most common—and easily avoidable—is the failure to reinvent. Those who feel the most secure in the status quo are in fact the most vulnerable. Many organizations, once great, wither and die as a direct result of their deep entrenchment in the past. They discover too late that success isn't about cracking the code once and then enjoying the spoils forever. Instead, it's a moving target that we have to hit again and again. And plenty of our competitors are aiming at the same prize. Kmart, Circuit City, and Blockbuster are just a few of the countless examples of once-great companies that had every reason to continue their winning streak, but they were brought to their knees by the disruptive imagination of a competitor or start-up.

How do I know this? Because I'm the guy on the other end of the disruption equation. For the past twenty years, I've been that entrepreneur who's haunted you, eager to dislodge you at every chance I had. I started my first company at the age of twenty and sold it at twenty-two. I founded, built, and sold four technology companies for a combined value of over $250 million. I've hired thousands of employees, fought through brutal setbacks, and landed the world's biggest brands as customers. I've spent my career disrupting the way things are by realizing what they *can* be.

The common thread running throughout my success is disruptive creativity. All of my critical wins and recoveries hinged on a willingness to take on the status quo with reckless abandon and a focus on desired outcomes that I imagined and then achieved through relentless perseverance. Today I run a venture capital firm and back the next generation of innovators who are, as I was throughout my earlier career, dead-focused on eating your lunch. In nearly every industry, start-ups like those we're backing are taking on previously untouchable industry giants, whose advantages of time and money no longer protect them from competition. And we're on the winning side. The disruption of ongoing innovation eventually topples any organization that fails to keep moving—to reinvent.

The good news about reinvention is that you don't need magic, genius, good looks, or vaults of cash to transform your organization or career. Instead, the required elements are open-mindedness, courage, and imagination. I've written *The Road to Reinvention* to explore the entrepreneurial mind-set and help you find it within yourself. Throughout this book, I offer stories of triumphant victories and crushing defeats—from personal experience, small businesses, and giants alike—that will serve as models for your own reinvention. This book will provide you with a framework for the accessible process of reinvention, along with big-picture examples and detailed techniques that will help you avoid gut-wrenching setbacks, accelerate growth, and unlock enormous rewards.

My previous book, *Disciplined Dreaming*, was all about an organized system for harnessing raw creativity and making the most of its energy. In this book, we tackle the next step: putting that creativity to work in the ongoing reinvention of your business, career, and personal legacy. Reinvention can take many forms: the seismic upheaval of revolutionary product innovation; the tiny process tweaks that send ripples of change throughout an industry. Disrupt just one element of the current structure, and you can make a world of difference in your results. In this book, I show you how to master the process of reinvention so you can move the needle of achievement dramatically upward—at every phase. Here's how the book is organized:

The first two chapters lay the groundwork for the journey ahead. In chapter 1, "Disrupt or Be Disrupted," we take a first look at the essential role of reinvention in building sustainable success and the risk you run if you choose to stagnate. Chapter 2, "Embrace the Reinvention Ethos," explores ways to adopt the mind-set and spirit of ongoing, disruptive innovation, necessary for transforming anything, big or small.

Each of the next six chapters highlights one element of your business that's ripe for disruption. In chapter 3, "Cannibalize Your Own Product," we cover a wide range of ideas for reinventing core products and services. Your customers know you by whatever it is that you sell, so it's an obvious starting point for disruptive change. Chapter 4, "Retool Your Operations," offers tactics for effectively upgrading the way you do business. As you learn here, innovative processes behind your offering can be as important to your success as the offering itself. Chapter 5, "Create Vivid Experiences," explores the rich territory for reinvention within your customer experience, and chapter 6, "Tell a Memorable Story," offers some keys for keeping the public face of your organization or offering fresh and compelling in a crowded marketplace. Chapter 7, "Overhaul Your Culture," dives even deeper into the process of overall reinvention as it examines how your organization's corporate culture guides its outcomes, along with some surprising new ways to upend old habits and bring fresh thinking to your sales and distribution processes. And, in chapter 8, "Reimagine Your Customer," we enter into some of the least explored and potentially richest territory for reinvention: your targeted customer base. By challenging prevailing notions about not just who you are but who you're marketing to as well, you can open up entirely new areas for growth and opportunity. In fact, by inserting creativity and innovation into any one of the areas discussed in these six chapters, you can catapult your business to a whole new level.

The final two chapters of the book focus on the critical work of personal reinvention. Chapter 9, "Transform Your Career," offers insights into the ever evolving challenge of mastering the forces that can drive you forward, and then hold you back, on your path toward professional achievement. The final chapter of the book, "Forge Your Legacy," trains its focus on the long view of that path as it examines how the influence of ongoing reinvention can extend well beyond our own experience to reshape the outcomes of individuals, organizations, industries—even economies—around the world.

Reinvention is more than a good idea: it's an essential practice. To help you build and maintain your own system of creative disruption, I've packed this book with examples, methods, and step-by-step techniques for applying the innovative ideas it contains, including the Tools for Transformation section at the end of each chapter.

I hope that you'll be able to return to this book frequently and use the tools it offers to regularly uncover new areas of your life and business where you can inject creative disruption. That ongoing spirit of reinvention will serve as a catalyst for the types of changes necessary for taking on tomorrow's challenges and claiming as-yet-unseen opportunities.

I also made sure that you won't have to rely on your imagination to understand how reinvention plays out in the real world. Throughout this book, you'll be reading about the transformative wins and heartbreaking flameouts of individuals and organizations caught in the never-ending momentum of creative disruption. Some of these stories offer fresh insights into legendary people and events; others focus on incredible innovators you may have never heard of before but whose game-changing creativity has the power to reshape our world in significant ways. I hope these stories will serve as inspiration and guide as you fold the processes of ongoing reinvention into your personal and professional life.

Throughout this book, I've also woven stories about my hometown of Detroit, Michigan. Perhaps no other place embodies the spirit of reinvention—both its powerful potential as an engine of growth and the dire consequences of neglecting it—more than this city that I love. Over its three-hundred-year history, Detroit has reshaped itself multiple times, from fur-trading settlement to nineteenth-century industrial center to the manufacturing capital of twentieth-century America. The forces of reinvention that transformed Detroit over the years didn't stop at its city limits. For all practical purposes, the automotive industry was born in Detroit and went on to reshape the rest of the world by providing the manufacturing processes that helped win World War II and build American prosperity for decades to come. The city's roots were nourished with cultural diversity as people from all over the world came to work in its factories and develop its neighborhoods. Not content to be merely a center of industry and manufacturing, Detroit built some of the nation's greatest architectural gems, cultural centers, and public parks and spaces. Through its hit-making Motown music studios, Detroit even reshaped America's relationship with popular music.

As a hometown boy with great admiration for this city, I also know that Detroit suffered immensely from a failure to reinvent. The effects of that failure have transformed Detroit as markedly as any of its triumphant reinventions. After decades of neglecting its creative fire and allowing the world to pass it by, Detroit entered the twenty-first century in shambles. In 2013, it became the largest city in the United States to file for Chapter 9 bankruptcy protection. Unemployment clocked in at 11.3 percent, nearly 50 percent worse than the national average, and the high school graduation rate was a shocking 32 percent. Expenses and violent crime were up, revenue and morale down. Elected officials and community leaders scrambled to stabilize a highly volatile situation. Detroit had become the poster child for the self-inflicted wounds of corruption, racial divisiveness, and a lack of economic diversity. But that series of staggering problems represents just one chapter in Detroit's history. Now the city is busy as it continues the story.

Emerging strong from such a devastating "reset" is a seemingly insurmountable challenge that Detroiters are miraculously achieving through the power of disruptive creativity and a collective willingness to overcome adversity. Courageous entrepreneurs and community leaders are fighting from behind to restore Detroit's mojo and prepare the city for the next phase. These creative disruptors are my friends, many of whom you'll read about in this book. I was born and bred in this great city, and I've woven its cast of characters, its triumphs and failures, its darkest periods of failure, and its most shining moments of invention and reinvention throughout this book. I'm confident that the rich history of my city and its incredible achievements of reinvention will set your own passion ablaze in whatever form it may take.

In the following chapters, I push you outside your comfort zone and challenge you to turn nearly everything you've come to know upside down. I'll make the case that unleashing your imagination is no longer optional and, in fact, will become the lifeblood of your success. I hope to change your thinking on courage, creativity, and risk taking, to help you embrace your role as chief disruption officer, no matter where you sit on the organization chart. In fact, your company and your career depend on it. It's time to architect your own future.

Let's get started.

CHAPTER 1

Disrupt or Be Disrupted

When I let go of what I am, I become what I might be.
—LAO TZU

The year was 1993, and Lee Kun-Hee, CEO of Samsung, had absolutely no rational reason to be unhappy. Since he took over the company after his father's death just six years earlier, Samsung's revenues had soared by an astonishing 250 percent. But Lee wasn't running victory laps. He wanted to help Samsung do even more. So he left South Korea to embark on a world tour to examine how his brand and company were doing internationally.

Lee's first revelation came early in the trip. At an electronics store in California, he was shocked to see Samsung TVs collecting dust on the back shelves, while the store prominently displayed those from competitors like Sony and Panasonic. This visit became Lee's moment of truth; although Samsung's brand was performing well in certain aspects, he believed the company was headed for problems. Samsung had excelled at producing large numbers of low-quality goods, but it offered little in the way of high-quality merchandise. Looking at his products in the competitive context of that California retail store, Lee understood that his company wasn't prepared to compete in the new era, with consumers the world over demanding a sense of luxury and high-quality craftsmanship in their home entertainment.

Samsung's near-term results were strong, yet Lee refused to coast while his competitors led the consumer trend toward high-quality products. Instead he was about to launch one of the most extensive companywide reinventions in business history.

When Lee's global tour took him to Frankfurt, Germany, he decided he was ready to strike. He called in hundreds of Samsung's top executives from around the world and conducted a session that would forever change the face of his company. He delivered a three-day manifesto that laid out the vision for the company's reinvention and path to his vision of success. In this powerful and emotionally charged call to arms that demanded reinvention of every aspect of the business, Lee famously exclaimed, "Change everything but your wife and children." The speech became known as the Frankfurt Declaration of 1993 and marked the company's most significant turning point. Samsung later began distributing a two-hundred-page transcription of the speech to all of its employees.

Today the spirit of reinvention and creative energy sparked by Lee's Frankfurt Declaration continues to reshape Samsung. One division of this massive organization is known as the Future Strategy Office (FSO). This elite group comprises top-performing employees, each a former employee of a separate division of the Samsung Group. Their job in the FSO is strictly preventative: they monitor diagnostics that might reveal mistakes or potential dishonest actions by employees, but also, and more important, the team looks for ways Samsung could fall behind by maintaining the status quo. In this light, their goal is to shed an "outsider's" light on areas where the company risks stagnation.[1]

Samsung's commitment to quality still shines brightly as the company continually pushes for better results. In 2012, prior to a smart phone release, inspections revealed that the product's cover texture was off. At the last minute, Samsung workers remade 100,000 covers, finishing the job before shipment and underscoring the company's ongoing push for continuous improvements in quality and design.[2]

Lee's determination to reinvent his organization has led to incredible growth and prosperity. As of 2013, Samsung was the largest TV and smart phone manufacturer in the world. Revenues topped $250 billion and net income was reported at nearly $20 billion. If this wasn't enough to be proud of, the company represented 17 percent of the entire gross domestic product of its home country, South Korea.[3]

As a leader, it's your responsibility to prioritize reinvention. If your organization has become intoxicated by its own success, your job is to infuse at every level the same creative hunger that launched it in the first place. The market no longer leaves room for me-too players, a principle that applies to both companies and individuals. Remarkable category-of-one products, services, and processes are the driving force of our fist-fighting economy. The choices are clear: disrupt, or be disrupted.

Global markets and rapidly evolving technologies have turned the rules for winning upside down. Hard skills born in the Industrial Revolution, including manufacturing expertise, strong customer service skills, and even accounting excellence, are now outsourced or allocated to technology. As a result, these once-prized skills have become merely the ante to play. Today's victors are turning their winning trump cards in the margins. Creativity is the new, most effectively sustainable competitive advantage; it's the one thing that no company can outsource. That makes disruptive innovation your most valuable natural resource, even though it isn't displayed on the balance sheet.

Reinvention isn't a single event, it's a way of life, a constant process of discovery and imagination. Change is inevitable. The question is, will you drive that change or be driven by it? You can choose to adopt the spirit of reinvention and, in the process, set the tone for both your company and your career. No matter how successful you are, no matter how many awards you've won, no matter how great last quarter's earnings may have been, you are risking it all if you expect your winning streak to automatically continue. Someday another company *will* come and put you out of business. It might as well be you.

Make the Leap to Reinvention

With global financial crises, increasing complexity, and crumbling competitive advantages, I've seen all too many people freeze in the face of oncoming upheaval rather than act. They worry about the negative consequences of change. They overestimate the resilience of the status quo and underestimate the driving need for innovation. They make excuses, close their eyes to the world around them, and lull themselves to sleep with naive clichés such as, "Things will get better on their own," or, "I'm sure the worst is behind us." When those phrases begin floating around your mind—or your organization—you can expect that the calamity of unforeseen change is barreling forward, and ready to mow you down.

When it comes to reinvention, getting started is the hardest part of the task, but it's also the most important. In today's warp-speed world, swiftness wins. If you wait to try a new idea until you've carefully orchestrated every possible maneuver, the world will pass you by while you're busy planning. As Rupert Murdoch said, "Big will not beat small anymore. It will be the fast beating the slow."[4]

The clichéd deer-in-the-headlights meets an untimely death not because it lacks capability, but because it lacks the courage to move. It doesn't really matter which direction the deer moves in as long as it unfreezes and gets moving. Individuals and organizations face the same challenge as they approach the process of reinvention. The first step is always the hardest to take, but it unleashes the momentum you need to overcome stagnation's looming threat and enact meaningful change.

Myth: Achievement occurs through a gigantic epiphany or an all-at-once breakthrough.
Fact: Most things worth accomplishing involve a persistent stream of small advances that lead to something transformational over time.

Even after making a first leap toward innovative change, many of us get discouraged when we can't reach our goals at Internet speed. We get frustrated with the slightest pothole or delay and are too quick to stop trying. We fail to understand that reinvention isn't an event; it's a lifelong process. The process of creative breakthroughs is marked by the same pattern, one that is so often completely misunderstood. Sure, there are bursting moments of creative insight, but the research shows that most creative breakthroughs come by chipping away at a problem. The creative act isn't some magical inspiration that arrives in the form of a lightning bolt. Rather, it typically is a series of experiments and techniques, trials and errors, through which inventors, artists, and musicians crack the code. Even the light bulb, the very symbol of fresh ideas, was the result of over one thousand attempts. That's why the most common traits among successful people are ruthless determination and unwavering persistence.

That's also the reason that the strongest organizations are constantly reinventing. Their executives realize that we live in an era with a rate of change like none other in history and that no one can count on what worked in the past being sustainable. Great leaders view reinvention as mission critical to ensuring their company's survival and prosperity, even during times of strength.

Maybe a first step in harnessing the power of reinvention is to truly shape your understanding of the term. Merriam-Webster defines *reinventing* as "to remake or redo completely."[5] The Oxford dictionary version is "to change (something) so much that it appears to be entirely new."[6] For me, a good way to think about reinvention is as the necessary process of proactively crafting a new future.

Too often, people use the words *reinvention* and *turnaround* interchangeably. In fact, these are radically different concepts. Turnarounds are generally reactionary, desperate responses to crushing challenges. Much like a drowning swimmer who will scratch and claw at anything in order to live another day, the goal in a turnaround is simply short-term survival.

The Difference Between Turnarounds and Reinvention

	Turnaround	Reinvention
Timing	After something devastating happens to the company, community, or individual (reactive)	Ideally when a company or person is thriving (proactive)
Characterization	Digging out of a hole, often through spreadsheet-based cost cutting, layoffs, and control by executives or outside consultants	Doubling down on innovation, nurturing a creative culture, letting go of past success, and architecting for the future
Outcomes	Destroys morale and is largely ineffective	Breathes new life, opens new possibilities, drives sustainable growth

There are two key problems with turnarounds. First, the reactionary, shortsighted mind-set driving any turnaround is the exact opposite of the thinking needed to sustain long-term growth and innovation. As a result, turnaround specialists slash costs, crack the whip, and generally put all innovation efforts on hold. Although this is effective in keeping a drowning business afloat, the turnaround mind-set typically damages the organization by stripping away its creative flair.

Second, by the time a turnaround is necessary, it is often too late. Once organizations have stumbled enough to necessitate a turnaround effort, only 10 percent ever regain their market leadership. In other words, a company may make it until the end of the fiscal year, but the scar tissue from failing to reinvent may not be reversible.[7]

Your job is to make sure that your organization never gets to the point that it needs a turnaround. Executing last year's (or last decade's) game plan with precision may work for a while, but remember: decay, like growth, rarely moves in a straight line. Unfortunately, many leaders skate through the days without recognizing the eroding force of deterioration until it's too late. Unfortunately, deterioration can be easy to ignore.

We start learning that lesson early. Remember how easy it was to forget about your dental hygienist's warnings about brushing and flossing after every meal? After we blew off the advice a few times and saw that our teeth hadn't rotted away, it became easier to forget about the warning altogether—until that fateful dentist visit months or even years down the road when we learned that we had developed cavities or, worse, gum disease. Then in indignant outrage, we asked, "How did this just appear out of nowhere?"

As adults, we understand that tooth decay is a slow process. We can go for years with hit-and-miss dental hygiene before our negative behavior produces a most unpleasant outcome.

Your organization's decay is just as insidious: it may not be noticeable until it's deeply problematic. The only way to ward off the decay of stagnation is to continually practice the organizational "hygiene" of ongoing reinvention. Today's reinvention efforts, in any (maybe every) aspect of your business, are your surest way to avoid unforeseen problems and speed healthy progress down the road.

Leaders understand this prevention concept intellectually, even though many of their actions seem to fly in the face of its message. In the early 1980s, for example, Kmart was heralded as a far superior retailer to Walmart. It was the second largest retailer in the United States, riding high on the seas of its past success: more stores, more merchandise, bigger company, more profits. Yet under the surface, erosion was taking its toll. As Kmart snapped up one discount outlet and competitor after another, it began to lose its brand identity as centralized leadership shifted its attention to other brands under the umbrella conglomerate.[8] That lack of brand focus and a failure to update stores joined other small, undetected acts that ultimately led to the company's undoing. The depressed chain filed for Chapter 11 bankruptcy in January 2002.

Even the smallest acts of neglect can trigger decay, so you have to be proactive, not reactive, to ward off lasting problems. What's going on behind the scenes in your own company that could be systematically unraveling your competitive advantage? What small details did you stop caring about in your team that could be leading to a painful crash? The more effectively you drive ongoing innovation and reinvention throughout your organization, the more routine these examinations will become—and the more opportunity you'll have to make a course correction before it's too late.

We all have to accept the fact that change in our business is inevitable. The earlier you can drive reinvention in your organization, the better; delaying only makes your challenge more difficult. Just as it's easier to blow out a match than to extinguish a four-alarm fire, your odds of success are directly correlated to the speed and consistency with which you reinvent.

Learn the Lessons of the Fall

We can learn a lot about the crippling force of complacency and stagnation from the story of two retailers that once commanded a substantial chunk of their marketplace, Borders Books and Circuit City. Both of these organizations suffered what might have appeared to be a relatively rapid decline before they folded. In fact, their downfall rolled out over a period of years, born and fed by a failure to reinvent.

Borders Books was founded in 1971 in Ann Arbor, Michigan, less than thirty miles from my home. It grew to 1,249 stores and employed nearly 25,000 people. In 2009, the company generated nearly $3 billion in annual sales. Just a few years later, Borders didn't even exist, having filed for Chapter 7 liquidation in 2011.[9] What went wrong?

At several critical steps along the way, Borders failed to reinvent. When you study the company's demise, you see a series of head-in-the-sand blunders that led to its undoing, including these:[10]

- *Outsourcing its online book sales to Amazon in 2001.* What needed to be a core competence of the company was handed over instead of developed.
- *Failure to enter the e-book market fast enough.* Unwilling to fully embrace the idea that books could be enjoyed digitally, leaders

at Borders hesitated at a critical time. As a result, they could never catch up.

- *Betting on the physical distribution of content (both music and books).* Failing to capitalize on the trends in downloading and streaming, Borders continued to put its bet on CDs and DVDs. Its investment in this shrinking market cost it dearly.
- *Overinvesting in physical stores.* In the same way a fancier carriage couldn't compete with the automobile, expensive retail stores were no match for digital competitors. A bet on bricks and mortar that may have made sense in the 1970s became a liability in an age when consumers moved much of their purchasing power online.

When Borders began hemorrhaging cash in 2006, it was already in a near-impossible turnaround crisis. A once-great brand had succumbed to its own apathy and inertia. Borders could have saved itself by taking action to reinvent its operation while the company was still healthy and strong, when it could afford to take bold moves to strengthen its relevance in a changing marketplace. Had its executives assessed the challenges facing them with the critical sense of urgency necessary for ongoing reinvention, their market position could have been dramatically different. The lesson is clear: quickly adopting future trends rather than clinging to yesterday's success is the only way to ensure long-term survival.

Circuit City, once the nation's number 2 electronics retailer, fell in a similar way.[11] Circuit City's crash played out during the first years of the new century, so it would be easy to blame the company's demise on a tough economy or other external factors. But during those same years, direct competitors like Best Buy continued to flourish while Circuit City crashed and burned. Like Borders, Circuit City flamed out from a failure to reinvent.

The company's complacency and shortsightedness was its greatest weakness. Circuit City had been successful for decades prior to 2000, but it failed to manage innovation wisely in the face of larger changes in its industry. As a result, everyone else caught up—and then left it in the dust. Leaders lost their customer base by missing important trends, such as a full embrace of the market for gaming devices. They stood still while competitors reinvented physical stores, sales promotions, and even customer service. Inventory management never evolved at Circuit City, so competitors were able to stock newer, more attractive items. As Amazon and others built sophisticated e-commerce sites, Circuit City ignored the Web retailing movement instead of viewing it as its biggest opportunity. As executive pay increased, sales and profits plummeted.[12]

A once-great retailer with more than sixty years of success, Circuit City closed its final store in 2009. Had its leaders embraced a continuous process of reinvention and built a culture that celebrated and leveraged innovation instead of ignoring it, the company might still be alive and kicking.

Stories like these seem obvious with the benefit of hindsight, yet the vast majority of organizations continue to operate with the same tunnel-vision thinking that led to the end of Borders and Circuit City. "That isn't happening in *my* organization," leaders rationalize. But small, incremental tweaks don't relieve you of the responsibility of wholesale reinvention. If you are not the driving force of comprehensive change and innovation, you run the risk of being dislodged from your favorable market position. A fall from grace for a multibillion-dollar corporation is exceptionally disturbing, but it leaves behind a powerful lesson. The sinking of a small operation is no less unsettling, especially if you're the one caught in its downward plunge. No matter what size or type of business we're piloting, we can use the lessons of these two one-time industry giants to help avoid their fate.

Think Small

The most powerful disruptive innovations often come from start-ups. While big companies are busy protecting the golden goose, entrepreneurs have nothing to defend. Their every thought is focused on breaking norms and inventing a new, improved approach to business.

The good news is that we can all think like entrepreneurs. We can all think small, since this approach is a mind-set and has nothing do to with the size of your balance sheet or worldwide head count. Let's examine the difference between small-company thinking versus its bloated counterpart:

Small-Company Thinking	Big-Company Thinking
Embrace risk	Avoid risk
Urgent	Slow moving
Create new ideas	Protect old ideas
Bottom-up (everyone contributes)	Top-down (executives' ideas only)
Idea-centric	Rules-centric
Nimble	Bureaucratic
Fire-in-the-belly	Complacent

If you represent a larger organization, driving the philosophy in the left column is your prescription for long-term growth and success. Creating a culture that supports innovation at all levels is a key priority for leaders in today's fierce business battlefield. If you're part of a smaller organization, these are your main weapons in displacing the complacent giants.

Join Reinvention's Rise

Why would the guy who led the first eighteen generations of the iPod and first three generations of the iPhone leave Apple to build thermostats? How could someone ditch one of the most exciting companies and industries in the world for the staid arena of home temperature control?

Tony Fadell didn't ask that question. Instead, he saw an old-school, stale industry ripe with opportunity for the disruptive force of the design, engineering, and creativity skills he honed at Apple. Tony was a tech devices disruptor for years, and in 2010 he thought it was time to reinvent a different category.

Out of a rented garage in Palo Alto, California, Tony and Matt Rogers set out to create radical change in an industry that hadn't gone through much ground-breaking evolution since the late 1800s. According to Fadell, "The more we dug, the more we realized, this is a company we must go start. We could save 10 percent of energy costs, and solve an epic problem in a no-innovation, multibillion-dollar market. Why would we not do this?"[13]

From its humble beginning, the Nest Learning Thermostat represented pioneering disruption. In a dramatic departure from the traditional plastic rectangle most homeowners recognize as a thermostat, the Nest device is a beautiful, elegant-looking unit that resembles a round iPod. Its innovation goes well beyond looks; the device uses sophisticated technology to pack a punch with extraordinary simplicity. The Nest "learns" your patterns and begins to automatically adjust to save energy. It has sensors that detect movement so it makes sure it isn't heating or cooling an empty house. It has a live connection to the Internet, monitoring weather patterns and the arc of the sun so it can make smart decisions and adapt in real time. You can even connect with your Nest remotely from a smart phone if you want to check in, make changes, or see how much energy you are using. Through these features, the Nest saves homeowners 10 to 20 percent on energy bills, and it also makes a big environmental impact.

The Nest, which retails for $249, sold out within one week of its release in late October 2011. Due to incredibly high demand, its developers said it wouldn't be available again until 2012.[14] Meanwhile, the basic Honeywell programmable thermostat that we all know was widely available for $23.49. An unknown new start-up with no brand recognition or giant marketing department launches a new product in an industry it knows nothing about. The innovation is so compelling that the product sells for more than ten times the price of a directly competitive unit. And it was instantaneously so popular that it remained sold out for months. When Honeywell was busy making a slight incremental improvement by rounding the corners on its uninspired device, Nest completely changed the playing field by reinventing the category altogether.

What makes this reinvention effort all the more impressive is the Nest team's fundamental urgency. The thermostat shipped just eighteen months after Fadell and Rogers first set up shop in that garage. The two innovators recognized that speed is everything.

Distractions give way to the importance of the task at hand, when people with an urgent calling, as those two did, feel compelled to get the job done. An ambulance driver would never stop for a burger on the way to an accident. A star athlete wouldn't take a call to chat with his grandmother in the middle of an important game. Firefighters waste no time: as soon as the alarm rings at the fire station, the brave men and women respond with instinctive urgency. You can't hesitate on the road to reinvention.

We know that urgency saves lives and wins championships. Why, then, do we allow apathy and sluggishness to slow so many of us down? We can no longer afford the luxury of being laid back: leisurely skating through the workday is robbing you and your company, just as does stealing merchandise from the backroom. Worse, as your competitors wake up and begin to charge ahead with force, you run the imminent risk of getting plowed over. Today the slow lane is reserved for those on the fast path to obsolescence. In order to build healthy careers, companies, and communities, we need to leap into action.

Think about when you have real urgency in your own life: when you are late for your kid's baseball game or piano recital; when you have an assignment due in two hours but still have four hours of work to do; when you haven't eaten all day and you're racing home to dinner. In these situations, you have a heightened level of focus and purpose. To elevate the results in other areas of your life, unleash the same intensity as a firefighter and you'll drive outcomes to new heights.

A New Spin on Reinvention

With nearly 70,000 employees, $19 billion in annual revenue, a 135-country footprint, and a 100-year legacy, Whirlpool is about the furthest thing from a start-up.[15] Nevertheless, the company believes the most important priority is innovation, so in 1999, it set out on a quest to reinvent itself. Whirlpool's CEO at the time, Dave Whitwam, was convinced that the company needed to escape what he described as the "sea of white," the nearly indistinguishable grouping of competitive products. Fervent with this belief and a goal to stay relevant to consumers while enjoying profitable growth, he launched a wide-sweeping overhaul of Whirlpool that changed the company. According to Moises Norena, global director of innovation, "he insisted that every employee would be part of the innovation effort: it would not be exclusive to engineers . . . Innovation would come from everyone and everywhere."

A great example of Whirlpool's reinvention efforts was its exploration into the garage. Traditionally the company supported appliances in the kitchen and laundry room to the delight of customers worldwide. But a group of Whirlpool team members had a powerful insight: they realized that many people have well-kept homes but garages that resemble the aftermath of natural disasters.

In research visits to homes, consumers were ashamed of showing Whirlpool's employees their garage. It became clear that there was no logical way to organize things in the garage, and as a result, the standard for organization was completely different from that of the rest of the house. The garage was a source embarrassment instead of pride.

Whirlpool seized this insight and launched Gladiator Garage Works, a modular approach to garage organization. Beautifully designed workbenches, cabinets, wall systems, tool storage, flooring, and organization systems allowed this innovative company to find wide-open opportunity. Launched in 2002, the brand was earning over $300 million in revenue less than a decade later while still growing at a significant clip.

Jeff Fettig continued the momentum when Whitwam retired. As CEO, he was driven to unleash innovation and put the full weight of the company behind his efforts. The last thirteen-year innovation sprint by these two committed leaders was one whirling ride for investors too. Revenue more than doubled and the stock price tripled despite two economic crashes and fierce global competition.

Whirlpool leaders expect at least 20 percent of annual revenue to come from new products (less than five years old) for the foreseeable future. Fettig summed it up: "We know that we can best compete by focusing on introducing new and innovative products."[16]

Fighting Crime with Jewelry: The Reinvention of Social Responsibility

Jessica Mindich is a remarkable entrepreneur. Her company, Jewelry for a Cause, designs and sells jewelry and accessories not only to help customers but also to help humanity.

With unbridled curiosity, she stumbled on a program in Newark, New Jersey, in 2011 that was focused on getting guns off the streets.[17] Newark mayor Cory Booker had launched an effort that paid cash for firearms turned in to the city—no questions asked. The program was gaining traction and collecting thousands of firearms (and getting them off the streets),[18] but it faced two big challenges: it lacked enough funding to continue in full force, and storing thousands of illegal firearms was becoming a real issue.

Jessica saw an opportunity to help the community while driving her business. She approached the mayor and offered to take the stockpile of firearms off his hands. Working with local authorities, the guns were sorted, catalogued, and melted down, ready for reinvention. She then launched a new line of jewelry called Caliber, made from the metal of recycled weapons. The jewelry line offers pieces from $150 to $5,000, each proudly displaying the original gun's serial number and its origin: Newark. Demand is high, and gun violence is reduced with each sale: 20 percent of every dollar goes immediately back to fund the buybacks for Newark's gun amnesty program.[19]

In addition to driving real social impact, her business has grown dramatically from her creative insight. Although she was enjoying strong momentum before the new line, she refused to become complacent and had the courage to try something fundamentally different and truly unique. Her willingness to embrace fresh ideas led to her big breakthrough. That same groove will also lead to yours.

Avoid the Riskiest Move of All

All our lives we've been taught to avoid risk. Follow a traditional career path. Invest cautiously. Don't talk to strangers. Yet ironically, most of us live in an irresponsibly hazardous fashion, and without even knowing it. It turns out that playing it safe has become recklessly dangerous.

Since the start of the twenty-first century, the world has changed dramatically. Global financial crisis, technological breakthroughs, geopolitical turmoil, and other tectonic shifts in our world should have shaken our belief in the old-school ideology of success through risk aversion. We've had ample illustration of how dangerous it can be to sit back and watch the world move forward without us. And yet, shockingly, most people still play by the old rules, wondering why their results are plummeting as they faithfully follow their old formula for success.

In school, we were taught to follow the rules, guess what the teacher knows, believe there's only one correct answer, and, above all, not make mistakes. Maybe in grade school, it was useful to keep our heads down, do what we were told, and never question authority. But doing that in today's hypercompetitive, constantly changing world is a surefire path to mediocrity. Those who were lulled into a false sense of security were blindsided when corporate downsizings swept through and supposedly loyal customers defected to upstart competitors. It turns out that in this century, playing not to lose seals a fate of crushing defeat. Blandness has given way to boldness, with copycat-boring conquered by originality. What the world now demands and pays handsomely for is remarkable and creative thinking—in businesses, politicians, communities, education, and, of course, individuals. In the past, your job was to do what you were told. But today your organization may be looking to you for answers. The only place that mute obedience will get you to is a field of unmet potential with an abundance of regret.

In addition to the job title on your business card, you need to add the title of *disruptor*. Disruptors challenge assumptions. They shake the status quo. They are curious and creative. They adapt and improvise. They push the boundaries and shatter conventional wisdom. They'd rather forge new ground than blindly salute the flag of the past. Disruptors squirm at phrases such as "we've always done it that way," "that's just the way things are done in our field," and "if it ain't broke, don't fix it." They know that speed and innovation now trump rigidity and conformity. They know that discovering fresh solutions and unleashing new ideas are top priorities for both success and sustainability.

Disruptors wonder. They dream, explore, harass, discover, challenge, vex, disturb, rattle, break, upset, imagine, push, shatter, drive, offend, risk, and poke. They also win, get promoted, earn more, make a bigger impact, reach their dreams, and change the world. In the words of Jack Welch, the former CEO of General Electric, "If the rate of change on the outside exceeds the rate of change on the inside, the end is near."[20]

The story of creative disruption unfolds before us all the time, yet few of us truly embrace the seemingly obvious concept. The creators of the iPod disrupted the music industry, while the masterminds behind the Kindle and other e-books disrupted traditional publishing. These disruptors are changing the game in every industry; yours is no exception. And more than likely, the disruptors in your company are the ones who are getting promoted and reaching their dreams while the rule-following automatons remain frustrated in their cubes.

If you want to avoid life's biggest risks—mediocrity and regret—you must bring your guard down and raise your creativity. Driving disruption may be outside your comfort zone, but it's one of the safest things you can do. It's time to get in the fast lane of original thinking, innovation, and possibility.

Detroit: Catalyst for Change

If history has taught Detroit anything, it's the inevitability of disruption and the dangers of standing still in the face of change. In 1805, a sweeping fire nearly completely destroyed the village of Detroit. In its aftermath, instead of just rebuilding what it had lost, the village planned a new beginning. Inspired by the design of the nation's new capital in Washington, DC, Detroit began its transformation from former fur-trading settlement to a real city by laying out its streets in diagonal arteries extending away from a hub just north of the Detroit River.[21]

In the decades that followed, nineteenth-century industrialism took hold, and wealthy industrialists dramatically changed the face of the city once again, building lavish private mansions and impressive downtown commercial buildings. By the end of that century, Detroit's population, just 770 people in 1810, had climbed to almost 286,000, and it was the thirteenth largest city in the United States. The city had its first skyscraper and an electric trolley, and Henry Ford, just one of Detroit's growing number of entrepreneurs, innovators, and inventors, had driven his first test car down the city's streets.[22] Detroit had become a cosmopolitan capital known as the Paris of the Midwest, with art museums, opera houses, and grand public spaces, including Belle Isle Park, the work of Frederick Law Olmstead, who had also designed New York's Central Park.[23]

During the first decades of the twentieth century, the automotive industry exploded in Detroit, and so did the city's population. Detroit began another transformation, eventually sprawling out to fill a nearly 140-square-mile area with residential neighborhoods, shops, and businesses.[24] But by midcentury, yet another wave of disruption began to gather force as many white, middle-class Detroiters and even some factories began leaving the city and relocating to its suburbs. Among their reasons were increasing crime, additional city taxes that were not required outside the city limits, racial tensions, failing schools, and an unsupportive city government that created endless red tape for things like permits, licenses, and inspections. This time, Detroit wasn't already moving on to its next great moment, its next great innovation, its next creative transformation. As wave after wave of disruptive change swept over the city—energy crises, globalization, outsourcing, and automation—Detroit's jobs and population continued to dwindle, taking with them the city's tax base and other revenues.[25] Between 1950 and 2012, Detroit's population fell from its peak of nearly 1.8 million to just over 700,000.[26] While its revenues remained relatively flat over that period, Detroit's debt had grown to over $18 billion.[27]

The disruptive transformation of Detroit's depopulation didn't play out as quickly as the fire of 1805, but it certainly did leave destruction in its wake: abandoned houses, empty neighborhoods, whole stretches of the city lacking even basic services. Detroit once again began the process of clearing away ruins and reinventing itself, almost from the ground up. Stoked by a new fire of entrepreneurialism, civic responsibility, and calculated risk taking, Detroiters have learned that standing still is no way to survive, let alone thrive. Hungry new-tech start-ups snapped up suddenly affordable space in downtown skyscrapers, bringing new life and energy to its downtown. Pop-up shops take advantage of once-empty storefronts, alongside restaurants and producers of artisanal foods. The reinvention of Detroit is not limited to its downtown corridors. Neighborhood gardens and commercial farming operations now fill some of Detroit's estimated thirty thousand acres of distressed space.[28]

No single initiative or movement will make everything better in Detroit, but these artists, tech start-ups, visionary business leaders, urban farmers, and other game changers are making a difference as they tackle the rebirth and rebuilding of this city through their own disruptive force. The city will rise from the ashes, just as it has in the past, this time with a new understanding that the fire of change is always smoldering; you can either stoke it to power your own engine of innovation, or stand still and be consumed in the blaze. Disrupt or be disrupted.

Tools for Transformation: Rapid Reinvention

Pretend you are a business reinvention artist. Your job is to come into companies and help them invent the future. Unfortunately, your big presentation is due in ten minutes and you haven't even started brainstorming ideas. You'll have to use one of your favorite techniques: the countdown.

Set a timer for ten minutes and imagine you have $100 million at your disposal. Resources are nearly limitless, and your job is to dazzle your client, the CEO. Who is the client you're working for? Your neighborhood diner. That's right, the local burger joint that's been doing things the same way for decades. Have fun and imagine all the possible ways you could shake things up. Shoot for quantity instead of quality, and don't let costs or execution risk inhibit your thinking. See if you can generate thirty-five or more big ideas in this short time. Consider everything from new menu items to overhauling the experience, to new economic models such as a subscription service instead of per item charge. As a business reinvention artist, think of all the ways you could disrupt this simple and stable business.

Extra credit: Do the same exercise for your own real-world company. Pretend you're an external business artist instead of your current internal role, and see what you can imagine by taking an outsider perspective with tons of capital to invest.

CHAPTER 2

Embrace the Reinvention Ethos

Twenty years from now you will be more disappointed by the things that you didn't do than by the ones you did do.

—MARK TWAIN

Nike is innovative. Sure, you might say, Nike was innovative back in 1964 when it invented the modern athletic shoe. But is the company still a strong example of reinvention today?

You bet it is.

In fact, since the 1960s, Nike has strung together a series of innovations in the same way Motown Records kicked out hit after hit. Reinvention is in Nike's bones, and the company hasn't slowed down since that original waffle shoe.

Fast Company ranked Nike the most innovative company of 2013, beating out tech giants like Apple and Amazon because of two breakout Nike products that year.[1] The first is a wearable rubber wristband that measures physical activity throughout the day, helping consumers reach their health and fitness goals. The Fuel Band boasts a clean design, easy-to-read display with 120 LED indicators, and, of course, full sync capabilities to your smart phone. Nike's second big product breakthrough of the year was the Flyknit Racer, a completely reimagined shoe that is created from knit threading instead of multiple layers of fabric. The design challenged engineers to rethink their entire production system, but yielded a high-demand breakthrough in sports shoes that weigh significantly less than anything else on the market.[2]

Nike's CEO, Mark Parker, reaffirmed his commitment to innovation: "One of my fears is being this big, slow, constipated, bureaucratic company that's happy with its success. Companies fall apart when their model is so successful that it stifles any thinking that challenges it."

The business results are as impressive as the innovations. In 2012, Nike's revenue was up 60 percent since 2006 to $24 billion and profits were up 57 percent. Wall Street took notice, and gleeful investors celebrated the doubling of Nike's market capitalization.[3]

How has Nike been able to stay relevant, continue to innovate, and remain a force that tops the most-admired lists? The simple answer is "its culture." Nike's forty-four thousand team members feel empowered to take responsible risks and let their imagination soar. They focus on where they are headed, not just where they've been. The company invests heavily on making work fun and a place of creative expression, which helps it attract and retain the best team members. Cultural phrases such as "be a sponge" and "always offer something new" are burned into the company's collective consciousness with religious fervor.

Nike will continue to deliver incredible results because it has hard-wired reinvention into its DNA. The culture worships new ideas and shuns standing still. If a fifty-year-old, $24 billion, forty-four-thousand-employee company can continue to reinvent itself with such stunning consistency, you have zero excuses to stagnate.

Like Nike, your mandate is to operate in a state of constant reinvention. Organizations—and individuals—that refuse to get comfortable are the ones that win over the long term.

Eight Principles That Define the Reinvention Ethos

Study any supremely successful organization or individual, from Nike to 3M or from Madonna to Tom Hanks, and you'll encounter a consistent theme: an ethos of reinvention whose principles embody the disruptive mind-set. In this chapter, we look at eight of the most important principles of that reinvention ethos. You can embrace these principles and adapt them to your own circumstances in an effort to reinvent yourself, your career, your company, and your community.

The Eight Principles

1. Let go of the past.
2. Encourage courage.
3. Embrace failure.
4. Do the opposite.
5. Imagine the possibilities.
6. Put yourself out of business.
7. Reject limits.
8. Aim beyond.

Taking on these new principles may require you to abandon some ideas you've held for years. That's good. Letting go of deeply held beliefs and venturing into uncharted waters is a difficult task, but it's an essential one for innovators (and that group includes any company or individual engaged in building ongoing success). Most of us are ill equipped to meet the challenges we'll face in the next five years. Due to the rapid rate of change, we reach adulthood in a much different era from the one in which we are born. And a lot of what we learn in between is aimed at controlling our behavior, not promoting our innovative thinking. As kids, we're taught to comply— to follow rules, "get along," respect authority rather than challenge it, and avoid mistakes at all costs. Many of us also learned at an early age that it was wrong to be disruptive; we should blend into the crowd and not make any waves. These ideas may be useful for crowd control, but they're precisely the wrong principles for prospering in the innovation age. That work requires you to throw away the fear of failure, forget about safety in numbers, and embrace a mind-set of ongoing disruptive change.

Mercifully, you can reprogram your thinking to this new and improved mind-set. You can make a smooth transition into the ethos of reinvention with open-mindedness and a willingness to shed outdated beliefs. You have every necessary tool right now to make the positive shift. By reinventing your own ideas and approach to innovation, you will be able to contribute to the same spirit of reinvention in your business, community, family, and life. Embracing the reinvention ethos may feel a little daunting at first, but that fear will fade as you discover how using a disruptive, creative philosophy rockets your success several levels forward.

Principle 1: Let Go of the Past

We all face incredible challenges in our lives: difficult people, ruthless competition, time constraints. But so many of us succumb to an imaginary demon that somehow manages to strangle our potential and restrict our progress. This fictitious monster is called simply *the past*.

The past is a great teacher, but it's a horrible master. Living in the clutches of the past can shackle your imagination and relegate you to thinking small. Imagine carrying around a backpack full of rocks, each representing some past injustice or setback. You'll never be able to play your best game unless you release the burden of the past and liberate yourself from its heavy load.

Regret is the worst human emotion, since there is absolutely nothing we can do to change history. Dwelling on your past mistakes can eviscerate your ambition and is a fast path to unachieved dreams. At the same time, clinging to past successes is another sure way to stop any forward progress. Many businesses fall into that trap. Executives rationalize stagnation with myths such as "history repeats itself," "if it worked then, it will work again," and "it's just a cycle." The new rules of engagement are quite the opposite. Predicting the future based on the past is like betting on a football team simply because it won the Super Bowl a decade ago. Cycles are no longer two-dimensional; they may not exist at all. Instead of looking backward, it's time to focus on the present and commit to a brighter future.

Letting go of the past doesn't mean you have to pretend it never happened. The past may have given you a head start to fight your next battle by arming you with talent, resources, brand equity, and information. Now your job is to use these assets as tools for innovation, not crutches for repetition. The trick is not to feel emboldened just because you scored points last year or last quarter. In the words of Bill Gates, "Success is a lousy teacher. It seduces smart people into thinking they can't lose."[4]

Letting go is never easy, especially when things are "okay." Many people find themselves in "okay" jobs, "okay" relationships, and living "okay" lives. It takes boldness and courage to let go of the status quo to pursue the wonder and magic of what's possible. The more success you've enjoyed, the more painful and unnerving it feels to change course. But letting go early, before it's too late, and making a thoughtful leap to the next adventure can be the difference maker.

After I graduated from college in 1994, I launched my second business, Innovative Computer Solutions. We sold computer hardware, installed networks, and provided other computer-related services. After eleven months of business, things were good. But with less than one year of operations, I decided to sell a business that appeared to be successful and full of promise. This was a hard decision, since the business was profitable and growing rapidly. An introspective look in the mirror had revealed a company that was on the path to mediocrity. I was making money and winning clients, but our products and services were a commodity. The industry was heading toward a price war in which giants such as Dell and Compaq seemed unbeatable. I knew that I needed to let go of one opportunity in order to seize a bigger one. I was right. Letting go of that business enabled me to launch my next one, which became exponentially more successful.

As human beings, fear often immobilizes us and keeps us grounded to the shelter of what we know. However, none of us wants to eventually look back at our sheltered life and be filled with regret that we never went for it. Never took that big risk. Never chased down our true potential. We end up playing it safe, only to realize that that choice got in the way of our real trajectory and robbed us from reaching new heights. Living in the past results in a stunted life. If you want to explore your real capacity for living, you have to keep moving forward toward new successes. What are the things you need to release in order to make room for the new? What are you clinging to, out of habit or perceived safety, that has lost its enduring value?

The one thing life teaches all of us is that the world turns in only one direction: forward. We can't go back, and we don't need to. If you find yourself clinging to the past because you're afraid of what the future might bring, let it go. Your own grit and determination will become your new safety net. You'll liberate your spirit from the limitations of what was, and in the process, you'll make room for the opportunities of the present and the possibilities of the future.

Principle 2: Encourage Courage

Think back to the last time you were in a group brainstorming session. Perhaps you came up with a great idea, but instead of sharing it, you held back. You talked yourself out of sharing with poisonous self-chatter: "If it was such a good idea, someone else probably would have already said it," or, "My ideas are never good. I'll probably just look foolish." This awful soundtrack that plays in our head continues with more fear and doubt, and we might wonder, "What will my boss think? Who will fund my idea? What if it doesn't work out? What will it mean to my career?" Ultimately many stumble on the same action plan: "I better just keep my mouth shut."

If this is the vibe in your company, you are in more danger than you realize. The best organizations do the opposite: they encourage courage. They focus on celebrating new ideas instead of punishing them, and their ideation process flourishes without judgment.

As a busy leader, your instinct may be to quickly dismiss a team member's less-than-wonderful idea with impatient criticism, sending the would-be innovator scuttling back to his or her cube in embarrassment. You've just trained that person to never again come forward with an idea—good or bad. A more productive approach would be to take the time to engage with others about their ideas and keep negative judgment out of the picture. If you truly think the idea is bad, I'm not suggesting you lie and tell the person otherwise. Instead, have a thoughtful, judgment-free conversation to explore the thinking behind the idea. Remember, you *want* your team to be curious and innovative and bold in their thinking as they generate new ideas. And you want every member of your team to feel comfortable expressing those ideas.

We've all been shot down for our suggestions, so when someone brings you an idea that seems like a nonstarter, take a minute to understand the vulnerable position that person is in before you reply. Then, instead of chastising, ask questions. "Tell me more about that," you might say. "What was the thinking that led you to that conclusion? Where do you see this headed? Is there something else you could add to make it even better?" Often it takes some unpacking to really understand another person's thinking. By taking some time to let the person fully articulate and explore his or her idea, you may find unexpected value in it. In fact, the experience of considering ideas with others is almost always valuable. Those discussions strengthen bonds of understanding and encourage everyone involved to think deeper and imagine more fully.

After that kind of thoughtful discussion, the person returns to her desk feeling understood, and she's primed for digging deeper into her ideas rather than walking away from them in shame. The same person may return with eight more lousy ideas in a row. So what? Maybe one of those bad ideas will trigger something useful in your own thinking. Or her tenth idea might turn out to be the game changer you've been praying for: a powerful and disruptive concept that transforms your organization.

Those game-changing "tenth ideas" will never surface if you respond with harsh judgment and dismissive critique to the first, second, or third time a bad idea comes around.

You'll never instill the spirit of reinvention in your team by making people afraid to express their ideas. Instead, encourage the people you work with to be bold—confident in their ability to innovate and courageous in their vision. Your whole organization will benefit from their bravery.

Principle 3: Embrace Failure

"Every bull's eye is the result of 100 misses," the old saying goes. Yet we harshly condemn setbacks or any signal that doesn't indicate immediate success. Failure in fact is an essential part of the discovery process. As a leader, it's critical that you teach your team to consider mistakes and missteps a natural part of the pathway toward reinvention.

Unfortunately, most of us have a delusional view of how ideas are formed and come to life. We believe that a lightning bolt of creative genius strikes a select few, who then launch perfectly developed ideas. That's not the case. When you study innovative breakthroughs in just about any area, you find that some of the biggest advances are the result of someone toying with the seed of an idea, then developing it through a series of stumbles, missteps, and failed experiments that eventually bear fruit.

WD-40, the leading cure for all things squeaky, earned its name through a series of failed trials. The name actually stands for: "Water Displacement, Fortieth Experiment." It could have just as easily been named WD-31. What the makers of WD-40 know, and what we all need to embrace, is that mistakes are not fatal; they're part of the process of discovery.

No matter how quickly it may seem that great start-ups succeed, just about all of them first go through their own series of failures. The goal in the start-up world is to "fail fast": reach the inevitable sticky points as quickly and cheaply as possible so you're able to learn, adapt, and try again. This was the path that led to incredible success for an entrepreneur named Beck Besecker.

Beck, who had founded and sold a company before and had also worked as a senior executive at a large corporation, approached me about funding his new start-up. I had known Beck for a while and held him in the highest regard: he is smart, tenacious, and focused. He gave me his pitch, and frankly the idea was just fair. I challenged him to refine and adapt the idea before DVP would agree to fund it.

After a few months of tinkering and exploration, Beck was ready to go. We signed a term sheet to invest in his company and were preparing to close when I got a call that is most unusual for those of us in venture capital. Beck said that he went to an industry conference and found many competitors launching similar businesses. He felt he had to go back to the drawing board and refine the concept before taking our money. I was impressed.

Beck came back a few months later with a new version of his company, Blirt, which was to be a mobile app that allowed people within close proximity to chat anonymously. We were so enthralled with Beck and his approach that we funded the company and saw a clear path to growth and success. Naturally that path changed when Beck told us he needed to pivot the company a few months later. Being keenly aware of market trends, competitive threats, and technology advances, Beck no longer felt comfortable with Blirt. Instead, he decided to make a sharp left turn and change his company to a mobile shopping and review concept called Favers. He outlined for us a thoughtful and deliberate change in direction, not a knee-jerk response to a setback. Again, he had our support.

In the process of building Favers, it became apparent the model needed help. Originally a tool that would be sold to retailers, the app began to make more sense as one that targeted consumers directly. That realization triggered yet another pivot: Beck abandoned Favers and morphed his company's product into a retail shopping companion called ShopWith.It. This cool app would allow consumers to access online reviews and advice from friends, shop for competitive prices, and learn more about products while at a mall or retailer. It gave in-store shoppers the same power they enjoyed while online shopping. Brilliant. We figured this was finally it.

Except the market didn't embrace it. Perhaps it was too soon, or perhaps the app was too hard to explain. But Beck was in a tough spot after releasing his fifth pivot, each abandoning the business model from before. Its release was greeted with a yawn from customers. This failure was a tough one; most business leaders would blame others and throw in the towel. Not Beck. Throughout his exploration into the intersection of technology and retail shopping, he become increasingly curious about a new technology trend called augmented reality. Using this technology, a consumer can hold a mobile device or tablet up, look "through it" (using the device's camera), and see the physical world transformed. For example, you could look at a product picture in a catalogue and watch it come to life in 3D views, multiple colors, and different settings. Beck realized this uncharted territory had many applications from commerce to medicine. He became obsessed with the possibilities.

I'm sure you can guess what happened next: yet another change in direction and Beck decided to bet the company on this new field. It was his sixth pivot and fourth name change in less than a year. Marxent Labs was born in 2011 and has been unstoppable since. Instead of the friction Beck experienced in earlier iterations, customers and partners wholeheartedly embraced his new concept. The company built an incredible technology platform called Visual Commerce that allows catalogue companies, retailers, and print advertisers to bring their flat offering into a high-definition, three-dimensional, fully immersive experience. The phone started ringing off the hook with eager new customers. The product started to win awards, media coverage, and industry accolades. Partners from around the globe called wanting to form joint ventures. Revenue soared into the millions, and the young, creative team enjoyed explosive growth.

The average entrepreneur would have felt the sting of failure many times over in Beck's situation and run with head hung low back to his day job. Beck instead embraced the reinvention philosophy that each setback is a powerful opportunity for learning and growth. In his case, each failed experiment led to insight, which led to his ultimate success.

Not every innovative idea or reinvention process goes through as many iterations as Beck's example. Some go through more. Reinvention and innovation typically are processes, not events. As you work to develop the ethos of reinvention, remind yourself that worthwhile ideas are an investment—of time, energy, and other resources. Living in a time of fast-fire change and rapid technological advancement can encourage us to believe that those kinds of investments are a losing bet, but in fact the opposite is true. We have to carefully nurture ideas through numerous trials and adjustments to bring them to harvest. Therefore, you need to encourage everyone on your team to think of failure as essential nourishment for innovation. The only truly nonproductive type of failure is the failure of courage we suffer when we're afraid to explore new ideas.

Principle 4: Do the Opposite

Throughout time, some of the biggest breakthroughs have come from innovators implementing a contrarian approach. Leaders who have experienced the pinnacles of success have dared to zig while everyone else zags. Doing the opposite—upending expectations, pushing through boundaries, running toward the thing everyone else is running from—is critical to stand out from the crowd.

Living by this principle of the reinvention ethos takes courage, but at least it offers a clear starting point. That's because most markets are flooded with me-toos and wannabes, which offer a clear profile of what you don't want to be. In the beauty industry, for example, the formulaic marketing approach is abundantly clear. Step 1: hire an anorexic supermodel. Step 2: photo-enhance any pictures taken. Step 3: run a bunch of very expensive ads. Step 4: hope for the best. In an attempt to get its message heard above the noise of the beauty industry herd and communicate with consumers in an authentic, compelling way, Dove decided to do something completely different. Instead of showcasing digitally edited fashion models in its ads, the soaps, lotion, and beauty products manufacturer decided to applaud real women with ads that celebrated inner beauty.

Moving into this polar-opposite approach, Dove took a huge risk and produced a video that exposed the rest of the industry as imposters. The video showed a model getting transformed through makeup and stylists, then having her picture taken for an ad. Next, the video showed the pictures being altered with computer technology, removing every perceived "flaw" until the model's image represented a level of Barbie doll-like artificial perfection that few actual living people can match. The video concludes with the distorted photograph appearing on a billboard beside a crowded city street. We walk by similar billboards all the time, right? All that "perfection" has become so common, it hardly rates a glance.

Exposing the behind-the-scenes approach of beauty industry marketing, however, was groundbreaking. Dove had demonstrated how greedy marketers would showcase impossible standards of beauty to sell their products, even if their methods were crushing the self-esteem of their own customers. Dove bared the ugly side of the beauty industry, and the world took notice. Over 32 million people around the world watched the online video before Dove ran a single paid ad. When the marketing team at Dove realized that the company had launched a movement, they shifted their entire budget into the Real Women campaign (and later added Real Men). As the rest of the competitive pack was clawing and scratching for single-digit growth and blaming market conditions for poor performance, Dove's sales soared, returning three dollars for every one dollar spent. As the Real Beauty campaign expanded and featured specific Dove products, the results were equally astounding: US sales for the products featured in the ads increased 600 percent in the first two months of the campaign's release.[5] This completely opposite idea went on to become one of the most successful and enduring ad campaigns in history. Dove won not because it blended in; it won because it did everything possible to stand out.

Instead of struggling to fight your way to the front of a stampeding herd, try turning the other way. By freeing yourself from the expectation to conform, you've taken a fundamental first step in adopting the do-the-opposite principle of reinvention. Even thinking like a contrarian can help you find new directions. A powerful exercise is to list all the things you are currently doing—all the things that are industry standard, all the things that the competition does—and then brainstorm a 180-degree opposite approach. If your competition does face-to-face selling, what if you sold over the Web? If your competition offers the lowest price, what would you need to do to offer your goods or services at the highest price (quality, scarcity, luxury, status)? Explore the uncharted territory that is far outside your comfort zone, and you may end up discovering a formula for growth and reinvention that is both powerful and unique.

Principle 5: Imagine the Possibilities

With eyes wide open, you notice your physical surroundings. You can't help but see the world the way it currently exists. The obstacles, barriers, and roadblocks are painfully clear. But when you close your eyes, your mind can transcend reality and explore what's possible. When you're looking for powerful ways to reinvent your business, your team, your life, you have to be willing to close your eyes sometimes and imagine possibilities that don't yet exist.

Too often organizations and individuals are so worried about boundaries that they neuter their own creativity by blinding themselves to the infinite opportunities that lie beyond those limits. When you close your eyes, you are able to imagine much greater possibilities. Bold dreamers envision what can be instead of settling for what is. Incremental gains may come from open-eyed thinking, but to take truly great leaps of innovation and reinvention, you have to be willing to loosen your grip on the concrete realities of the here and now and venture into the unknown.

Dan Gilbert, founder and chairman of Quicken Loans, shares this belief. Deeply committed to philosophy and corporate culture, he takes a full day each month to evangelize his eighteen "ISMs"—the "north star" that guides decisions and behavior—with all newly hired staff (at the time of this writing, that's approximately five hundred new team members each month). In one of his ISMs, he flips an old saying upside down, dismissing the traditional logic of "I'll believe it when I see it" in exchange for his own proclamation: "You'll see it when you believe it." Instead of the fear-based approach of doubting progress until it is tangibly apparent, Dan feels that one needs to first believe fully in something, and that belief will manifest and shape reality.

Disruptive thinking takes a certain amount of faith. You have to be willing to explore the unknown and imagine outcomes you've never experienced before. The human brain is hardwired for imagination; in fact, our ability to project possibilities is part of our survival system.

From our understanding of the workings of the universe to our knowledge of the microbes on our skin, almost every human advancement began as someone's wild dream. If we waited to see it first, we'd never have civil rights, advanced manufacturing, lifesaving medical treatments, or wireless Internet. Reinvention is born in the imagination. We have to unshackle ourselves from the bland realities of the present in order to imagine, and then create, a profoundly different future.

Principle 6: Put Yourself Out of Business

Software companies have a beautiful process of planned obsolescence. Each time a new version is released, the objective is to render the previous version irrelevant. It's the same with consumer electronics; the iPhone 8 will be designed to put the iPhone 7 out of business. Unfortunately, many companies and leaders don't embrace this important principle of continuous reinvention. They become entrenched in yesterday's version of success and do everything possible to preserve it, leaving themselves vulnerable to competitors who are working fiercely to innovate. Every success is eventually eclipsed by another. Ultimately companies that are unwilling to "kill their darlings" and create a new version of success either fail completely or evolve begrudgingly, after it's too late to capitalize on their previous success.

The best leaders today realize that their job is to put their own companies out of business. They know that ongoing, far-reaching reinvention—from products and services to production and technology—is mandatory for survival. Top-tier companies constantly examine their offerings and the way they do business to find new approaches with greater impact. They are obsessed with finding a better way to do their work and are on a relentless hunt for outdated systems, processes, communication, and frameworks. Sometimes this philosophy yields a series of strong, incremental improvements that collectively move the needle. At other times, the gains from this approach are transformational.

We all know and revere Warren Buffett as a disciplined, thoughtful, and patient leader. His company, Berkshire Hathaway, generated $22 billion in profits on $162 billion in revenue in 2012. It has delivered annual growth in market value of 19.7 percent for the last forty-eight years, more than double the performance of the S&P 500 overall.[6] This success has made Buffett one of the wealthiest men in the world, and he has donated billions to philanthropic causes.

What you may not know is that Berkshire Hathaway itself was a reinvention. The company's roots go back to a textile mill founded in 1889. In 1955, after a series of mergers, the company (by then known as Berkshire Fine Spinning Associates) merged with the Hathaway Manufacturing Company to form the namesake we now recognize. Buffett began buying stock in Berkshire Hathaway in 1962 and continued to buy when others were selling. By 1964, he controlled the company.

The textile business was not doing all that well in the mid-1960s, so Buffett reinvented with unbridled fervor. He began investing in insurance and other nontextile businesses because he believed the investments would provide a better return to shareholders than doubling down on the core business. Essentially he bet the company and took a completely fresh approach for the future.

The original textile business was finally shut down by 1985, and today the conglomerate has ownership stakes in a diverse group of businesses, including Coca-Cola, IBM, GEICO, and NetJets. Had Buffett stuck to his knitting, most of us would have never heard of the Oracle from Omaha.[7]

Berkshire Hathaway isn't the only company that achieved massive success through top-to-bottom reinvention. 3M, originally Minnesota Mining and Milling, today produces tens of thousands of products as a multinational conglomerate. The only thing that bears a resemblance to its original iteration is its headquarters, still in Minnesota. IBM, the pioneer of computer manufacturing, no longer makes computers; it prospers instead as a tech services business. Western Union started as a telegram company and became the world's giant in the service; as telegrams died out, the company reinvented and started offering money transfers. Today the telegraph service does not even exist, but Western Union is going strong.

These companies had leaders with the courage and imagination to seize new opportunity within changing times, and as a result, they continue to remain household names. For each one, however, there are hundreds of organizations that failed to embrace this principle of reinvention, became irrelevant, and folded. Instead of dying slowly through stagnation, successful companies put themselves out of business before the competition or market conditions do the job for them.

Principle 7: Reject Limits

A colleague approaches you with a radical new idea. What are the odds you will imagine the possibilities, build on her concept, and embrace this new vision: 18 percent? 3 percent? 0 percent? Grumpy professors, cynical parents, and finger-wagging bureaucrats have lured many of us into building championship "no" instincts. It's much easier and less risky to protect the current situation, right?

The problem with this stop-sign approach is that it completely undermines forward progress. It's a primary force that has led to the downfall of great leaders, companies, and cities, but so many of us continue to reflexively toss out "no" with rhythmic consistency.

In late spring 2013, I found myself on a call with lawyers and tax specialists that made my stomach turn. These "professionals" were remarkably adept at shooting down idea after idea. A concept that generated 2 percent risk. NO. Another approach that yielded a .5 percent risk? NO. Any idea whatsoever that would require judgment and creativity? NO, NO, NO.

The world is filled with naysayers, but if we accept the limits of their no-can-do thinking, progress as a society stops. Nearly every advance in civilization was met with an ice-cold reception. Thankfully, the best leaders have the courage to advance their causes despite the critics.

Are you one of those lost souls who act as the self-appointed idea police? Do you feel obligated to find flaws and overstate the risks? Do you find yourself playing the role of devil's advocate often? If so, you're denying your own spirit of innovation and strangling the ethos of reinvention throughout your organization. When "no" becomes your reflexive response to new ideas, take a hard look in the mirror and realize you've been brainwashed by the fearmongers. That's not who you really are. Saying no is much easier than yes, but it also chains you to mediocrity. Forget about "easy"; it's time to do the right thing and fight for the win.

The Streetfighter: Reinventing the Entrepreneur

The word *entrepreneur* comes from French and implies an aristocratic polish, straight from the bourgeoisie. It's probably time we discarded the word *entrepreneur* and coined a new term to the adventurous journey of building something out of nothing. Truth is, building a company is hard work. To me, a more fitting term for someone engaged in that effort is *streetfighter*, because it much more accurately describes the character and skills necessary for winning the fierce competition of a modern, global economy. Here are the streetfighter rules of engagement:

Rely on grit and determination. Be willing to get your hands dirty and do whatever it takes to succeed.

Get scrappy. Adapt quickly and figure out how to do more with less.

Ignore tradition. Find fresh new ways to achieve instead of being weighed down by dogma.

Use what you've got. Lacking formal training or fancy tools, streetfighters must use whatever is at their disposal. Often these are internal tools (heart, passion, courage) instead of external ones (fancy tech tools, academic degrees, country club connections).

Prepare to engage on a moment's notice. Make sure you're ready for battle and prepared for competitive attacks from any direction.

Have a chip on your shoulder. Embrace a healthy disregard for the status quo and a willingness to stick your finger in the eye of the current territorial leaders.

Learn and grow from adversity. Realize that your most important areas of growth are just outside your comfort zone.

Speed wins. Beating your competition to the punch is much more effective than waiting to craft the "ideal" solution. There's no time in a street fight to have ideas stuck in committee.

Fight from behind. Have an underdog sense of urgency. Be ready to outwork your competition ten-to-one.

The term *entrepreneur* has had a good run, but it may have lost its punch. If you're planning to win in today's intensely competitive and complex world, it's time to let your inner streetfighter out of the cage.

We've heard story after story about prolific leaders rejecting apparent limitations by refusing to accept the reflexive "no" from their teams. Steve Jobs insisted the iPhone be a certain size and feel without sacrificing a drop of tech wizardry. Walt Disney demanded never-been-done-before quality and realism while making huge leaps forward in the craft of animation. A common thread among those who change the world is a healthy disregard for limits. Great leaders put *yes* before *no*, *can* before *can't*, *will* before *won't*.

More often than not, the things that we think are limiting our companies and careers are imaginary. Self-imposed limits are the enemy of progress. By refusing to accept them, we can make all the difference in our lives.

There's the legendary story of a group of mountain climbers who got trapped in a small cave during an avalanche. Being sophisticated sportsmen, they were able to calculate how much oxygen was available and how much time they could survive, determining when a rescue would have to take place in order to for all of them to make it out alive. It turned out that only one member of the group of eight had a watch. To boost morale, that timekeeper routinely added thirty minutes to the clock without the others knowing. In other words, the one with the clock was the only one who actually knew how long the troubled group had to live. Long after the stranded climbers' time should have been up, a rescue expedition reached them. All were alive but one—the one with the watch. He had become so convinced that his time had expired that his body stopped fighting. The others, who believed they were capable of living longer, did.

As a disruptor, you will constantly be met with resistance. The path forward involves crushing supposed limits, refusing to accept the reflexive no, and unleashing an unwavering belief that you will prevail. If you're not willing to do that, are you willing to accept the alternative?

Principle 8: Aim Beyond

When I launched my third company in 1995, most people thought I was crazy. My business was building these bizarre, new-fangled contraptions called "websites." I would literally call potential customers and ask them if they'd ever heard of the Internet. Most people starting a business look at research and market data, which in this case revealed there was zero market for a website development company. That assessment was true at that moment, but I was aiming for something I saw in the future. Because of that future aim, my business was a success and I ended up selling it to a public company in 1999.

Whether you are launching a product, opening a fashion boutique, seeking a job, or rebuilding a broken community, your focal point must be ahead of you. You need to move forward anticipating trends and changes in the competitive landscape. A solution that is spot-on in the near term may completely miss when it's time to go live, even if it's only a few months away.

Misguided dreamers often develop their idea in the context of today's market environment without anticipating the momentum of competitors. It's as if the world will freeze for twelve months while they develop their new product. Yes, ideas have to pass through trials and adjustments, and they may take time to fully develop. But that development process needs to be targeted at where you think the market is heading, not myopically trained on ground that's already been covered. The world never freezes. In fact, we are in a state of perpetual motion, with new advances arriving on a more rapid schedule than in any other time in history: new political upheaval, new scientific breakthroughs, new regulation, new competitors, new natural disasters, new ideas. As you seek to realize your full potential in the work of reinvention, never forget that we are all aiming at moving targets. Don't let the past or even the present mislead you into taking a losing shot. Do your research, know your data, and then use that understanding to project your path forward.

Put It All Together

Courage; resilience; imagination; faith in your ideas: these are the threads that run through all of the principles of reinvention discussed in this chapter. And what's not to love about the ideas and characteristics involved in them? But understanding the spirit of reinvention—even admiring it—won't guarantee that you can live it. Adopting a new way of thinking is, like any other form of innovation, a process. You might have to kick some old habits and retrain your reflexes, and that takes practice.

It's easy to believe ideas that have become second nature to us are inherently right. If we've been conditioned to fear the unknown, to approach every new exploration with the certainty that we're going to lose our way, then it's going to take some concerted effort to retrain our thinking and awaken our inner disruptor. But if we don't go through that process, we'll always be traveling blind. The world is going to change; your marketplace is going to change; your business is going to change; you are going to change. Those are predictions you can make with absolute certainty. The question is, will you master the process of driving change, or will you be driven by it? By practicing the principles that give form to the spirit of reinvention, you're developing the innovative muscle memory necessary to lead change—in whatever direction you decide to take it.

Detroit: Catalyst for Change

For most of its over three-hundred-year history, Detroit was a beacon of innovation and industry. And after a decades-long period of decline that culminated in the city's 2013 bankruptcy filing, a bright light of reinvention is gaining powerful momentum. Detroiters are embracing the dynamic forces of this disruption with open arms.

The efforts are big and wide. In 2013, as I write, the city is finalizing plans for a light rail system to unite its disconnected city center—a system funded by a coalition of public and private sources.[8] Enormous "placemaking" projects—the process of creating squares, plazas, parks, streets, and waterfronts that will attract people because they are pleasurable or interesting—to activate pedestrians in the once-abandoned downtown streets are under way. The Project for Public Spaces (PPS), a nonprofit planning, design, and educational organization, is busy collaborating with Downtown Detroit Partnership and Rock Ventures/Opportunity Detroit (a division of

Dan Gilbert's Quicken Loans) to bring new businesses and employees in to fill downtown Detroit's empty commercial spaces.[9] PPS
also announced plans to help bring Detroit's waterfront back to
life, working on both the Detroit RiverFront and the city's green
island jewel, Belle Isle Park.[10] Among the attractions at RiverFront
are a hand-crafted carousel, gardens and walkways, fishing, cafés,
bike riding, and a concert venue. Belle Isle Park offers an aquarium,
greenhouses, historical building tours, picnic areas and walkways,
a Great Lakes museum, a golf driving range and putting green, a
nature center, a giant slide, a beach, and playgrounds. As I write,
big-name retailers are working with mom-and-pops to fill abandoned storefronts, and an emerging tech scene of young, vibrant,
create-class workers is breathing diversity and new life into a limping
economy.

Detroit schools are getting an injection of energy from dozens of creative programs in an effort to boost abysmal graduation
rates. In September 2013, for example, the UAW-Ford National
Programs Center, the Ford Motor Company Fund, and the Detroit
Public Schools Foundation announced that they would join forces
to contribute half a million dollars to restore arts and sports programs to Detroit's schools.[11] And in July of that same year, the
Chrysler Corporation and Detroit Public Schools announced their
plans for ARISE Detroit! a program of community service partnerships for Neighborhood Day. The agencies will combine forces to
upgrade libraries, repaint classrooms, and replant flower beds and
shrubs around Detroit's public school buildings to help make them
brighter, more effective, and more appealing places in the next academic year.[12]

Detroiters are wading into the work of rebuilding their city
with a bold spirit. We may have been slow to address our problems, but I don't see a lot of foot-dragging now in our community.
State and local governments, business owners, community leaders,
private citizens—Detroiters are tough people. And while you can
learn a lot of things from the experiences of my hometown, maybe
Detroit's most powerful lesson lies in its citywide embrace of the
reinvention ethos.

Tools for Transformation:
What If . . .

One way to embrace the ethos of reinvention and explore the infinite possibilities of innovation is to brainstorm questions instead of answers. Play twenty questions, each beginning with the phrase "what if?" It's a simple exercise that forms a powerful technique for escaping the limitations of conventional wisdom.

Ask yourself: What if . . .

1. We encouraged those around us to take risks and try new ideas?
2. You set out to leave your mark on the world instead of following conventional wisdom?
3. We taught our kids to follow their hearts instead of the herd?
4. You gave yourself permission to have more fun and let your creativity shine?
5. We celebrated new ideas as much as near-term financial performance?
6. You didn't let fear and imaginary barriers hold you back from reaching your true potential?
7. You committed to becoming a lifelong learner?
8. You injected your coworkers with positive energy three times a day?
9. We removed regret and realized that setbacks are simply the pathway to progress?
10. We prioritized creative thinking over tasks?
11. You tapped your full creative potential?
12. You let go of the rules and followed your dreams with unapologetic vigor?
13. You refused to accept mediocrity?
14. Our kids learned that creative problem solving is more important than rote memorization?
15. You tried something new every week?
16. We didn't take ourselves so seriously?
17. You seized this moment and committed to change?
18. You had the courage to stand behind your best ideas?
19. You laughed twice as much?
20. You realized that you had the power to change the world?

CHAPTER 3

Cannibalize Your Own Product

There are two primary choices in life: to accept conditions
as they exist, or accept the responsibility for changing them.

—DENNIS WAITLEY

The sting of crushing defeat. The agony of job loss. The collapse of an iconic brand. The Polaroid Corporation, once heralded as the gold standard of innovation, had suffered all of these dismal ends when it reached the unthinkable point of filing for bankruptcy protection in 2001.[1]

For more than fifty years, Polaroid had been the dominant player in instant photography. It prevailed in a patent battle against rival Kodak, which then abandoned its instant camera business in 1986. Instead of opening up new possibilities for innovation at Polaroid, this glorious victory seemed only to narrow the tunnel vision of the company's leadership still further. Confident that its win over Kodak had proved that Polaroid was a bullet-proof brand, the company, which had once reinvented the photographic process, became isolated and out of touch with its marketplace. Why bother creating new successes when your current version was surely going to last forever?

When researching the crash of this once-great company, I found story after story of valiant attempts to reinvent. Each suggestion of product innovation, whether from internal team members or external consultants, hit the same stonewall objection: "We can't do that. We can't *cannibalize* our core business!"

We've all heard this kind of conventional thinking. Oriented in a mind-set that sees limitations in every direction, where every marketplace, technological sphere, or other essential resource is finite, the folks who cling to the cannibalization myth can't possibly imagine creating some wholly new success. In their version of the world, survival is the only goal; forget about growing and thriving.

The idea behind this business school mainstay is that in order for a business's new idea, product, or service to gain market share, it will have to take it from another of the business's offerings. In other words, you have to kill your current golden goose in order to bring in a new one. That way of looking at the marketplace doesn't make sense to me. In a free market economy, innovation wins. Isn't replacing past successes with new ones the very nature of progress? Shouldn't we all be gunning hard to drive the next evolution of our industry or marketplace instead of using a fear of "cannibalization" as an excuse to slam the brakes on exploration?

Refusing to embrace new products or processes because they might prove to be more effective than existing ones is an illogical exercise in magical thinking. It assumes that we can prevent progress, that we wield some paranormal power to control innovation throughout our marketplace. We can't; we don't. Regardless of our industries, and no matter how powerful our organizations may be, we cannot prevent disruption. Those who focus all of their energy on simply holding on to what they have will never be able to reach out for more. By clinging to the past, they are choosing to become obsolete.

In today's highly competitive world, we must sprint toward cannibalization instead of trying to hide from it. If Polaroid had reinvented its product line to lead the way in embracing new forms and uses of photography, it could have opened up entirely new areas of its marketplace. With its brand power and resources, Polaroid ought to have been the company to launch a major innovation in the world of digital photography. Instead, it left that opportunity on the table, to be snatched up by a hungry new start-up called Instagram, a runaway success iPhone app that allows you to take pictures from your phone and easily share them with friends.

Ironically, one of the most popular features on Instagram is making digital photos resemble old Polaroids. Adding insult to injury, Instagram was sold to Facebook for $1 billion in 2012, two years after its launch in October 2010.[2] That's just about the amount of debt Polaroid cited as its rationale for requesting bankruptcy protection in 2001.[3] What about Snapchat, which enables people to send pictures (often silly, bizarre, or inappropriate) to friends who can view them for only five seconds before the picture deletes itself? In November 2013, Snapchat founders rejected a $3 billion all-cash offer from Google because they believed that amount undervalued their creation. Why couldn't Polaroid have been the source of that innovation? These are just a few examples of how, time and time again, the market rewards cutting-edge innovation and sharply punishes stagnation. That makes cannibalization a strategic choice, not a disaster.

Success can intoxicate even the most disciplined leaders and trick them into thinking their advantage is sustainable. Don't drink that moonshine. Your responsibility as a leader is to deeply instill within your organization the understanding that even its most profound successes are only temporary delights. Market conditions change faster than runway models change outfits, and your goal is to drive those market changes with ongoing innovation. We can become a consistent source of reinvention and reap the benefits of success. Or we can hide behind the fear of "cannibalization" and exist on ever dwindling scraps of the status quo while our competition feasts on the rewards of innovation.

See with Your Customer's Eye

Ongoing innovation demands deep and persistent exploration. In *The Importance of Innovation for Company Performance*, researchers Luuk Klomp and George Van Leeuwen conclude that "companies which perform R&D on a permanent basis or innovate in partnership have a significantly higher level of innovation output than other companies . . . [and] a significantly positive effect of the level of innovation output on sales growth."[4] This conclusion is critical. The minute you stop to bask in the glory of current success, you become a sitting duck, vulnerable to any competitor's innovation that offers a better option to your (now former) customers.

An ideal place to begin your exploration of comprehensive, ongoing reinvention is with your core product or service. That core offering is your company's identity, your most recognizable achievement and the thing that keeps your customers buying from you. But if your marquee offering doesn't adapt to the public's rapidly changing demands or the market's evolving opportunities, your customers will buy elsewhere. Casting a cold eye on your core offerings can be difficult. We all have filters of past experiences and expectations that can muddy our vision as we explore opportunities for core-deep innovation.

Going deep into its customers' perspective helped one company find an ocean of opportunity through innovation of its core service. In Hawaii, the scuba-diving industry was facing a host of problems after the economy took a dive back in 1989, including declining sales, increased competition for shrinking entertainment dollars, and new consumer alternatives. Scuba diving is an incredible experience, but it's also a lot of work for customers. It requires certification, carrying heavy tanks, and restrictions on when you can fly home after your underwater exploration—not to mention its high cost, an increasing deterrent in a bumpy economy.

As the industry fell into a price-cutting race to the bottom, one company dared to be different. Developers at SNUBA took a hard look at the obstacles that were keeping their customers away, then focused their creativity on making the process more customer friendly. They developed a radical new approach to pleasing their customers and were rewarded handsomely for the effort.

Instead of divers lugging heavy tanks, SNUBA keeps the tank up on the water's surface in a raft and connects to customers with a twenty-foot hose. Divers get a similar experience to scuba (breathing underwater), but SNUBA requires no certification, training, heavy lifting, or flight restrictions. Another plus? The activity is a fraction of the cost of the old-school model. The fusion of snorkeling and scuba diving created a fresh new category and allowed this company to blast off. Now considered the safest form of diving, over 5 million people have enjoyed SNUBA worldwide.[5]

Sometimes you can score deep product innovation by turning the common model inside out. But first you need to understand how that kind of dramatic transformation will work to meet your customers' real-world challenges and aspirations. That's what Veronika Scott did. For her senior project at Detroit's College for Creative Studies, Scott was challenged to design a product that could help the homeless. She didn't look for answers in existing research or media reports. Instead, she immersed herself in the world of her "customer." For months, Scott spent time visiting homeless shelters, observing and talking to people struggling to survive in some of Detroit's most challenging neighborhoods.

After being threatened with violence, berated with foul language, and exposed to a number of uncomfortable social situations, Veronika started to understand some of the day-to-day challenges her audience faced. She discovered that having autonomy and independence was paramount to this group. Certainly they needed shelter, but they often didn't want to go through the administrative burdens of and social realities of the system. Of course, she also heard complaints of Michigan's bitterly cold winters.

To create a product that could help address all of these issues, Veronika reinvented something inherently basic: the coat. She designed a winter parka that doubles as a sleeping bag when it is turned inside out. This invention gave her new clients warmth, shelter, and increased autonomy. Instead of simply turning in her paper and hoping for a passing grade, Veronika launched her idea into real-world life after graduation, starting a nonprofit that began as soon as she collected her diploma.

As if this coat production wasn't enough, she used her mission to create much-needed jobs for the very people she set out to serve. With some help from local Detroit philanthropists, she opened a small factory to manufacture the coats, staffed entirely by homeless women. Labeled as the Empowerment Plan, this inspiring humanitarian nonprofit effort has helped ended the vicious cycle of homelessness for her staff through steady wages and work and structured motivation. She not only empowered the end users of her product, she empowered her team by providing jobs that helped get them off the streets and into a new life.

After winning dozens of awards, meeting Oprah, and being applauded in countless media features, Veronika's mission continues. She is now providing thousands of coats around the country while employing a growing team of women in need. Her long-term goal is to sell the coats to those who can afford them (military, campers, outdoor explorers) and donate one coat to a homeless individual for every one that is sold.

Veronika Scott's innovative ideas are directly helping countless numbers of people and inspiring even more. The enterprise began with her ability to deeply connect with her customers' needs. She had the patience and determination to look past the obvious quick fixes and invent something truly remarkable. This is the type of curve-jumping, radical innovation that's needed in every company, career, and community. The creativity needed to reinvent a coat, sleeping bag, computer chip, life insurance policy, Broadway musical, or medical device—or any other product or service you sell—is yours for the taking. It starts with committing to change, listening to your customers, and then not stopping until you've achieved the blazing success that you imagined in those first sparks of creative fire.

When you are considering ways to reinvent your core product or service, don't limit your ideas to small tweaks and incremental shifts. As the examples in this chapter illustrate, world-beating products, companies, and individuals shun that uninspired approach. You should too. Go deep. See through your customers' eyes. Unshackle your imagination from the past and its restrictions so you're free to explore innovations that will upend your past successes. The only thing better than creating the best offering in the marketplace is creating the one that takes its place.

The Twenty Questions About Customers

To create any truly worthwhile innovation in your core product or service, you'll have to go deep in understanding your customers' perspective. At the end of chapter 2, you practiced playing twenty questions as a way to uncover and unleash your own creative possibilities. Here's another round of the game, aimed at exploring your customers' needs, aspirations, frustrations, and experiences with a quick list of jumping-off questions:

1. What has changed recently in your customers' lives?
2. What three big worries or concerns are they facing?
3. What will be different in your customers' lives three years from now? Five years?
4. What do your customers do for fun? For work?
5. What infuriates your customers today?
6. How do they currently use your product? What are their favorite and least favorite features?
7. If your customer could change any one thing about you, your company, or your product, what would it be?
8. Which is most important to your customers: time, money, or quality?
9. Why might a customer choose your competitor instead of you?
10. What alternatives does your customer have if she never wanted to work with you again?
11. How simple is it for your customer to make a change and buy from your competition?
12. What's one thing your customers want, but can't get, from any business in your industry? Why not?
13. What do your customers aspire to be? If they could snap their fingers and were living their dream lives, how would that look?
14. What complementary services or products would your customers buy from you if you offered them?
15. How does design or style play into your customers' view of your offering? How would a style makeover influence your customers' buying decisions?
16. If your customers could have a lot more of one thing you offer, what would that be? (This could be any product or service attribute you already offer.)

17. What materials, colors, smells, or other sensory touch points would your customers want if you could produce them at the same price point?
18. What three things would your customers remove from your offering if they could?
19. How have your customers' needs changed? How do they use your product or service differently than they did five years ago?
20. What would you need to offer in order for your customer to pledge lifetime support for your product or service?

Considering these types of thought-starter questions can lead to the core innovations you've been seeking. Use the twenty questions exercise to generate initial seedlings of ideas—as opposed to fully formed, ready-for-primetime innovations.

Launch a New Version

Your bolt manufacturer, version 3.1. Your landscaping service, version 2.0. Your bridal shop, version 5.2. Maybe if other industries embraced the practice of reinventing new versions of their core offerings on a regular basis, they would enjoy some of the other benefits that software companies have: talented people, huge valuations, fully engaged cultures, and deeply loyal customers.

Software companies are in a constant state of reinventing their core product. As soon as one version reaches the market, they start imagining the next. The goal each time is to blow their flagship out of the water with the new release.

The process goes something like this: even in advance of launching one version, the most successful software developers begin gathering insight and feedback from customers, vendors, the media, and team members. Software companies know they have to be tuned in to these audiences. Rather than shunting aside feedback on their most popular products, these companies want to know what went wrong in previous versions, what went right, and what was missing entirely. They also begin aggressive brainstorming sessions that explore the boundaries of what could be. They aren't there to fiercely protect the sanctity of their past offering and they aren't afraid of the unknown.

Whether your own organization sells cleaning supplies, packages free-range chickens, or assembles custom cabinetry, it's time to think like a software company and launch your next version. How could you bring a whole new set of competitive advantages to market? New value to customers? Better features? A faster supply chain? Your next feature must entail something that would be as remarkable and engaging as the spark that got your customers excited in the first place.

If you don't make your market successes obsolete, someone else will. That's why start-ups are often the driving force of disruptive creativity. A case in point is the disruption of presentation software. Bad Microsoft PowerPoint presentations have reached the same punch line status as lawyer jokes, but most of us still use this tool. Some have moved to other programs, such as Apple's Keynote, which has cool transitions and flaming bullet points, but it is still essentially the same thing: a linear presentation system.

A hot new start-up company, Prezi (Prezi.com), finally broke the mold. Rather than step-by-step sequential presentations, Prezi has an entirely different approach. Users begin with a giant canvas on which to post all kinds of content (e.g., text, images, video, sound, designs, graphs). Once the elements are on your canvas, you can easily move to any piece of content at any time. You can create a specific path if you want (or several different paths), or you can just improvise the order of your presentation based on your interaction with the audience. The tool also allows you to zoom in or out on any piece of content and, of course, make cool visual transitions. Instead of incremental improvement, Prezi architected the first truly revolutionary presentation tool in the past ten years.

So why did it come from a start-up instead of Microsoft? Why do most breakthroughs come from nimble and hungry entrepreneurs instead of well-established incumbents with endless resources? Why did the brilliant idea for Zipcar come from a start-up instead of Hertz or Avis? How come Red Bull didn't originate from Coca-Cola or Pepsi?

The answer is simple: most large organizations exist to protect old ideas, not create new ones. To them, innovation is about incremental improvements, not reinvention. Many of us punch the clock at large bureaucracies that are more focused on compliance than creativity. Obedience is valued over imagination.

It doesn't have to be that way. Whether we work in a big company or a start-up, the research clearly shows that all people have tremendous creative capacity.[6] We all have the opportunity to develop our imagination, shatter boundaries, and invent a brighter future. We'll never really take advantage of those opportunities, however, if we're unwilling to challenge our past wins. When you're exploring areas for innovation in your organization—or in your life—remember to go deep. Your most sustainable advantage in any marketplace lies in your ability to remain constantly engaged in reinventing your core strengths.

Getting H.O.S.E.'d

Throughout your efforts to reinvent your offering, stay focused on differentiation. You must ensure that your new plastic fastener, investment service, or entertainment venue is substantially different from all the others on the market. A good litmus test is to ensure you H.O.S.E. the competition by delivering a new product or service:

High value: Just because you can do something doesn't mean you should. Your new product must deliver exceptional value to your customer. Unless it solves a real problem in a meaningful way, forget about it.

Original: Getting confused with a competitor should be the greatest business insult of all. Keep your offering uniquely you so it always stands out.

Significant: A minuscule product improvement will go largely unnoticed. Go big by breaking the mold of the past and launching something that truly matters.

Emotionally charged: Product features may stimulate inventors, but they won't motivate your customers to leap into action. If your product evokes passion, customers will line up to buy.

Refocus to Reinvent

Ashifi Gogo, Dartmouth's first-ever PhD Innovation Fellow, was already engaged in the process of reinventing his core product by the time he graduated from the prestigious program in 2010. Gogo's first creative spark sprang from his realization that consumers had no way to check the authenticity of food labeled as organic since some greedy producers make false claims that their products are organic in order to sell more. To give consumers a tool for checking the organic bona fides of any food producer, Gogo came up with the idea for a scratch-off product label carrying an authentication code. Consumers would be able to text the code to Gogo's company, Sproxil, and would receive an immediate response as to the authenticity of the product.

The problem, according to Gogo, was that "nobody wanted to buy it." Even shoppers who always go to Whole Foods and other specialty shops weren't responding. Rather than shutting down the company, Gogo decided to reinvent its core approach. He was convinced that his solution for protecting consumers against fraudulent goods was solid; he just needed to move it out of the produce aisle. So he made his creative leap into the pharmaceutical industry.

In examining the broader reach of false claims by greedy producers, Gogo learned that consumers of medications are not always getting the real thing, especially in emerging markets such as Nigeria and India. In many cases, fake knock-off drugs contain chalk or even deadly ingredients such as road paint.[7] Gogo saw an opportunity to launch a product that met a real need for both consumers and manufacturers. When Gogo started pitching pharmaceutical manufacturers with the idea of stickering their medication with his mobile product authentication (MPA) solution, his willingness to reinvent his core product paid off. Sproxil was off and running.

In just four years after launching his new solution in 2009, Gogo's company has authenticated over 6 million items. He reinvented his own product, scratch-off authentication, to serve a different need and has reached undeniable success: his hypergrowth company was named number 7 on *Fast Company*'s Most Innovative Companies list for 2013.[8]

Sproxil isn't the lone example of a company that scored significant success by pivoting its original concept. One of the hottest tech start-ups to hit the scene over the past few years is a company called Zaarly. Visionary Bo Fishback launched the company to provide a marketplace for local services. Users could find people to take out the trash, babysit, or paint the house. Service providers and sellers could quickly pair up with eager customers, creating a whole new type of shopping bazaar.

The problem was that the idea fell flat on its face. What sounded great in theory was simply not embraced by customers. Bo had raised millions from A-list investors, and a crash could have meant an end to his professional reputation. Where others may have caved, Bo reinvented.

Bo was still passionate about local service and helping to drive commerce in individual communities, but he decided to refocus his concept on a smaller marketplace of handpicked local stores and specialized delivery services. Shopping for goods and services on Craigslist and eBay can be difficult for consumers, since it is hard to determine quality and service levels in advance. Zaarly members, however, know they are getting the best of the best. That layer of internal screening drives trust, which in turn drives sales. Zaarly is now enjoying millions of dollars of local commerce, helping consumers discover new goods and services in a safe and trusted format. And of course, Zaarly takes a small cut from every transaction.

Sometimes market changes trigger opportunities for changing your product's target market. That was the case for Mark D'Andreta, whose company, TDIC, made specialized covers for paint robots, which are largely used in auto manufacturing. The nifty custom-stitched covers protected the robots from harmful paint spray, reduced maintenance and downtime, and helped diminish contaminants that can ruin a job. His entrepreneurial efforts were rocking until 2008, when the economy collapsed and the auto industry took a dive. Like so many other businesses, D'Andreta's company was under attack by the forces of economic change.

A careful review of TDIC's core competencies led D'Andreta to the conclusion that the company could use its expertise and equipment to serve a broader customer base. While domestic auto manufacturing was on the decline, aerospace was taking off. A new division of TDIC was born, and the factory once again started humming. The momentum of reinvention became contagious as the company realized that another industry could also use its help. TDIC next launched sophisticated medical covers to protect medical robots and other advanced medical devices. Following the success of these new lines, D'Andreta turned to custom boat and car covers for enthusiasts, and followed that with specialty industrial covers. The more TDIC zoomed out from its original core market, the more success it enjoyed.

It was no surprise when D'Andreta made another creative leap by taking his company's core reinvention even further: he parlayed his know-how, experienced team, factory, and supply chain into an entirely new industry: fashion. Teaming up with high-end designers, he launched Motor City Denim Company, manufacturing high-end jeans that symbolized the grit and determination of Motown. Made in southeastern Michigan, Motor City Denim Co. has become one of the hippest denim lines in the country. There's no stopping this white-hot fashion brand, which produces shorts, jackets, hoodies, and accessories.

Like so many of us, Mark D'Andreta, Bo Fishback, and Ashifi Gogo faced a fundamental challenge: reinventing their core product model. Nothing in that model can be off the table when it comes to the process of innovation. The biggest opportunities sometimes demand change at the deepest levels even when that means remaking core areas of your business concept.

Bet Your Assets

Ford Motor Company, the iconic brand of America's automotive industry, was built through visionary leadership and game-changing innovation that helped launch America's twentieth-century industrial boom. But maybe the company's most powerful demonstration of disruptive thinking came in the twenty-first century, when the industry it had helped launch was suffering from its most crushing challenge. To meet that challenge, the company had to put almost everything it had built over its hundred-year history on the line.

In 2006, Ford suffered its worst loss ever: $12.7 billion. Toward the end of that year, the company made a drastic change, hiring the first person outside the Ford family to take the helm of the company.[9] Alan Mulally became the president and CEO and made it his mission to bring the automotive giant back to its former glory. Coming into a situation with uncharted waters, a plethora of finger-pointing and responsibility avoidance, and a history of silos within the organization, Mulally knew that Ford's reinvention would have to extend to the very heart of the business. He started with his direct reports.

Mulally began by establishing what he called the "business plan review," a weekly meeting for senior leadership held on Thursday mornings at 7:00 a.m. sharp. Mulally asked all the executives to come to the first meeting with color-coded reports: green if all was well in their division, yellow if there were any warning signs, and red if something was wrong. When he walked into that inaugural meeting and saw a room full of green reports—from leaders of a failing company that just posted billions of dollars in losses—he challenged the executives to own up to their own failures. It was obvious to Mulally (and to outsiders everywhere) that something had gone dreadfully wrong at Ford. He explained that owning up to failure is the first step toward fixing it and figuring out a better way. From then on, the colors were all mixed up in their weekly meetings, and he knew he had buy-in from the top.[10] Mulally had disrupted the complacency of Ford's leadership. Now he was ready to take on its operations.

Next, Mulally rolled out his vision for "One Ford"—one company, one shared vision, one goal for success, and one path to get there. Mulally understood that everyone had to be working toward the same purpose. He recognized, for example, that a Ford made in North America and Europe has the same target customer, but the company wasn't making those cars with the same components.

Ford's product lines were segmented, and divisional leaders didn't communicate with each other. Not only that, but Ford products felt stale to consumers because they hadn't kept up with drivers' needs—the designs were old and boring, they were lacking modern technology features, and interior styling was bland compared to that of the competition—and they didn't have a common platform.[11]

When Mulally stepped back and looked at Ford in its totality rather than just its individualized segments, he realized that great economies of scale could be leveraged in its product lines. That insight led to a disruption of Ford's core processes and products. As a result, multiple Ford models are now made on the same platform and share a variety of common parts, even when the final products are specialized to meet the needs of individual markets.

Mulally was willing to bet his company's most valuable assets on its reinvention. When he took the helm in 2006, he leveraged all of Ford's assets (including the classic blue emblem) in exchange for a much-needed cash flow. Fast-forward two years later to 2008: Chrysler and General Motors sought (and ultimately received) loans from the federal government, then went on to file for Chapter 11 bankruptcy the next spring.[12] Ford avoided bankruptcy without taking a government loan, making Mulally's assets-mortgaging strategy seem visionary.

That strategy wasn't just about saving face or differentiating Ford from its Big Three brothers. Because Ford had an extra stockpile of cash from the mortgage efforts, Mulally was able to continually invest in new, exciting products. While Chrysler and GM focused on recovering from bankruptcy, Ford's leadership team focused on design and technology. As a result, by 2010, Ford was the world's top automaker in terms of highest customer satisfaction and the fewest number of defects.[13] It also forged new ground with the use of technology. In a partnership with Microsoft, Ford launched an innovative technology solution called Sync. Pushing the boundaries of transportation software, Ford significantly enhanced the driving experience. It took giant leaps forward in embracing technology such as a joint project with Microsoft, Ford Sync. The designs, both internal and external, became significantly more exciting. Furthermore, the company began to embrace better manufacturing practices, which improved both quality and performance. It's no coincidence that the only CEO to deliver two keynotes at the Consumer Electronics Show, the largest annual event of its kind, was not the leader of a software or device company. It was Ford's own creative disruptor, Alan Mulally.

Breaking the grip of leadership complacency; reinventing core products and processes; betting the company's greatest assets on renewed market strength: Mulally's bone-deep reinvention of Ford Motor Company wasn't just about survival. His company in fact thrived in the wake of a recession that rocked businesses and economies around the world. Ford's embrace of disruptive change also helped change the way we think about the American automotive industry, which once seemed the very embodiment of slow-moving, behemoth organizations with more interest in preservation than innovation.

Throughout your career, you will inevitably be faced with an inflection point—which may come disguised as a crushing setback or even an unprecedented success. In every case, you will have a powerful choice to reinvent or stay the course. As Alan Mulally has shown, no product, process, or industry is too complex or deeply entrenched to disrupt. By making the choice to challenge even your most valuable core concepts, you can help to ensure that your organization will grow stronger as a result of innovation rather than being consumed by it.

Find the 10X Factor

When deciding which start-ups to back once we hear their pitches, my partners and I at Detroit Venture Partners ask ourselves, "Does this new solution solve a customer problem ten times better than the current market leader does?" Unless you are bringing a profound improvement to market, going head to head with a giant that has deep resources, a substantial customer base, and market-leading brand equity is a surefire path to doom. To slay those dragons, we advise entrepreneurs that they need something that will truly elicit a

"Wow!" The same applies to reinvention within existing companies: you must aim to be better than the competition's product and your own previous offering by a factor of ten.

To hit that level of superiority, you'll need to do something so compelling, so remarkable, and so brash that it can't be ignored. That's the only way to disrupt the status quo. And you can't achieve 10X factor success without being willing to unseat even your most highly prized product or service and usher in a new superstar to take its place.

When ink-jet printers hit the market, they all did one thing: print. Manufacturers were primarily competing on price and base-level product attributes, such as the speed of printing, print resolution, and the amount of paper the machines could hold. The commodity ink-jet business was in a downward spiral on price until Hewlett-Packard introduced a bold new feature: a printer that also doubled as a fax machine.

Within weeks of the release, there were all the other printers and then there was the multipurpose unit from HP—a bold product innovation that added a significant and high-value feature, making it rise above the noise. Sales—and profits—soared. As the ink-jet printer evolved, it encompassed more and more core utility features. It became a scanner, a copy machine, a photo printer. The manufacturers that focused on incremental change and bolstering the status quo got caught in a never-ending game of commodity price wars, while the innovators, who reinvented the very purpose of their devices, won the contest.

Your customers already have solutions to many things in their lives. They have a car insurance solution, an orange juice solution, and a favorite burger joint solution. Sticking to these familiar patterns is safe and easy. They don't have to think much, which allows them to focus on the zillion other things happening in their lives. As a disruptor, you must offer an exciting reward to entice customers to buy a new digital camera, shun their favorite grocery store, or switch light beers.

For years, pharmacists doled out their goods in the all-too-familiar identical pill bottle: round, amber base, and a white cap. This is a product that nearly every individual in America was using at one time or another, and no one seemed to be thinking about how well it worked. But these generic bottles were leading to problems. Identifying medications through the amber plastic body can be difficult, as can opening the bottles or reading the tiny print on their labels. The Institute of Medicine estimates that there are over 100,000 cases each year in which people are harmed by taking the wrong medication.[14]

This health risk, combined with the bottles' ho-hum style, led design student Deborah Adler to forge new ground. She tackled the redesign as her thesis project, which led to the invention of the ClearRx medication bottle. Adler rejected conventional wisdom and reimagined what a pill bottle could be. She started by literally turning the bottle upside down. Her new bottle is designed to stand on its cap, and the body has a rounded wedge shape that's easy to grip. The flat wedge of the body boasts a large, easy-to-read label with clear lettering and a big, bold font to avoid any confusion. The ClearRx design includes much more visible warning symbols and a small magnifying strip that can be inserted into the side of the bottle for those with troubled vision. Most notable, the bottles contain a color-coded rubber ring; customers can use a different color for each member of their household to help avoid the common mistake of taking someone else's meds.

ClearRx was a top-to-bottom overhaul of a product assumed to be unchangeable. Like most other powerful reinventions, the results were stunning. Target Corporation adopted this design for all its in-store pharmacies. Adler's design also won the prestigious Design of the Decade award from the Industrial Designers Society of America in 2010.

Massoud Hassani is another visionary who was able to leverage a mundane element of his environment to create a truly revolutionary product innovation. Growing up in Kabul, Afghanistan, Hassani was surrounded by mine fields. Land mine accidents occurred with harrowing frequency in his area. Hassani's big product idea didn't come by studying advanced weaponry strategy or reading journals and academic reports about military disarmament. Instead, he found inspiration in nature—tumbleweed, to be exact.

Hassani observed how tumbleweed blew freely in the wind, rolling gently across the ground. This moment of understanding led to the launch of the Mine Kafon ("mine exploder" in his native language). Made of two hundred bamboo rods and plastic feet, this invention rolls across troubled areas, detonating hidden land mines to prevent catastrophic injury. It is heavy enough to trigger the mines, light enough to tumble across suspected mine fields, and flexible enough to withstand multiple blasts per unit.[15]

The extraordinary products launched by Hewlett-Packard, Deborah Adler, and Massoud Hassani were transforming to their business, career, industry, and culture. A copy-cat solution to any of the problems these innovators faced would have barely made a difference. Frankly, the world doesn't need another me-too player or another me-too anything. What the world craves is breakthrough ideas and daring invention. The history books are reserved for people who changed the game, not those who improved margin by 3 percent or reduced defects by .07 percent.

When bringing a new product or service to market, don't lose sight of how much force is needed to shake things up. Your new mobile app that is only slightly better than the market leader isn't going to be enough for you to reach the promised land. It's going to take a sonic boom of innovation to grab attention.

Is your sales pitch 10X better than your competitors'? Is your theater performance 10X stronger than the others auditioning for the same part? Is the software code you just wrote 10X better than last year's version? If you want to remove chance and luck from the reinvention of your organization, explore every option, and then focus on the 10X factor. Even if you hit an unexpected speed bump, your determination to go deep in exploration and innovation will give you the momentum you need to win.

Detroit: Catalyst for Change

Henry Ford didn't invent the concept of the assembly line, but he did use it to change the world. Along the way, he went through some changes of his own as he continually chose to leave behind current successes in pursuit of an even greater future. In 1899, after eight years with the Edison Company, Ford walked away from the offer of a supervisor's job at $1,900 a month to become the owner of his own auto company (monthly salary, about $150).[16] Lacking good investors or competitive strength, the business failed in about a year. Ford's next venture failed too; his investors weren't interested in what they referred to as the "racing cars" he was designing.[17] But his third start-up, the Ford Motor Company, got the product right. Tossing his previous design focus, this time Ford produced a series of automobile models designed to be easy to operate, easy to maintain, and inexpensive. His Model T, introduced in 1908, was hugely successful, representing a revolution in the market for reliable, affordable cars.[18]

The transformative impact of Ford's product innovation wasn't limited to car design and didn't stop at his factory doors. Between 1903 and 1913, his company's increasing use of the assembly line swept away the traditional approach to manufacturing. Ford's development of the assembly line system transformed his business and reshaped industrial processes for manufacturing everything from toasters to vacuum cleaners. Then in 1914, Ford introduced a truly revolutionary change, one that would shake up conventional business wisdom and send ripples throughout the American economy: Ford Motor Company announced that it was going to double its workers' pay to five dollars a day and cut the length of their workday from nine to eight hours.[19]

Pay workers more? Shorten their workday? While it may have looked like a foolish willingness to cannibalize the success of his booming business and tear at the very heart of the American industrial model, Ford's move was a ticket to even greater profit and productivity. Mass production was repetitive, with low pay and long hours, and factories suffered a lot of employee turnover. In 1913, Ford had been forced to hire fifty-two thousand men just to keep the fourteen thousand slots on his assembly lines filled.[20] Ford's new model helped stop the bleed of attrition so he could keep the workers he'd trained. And it effectively folded his workforce into his marketplace. Workers could afford to buy the cars they were making, and they had more free time in which to drive their cars around. Ford also boosted his operation's productivity; the shorter hours enabled him to run three shifts instead of two.[21] Thousands flooded into Detroit in hopes of landing a job in Ford's factory, beginning an industrial and population boom that would take Detroit well into the second half of the century.

Ford's "$5 a Day Revolution" helped speed the development of America's manufacturing core and its strong midcentury middle class.[22] And as more workers bought automobiles, America's networks of roads and bridges expanded to accommodate the country's newly mobile masses. Henry Ford was a bold visionary, brave enough to tear down old successes, learn from defeat, scrap his product model, and forge a new path forward. His example illustrates an important truth about the power of disruptive change: sometimes the best way to see the future is to stand on the ruins of the past.

Tools for Transformation: A Practical Guide to Making Your Product Obsolete

Here are nine simple yet powerful approaches that you can use to springboard your own creativity when working to transform your core product or service. Any one of these tactics can take your exploration for fresh innovation to whole new levels:

1. *Trend spotting.* You don't have to follow trends to benefit from them in your search for core-deep innovations. Macrotrends in our society—an aging population, social media changes, environmental awareness, even dining habits—can open new areas for exploration. How can you incorporate the momentum of these trends in a new way into your line of work? Take a close look at your industry. What changes in consumer preference have emerged? How has legislative reform or new regulation affected your market? What are your customers demanding today that they didn't care about ten years ago? Which companies are moving into the lead, and which have fallen behind? Are new start-ups threatening your industry norms? If so, how are they doing it?

As a practical technique, conduct a brainstorming session with your team that lists out as many macro and industry-specific trends you can identify. Leave them up on the board and mix and match them as you explore where to take your product or service. Through this exercise, you'll quickly find new opportunities for disruption.

2.   *Add a new secret ingredient.* Start with your existing product, and conduct a brainstorming session around a simple question: "What is ONE thing we could add to our product or service to make it really special?" What could take our offering to a rarified level? It could be a new material or ingredient. It could be a new feature or attribute or a new packaging, pricing plan, or design. In this exercise, don't worry about creating a whole new masterpiece. Just keep trying a single addition at a time and evaluate how your customers would experience this spicy new flavor or unexpected attribute.

3.   *Borrow ideas.* The most profound innovations often come to life as a reincarnation, not a purely original thought. Borrowed ideas have been the source of product innovation for centuries. Your creative sparks can easily come from nature, other industries, art, or even science-fiction novels. Instead of being shackled to industry norms, look outside for inspiration, and you may just stumble onto your own mine field of opportunity.

4.   *Your magic wand.* For this exercise, you're best to leave the soul-killing, windowless conference room behind. Find a nontraditional location (outside in nature, art museum, music studio, elementary school classroom), and get ready to let your imagination soar. Start with a completely blank canvas and ask yourself, "If I had a magic wand and could invent the ideal solution to solve my customers' needs, what would it be?" This should be a no-holds-barred approach with total disregard for engineering constraints, costs, restrictions, legality, cannibalization, politics, or any other potential element of friction. Use the "magic wand" of your imagination to envision a radically new solution. If logic and reason start to creep in, zap them away. The objective here is to dream, and dream big. Many of the greatest inventors in history, from Edison to Ford to Jobs, refused to let practicality dilute their most novel ideas. They imagined their ideal solution, and then got to work with their teams to figure out how to implement it. Think like these visionaries. Don't let executional challenges shape your creative process. Imagine first; deliver second.

5.   *Extreme makeover.* Reality TV is loaded with style and design makeovers for people, houses, and even whole families. Today's demanding customers want both function and form, so giving the design of your product a makeover could launch you into a new level of success. What would upgrade your product? A new grip, sexier materials, or more stylish design? If you are in the digital world, could your user interface use

a whole new look? For service providers, what about the paperwork you require or the way you deliver your work product? Beauty may be just skin deep, but your makeover can go much deeper in offering new ways to appeal to your marketplace.

6. *Transform it.* The transformation of one thing into another can also be a powerful source of inspiration with respect to product reinvention. How could your product or service transform into something entirely different? Perhaps it serves a different use or delivers value to a different customer. Or maybe your product's delivery mechanism could be changed into a new format. A good approach is to brainstorm on this question: "If you had to morph your product to serve a completely different need, what could it be?" Perhaps the toothbrush manufactured by your company for decades could become a specialized jewelry cleaner. Or your restaurant could transform into a group meeting space. Perhaps your cupcakes normally sold on grocery shelves could be sold during live cooking demonstrations for VIP customers. Forcing yourself to look at your offerings in a new way can lead to significant innovation and help you discover wide open market opportunities.

7. *Make a bold statement.* When it comes to reinventing your core offering, packaging and presentation offer profound opportunities. Tiffany & Co. is famous for its blue box. That specific shade of blue communicates elegance, high quality, and class. It has been suggested that this consistent and distinctive package drives an additional 25 percent or more to the purchase price of all Tiffany merchandise.[23] Similarly, the sole of every single Christian Louboutin shoe is painted bright red—Pantone 187C to be exact. At up to three thousand dollars a pair, it's obvious that the quality of Louboutin's product is outstanding. But that's not what women buy: it's that alluring red sole that makes Louboutin shoes distinctive. What innovations to your core offering's packaging and presentation could make the kind of bold statement necessary to draw customer attention in a crowded marketplace?

8. *Add a new utility.* A good brainstorming effort is to set a timer for ten minutes and ask your team to use it to come up with as many new major features as possible for your product or service. Go for quantity, and avoid judging ideas as they surface. You'll end up with a long list of new ideas. You will discard many of them quickly after the session. What will remain is a small list of real opportunities to beat the competition. It's time to stop competing on price and start competing on imagination.

9. *Zoom in, zoom out.* Zoom in so close that you'll discover something you've been missing all along. What microcosm has been hiding

right under your nose this whole time? Zooming out is another powerful approach. If you currently cater to one customer base or use with
your product, try zooming out to see if you can create broader appeal.
Facebook started as a student-only effort and then expanded to serve a
mass audience (1 billion and counting). This same pattern can help you
uncover fresh opportunity; new fish are always waiting to bite, but your
hook needs to be in the water.

CHAPTER 4

Retool Your Operations

*You can never cross the ocean until you have the courage
to lose sight of the shore.*

—CHRISTOPHER COLUMBUS

At the peak of their success in 2011, with a record $30 billion in loan origination, the top twenty-five leaders of Quicken Loans gathered for an urgent two-day, all-hands-on-deck off-site meeting. Mobile phones were silenced. All other meetings were cancelled. This was a critical session in the company's evolution.

Most companies have meetings with this level of importance when things have gone very, very wrong: preparing for massive layoffs or facilitating damage control when the stock price tanks, for example. But this was a different kind of meeting. The leaders had cleared their busy schedules and gathered for one reason: to reinvent the company. Again.

The urgency for reinvention at Quicken Loans wasn't driven by setbacks, impending regulatory changes, or competitive threats. Instead, it came from the realization that successful reinvention can make a far bigger impact when it springs from a position of strength rather than when it struggles to come from behind. Finishing their most profitable year in the company's twenty-five-year history, the bold leaders of Quicken Loans set out to challenge every assumption: to aggressively explore the possibilities, let go of what *was* in favor of what *could be*, put themselves "out of business."

At that high-stakes meeting in late 2011, the leaders of this fast-moving company brainstormed how to apply technology to serve customers better. They unleashed their imaginations, discussing everything from mobile apps, social media, and webinars to text notices. Fueled by an ongoing commitment to disruptive change, they worked tirelessly to reinvent the Quicken Loans operation and, in the process, begin an entirely new chapter in the company's journey.

The following year, Quicken Loans racked up over $70 billion in closed loans, representing over 130 percent growth in just twelve months. Then in 2013, Quicken Loans made another gigantic leap forward as the company surpassed the $100 billion mark.

This hockey stick trajectory—and the company's prior success—had absolutely nothing to do with a transformation of the Quicken Loans product: mortgages are a commodity. It never was seduced into offering bizarre mortgage products during the go-go days leading up to the financial meltdown and simply continued to offer and sell traditional mortgages. But this company sells more of them online than any other company, and it is light years more efficient than any competitor.

What Quicken Loans does better than any competitor is reinvention—the ongoing process of transforming the way it does business. One of the company's publicly stated philosophies is "being obsessed with finding a better way." Realizing that they can't apply their creativity to the product itself, Quicken Loans leaders and teams push all their innovative efforts toward improving their operational processes. By the end of 2013, the company had won the highly coveted and independently ranked JD Power & Associates award for "highest in customer satisfaction for primary mortgage origination" for an unprecedented four years in a row.

Reinvention has been the lifeblood of Quicken Loans since its humble beginnings in a suburb of Detroit. Founder Dan Gilbert launched the small firm with the five thousand dollars he had saved from delivering pizzas and began selling mortgages in the traditional way. Dan wasn't content as just another player in an already crowded pack, however. He wanted to change the mortgage industry. After a decade of strong but unremarkable growth, he pioneered a radically new concept: online mortgage sales.

Gilbert's idea was an astonishingly new one in the mid-1990s, when the Internet was uncharted territory. To complicate things, every county in all fifty states had complex and differing regulations. Dan's vision of a centralized and highly efficient origination and processing center that served the entire country through the Web was wild, fanciful, and crazy, which is exactly why it was so incredibly successful.

"Mortgage in a Box," the company's original effort to move documentation and processing online, was a transformative leap forward in the mortgage industry and marked Quicken Loans' first major reinvention of the mortgage process. Once perfected, this concept rocketed the company to new levels of success.

In early 2003, Dan had another game-changing insight: a pilot wouldn't be expected to rebuild the plane while flying it. He realized that team members with direct line responsibility were busy delivering and couldn't be expected to holistically reinvent at the same time. He also realized that the skills needed for process engineering can be markedly different from those required on the front lines of business development, sales, underwriting, or marketing. So Gilbert launched the "mousetrap team," which had no direct production responsibility and was charged solely with "building a better mousetrap." This group examined and reexamined every process, big and small. It listened to feedback from those in the field and evaluated how to make effective change. Manifesting the company's obsession with finding a better way, the mousetrap team drove the company to new levels of efficiency, growth, and client satisfaction through better operational systems. When you ask Dan what he'd do differently if he were to start a new company today, he replies, "I'd start with two people: a CEO and a mousetrap leader [head of process engineering]." He links the ability to scale with a company's proficiency in developing fluid systems and processes that enable operating leverage and efficiency.

With this obsession on process, Dan had a great run—until, of course, the bottom fell out of the economy and mortgage bankers came to rank alongside violent criminals as objects of general repulsion. In 2007, the industry was in free fall. Capital markets slammed shut, and major financial institutions crumbled. Quicken Loans was in a battle for survival, as was most of Wall Street. As Dan Gilbert found himself in the prizefight of his life, his salvation rested with another process reinvention.

With ferocious urgency, the leaders of Quicken Loans leaped into action. They conducted a thorough investigation of the entire company, looking under every rock and challenging every assumption. Their work paid off as they redesigned the business from top to bottom—again. They employed new technology to automatically route inbound leads to the salespeople who would be most likely to close them. This process adjustment made the return on investment of purchased leads significantly higher. The company doubled down on business intelligence to bring in the kind of microscopic details necessary for making fast, sound decisions. The company's leaders challenged every assumption. They changed everything from the way they sourced leads to how they served customers. And as the rest of the mortgage industry crumbled, Quicken Loans' massive operational reinvention allowed them to weather the storm and emerge as the dominant player in the field.

We've seen how product and service reinvention can transform an organization, but the opportunities for disruptive change don't end there. Just as Quicken Loans crushed its competition with zero product innovation, you have the ability to drive your own organization forward through an overhaul of your processes, systems, procedures, rules, and approaches. You can win by reinventing the way you do your work even if the business itself remains unchanged.

Clear Away Cannonballs

Your efforts to rethink the way you do business will likely be met with resistance. There are probably people in your organization who are fiercely committed to protecting the status quo. You'll need to make the case for change, but it is easier to do that once you have a proposed solution. Asking people to let go of their current operational bedrock and move on to a complete unknown is not an easy sell. Once you have a concrete plan to propose, it becomes much easier to convince others to join the movement.

Of course, any bureaucrats who have burrowed their way into your company will have a vested interest in resisting change. These folks often rely on creating and maintaining complex processes to justify their own existence and feel important. Their arguments for sticking with outdated, unfriendly traditions may be weak, but they still can dampen your organization's innovative fire and weaken its position in the market. To identify the sources of stagnation in your organization, you'll need to ignore such rationalizations and examine every aspect of its operation.

To begin the process of reinventing the way you do business, take a look at your operation's most deeply held traditions. As you might imagine, the US military is the mother lode of outdated traditions. One of my favorites is the requirement that three men are needed to fire a cannon. According to the detailed military operations manual, one soldier holds the cannon, one loads the ammunition, and the other literally just stands there. Sounds wasteful, right? Originally the third man's job was to hold the horse so that it wasn't spooked by the sound of the cannon's explosion. Of course, when the manual was written, you had to have a horse pull a cannon to the top of a hill. That meant that you also needed someone to stand there and hold the reins so the horse couldn't run away when the two others started firing the big gun. This made total sense for maybe the first two centuries or so of our military history, but do we really still need *three* soldiers to fire a cannon successfully? Presumably the person with no active role may have some ceremonial or backup value, but in reality it is a total waste of resources.

With that, let's define a new noun for the reinventing vocabulary: *cannonball*. This could be a system, process, or way of doing business that made all the sense in the world at one point but today is a relic. What are the cannonballs in your organization? What do you do as a matter of routine that could be radically improved by taking a fresh look? In sharp contrast to the typical tradition-bound military leader is Commander Michael Abrashoff. In 1997, Abrashoff took command of the $1 billion warship the USS *Benfold*, becoming the youngest leader to assume such a post. The honeymoon was short-lived, however, when he realized what he had inherited: the worst-performing US Navy ship in the Pacific Fleet. Morale was perilously low, expenses were high, safety was abysmal, and the ship held low scores in nearly every measurable category. Within one year, Abrashoff had transformed the operation to rank as the top-performing ship in the region. He did it with the same crew, no additional funding (he actually came in significantly under budget), and no new technology advances. Abrashoff attributes his success to reinventing the way the crew members approached their work. "Why spend time doing the $10 per hour work, when you can be doing $100 per hour work?" he challenged. Accordingly, he grouped each of the thousands of tasks on the ship into two categories: non-value-added chores and mission-critical work. It was a great area to start on the ship and is a great area for you to start in your own organization.

A key part of Abrashoff's strategy was to listen carefully to what the people doing the actual work had to say. One of the biggest low-value time drains was the constant painting and repainting of the vessel. Saltwater was taking a heavy toll on the metal ship, making the ship's appearance abysmal. Since a disheveled presentation isn't acceptable, the crew spent eight months each year in painting mode, at a cost of several hundred thousand dollars. Much of the rust and cracking came from the bolts and fasteners that corroded and then tarnished the paint. Once Abrashoff made it clear that he was truly open to new ideas and wanted the input of the crew, one sailor came forward with a simple solution: use stainless steel fasteners instead of the standard-issue material that was used on every ship in the US fleet. The bolt replacement cost under twenty-five thousand dollars, which resulted in savings of more than ten times that amount each year, not to mention the countless hours of non-value-added work that the crew had performed over and over again. Once central command heard of this improvement, it ordered the change on every Navy ship.[1]

This idea would have never surfaced in a typical command-and-control culture. The Navy in fact had previously accepted the rust as part of ship life, but the courage of a young commander to challenge conventional wisdom led to a simple improvement that today saves taxpayers millions. Dozens of other process improvements of this nature led to Abrashoff's success. The same holds true for you. The answers are often not hard to craft if you simply ask the right questions. Taking a careful look at every aspect of your operation and exploring areas for improvement in your model will help you reinvent your business and gain competitive advantage.

The Beauty of Forest Fires

There are few things in nature as powerful as a forest fire. Once they gain momentum, these vicious fires can consume hundreds, even thousands, of square miles, leaving behind a trail of destruction and scorched earth—not a symbol of beauty. Yet I see magic in what can be an act of tragedy. Forest fires are an important part of nature and serve a critical purpose. They clear out the old, making way for the new. They reset the conditions so new life can form, often removing previously restrictive limitations. This process begins in a difficult way. The charred land takes a long time to heal—sometimes generations. But in this process, the forest gets a fresh start.

A new, picturesque plant species is able to thrive since it no longer competes for sun with the previously tall, dead trees that hoarded the light. A new redwood is able to climb majestically to the sky because room has been made for its roots to expand. Although forest fires are painful in the moment and for some time after they've run their course, they are a vital aspect of evolution. This applies not only to nature but also to your company, career, and community.

Often the biggest impediment to success is the stubborn overgrowth of the past: restrictive rules or polices that long ago ran their course, leaders who cling to the days gone by and are ill equipped to lead into the future; mature products and services that consume company attention and resources that often linger, starving out fresh, more innovative ideas in the process.

While I don't suggest setting your building ablaze, it is critical for leaders to break free from the shackles of the past. We can't get on with the hard work of creating if we are chained to yesterday's priorities.

Establish what "dead trees" are hanging on in your organization. In a forest fire, these are the first to burn because their dry, airy wood crackles and pops and is ablaze in an instant. When these processes are removed, the way is clear for new ideas, akin to their forestry counterparts. Once your team has made the often difficult decision to make room for new life, it's time to focus squarely on using your new, fertile soil to plant the seeds of your future.

Reinvent Your Market's Model

Many people shy away from the idea of making large creative leaps because the competition seems unbeatable. "Sure, someone can break new ground on a mobile app," the logic goes, "but not in *my* industry. I'm up against deeply entrenched competitors and complex supply chains. I can only hope for small, incremental advances."

Tell that to Michael Dubin, founder and CEO of Dollar Shave Club. His idea was to shake up the mature world of razor blades, a daunting task. To the horror of his friends and family, he decided to take Gillette head-on. Calling Gillette a "market leader" is an understatement. The company enjoys a 70 percent market share, has hundreds of millions to spend on advertising, and has locked in shelf space at every retailer from Akron to Zurich. How can someone possibly take on a giant of this magnitude and expect to live through even the first round?

Mike's approach was to leverage his background as a stand-up comic. He launched a hilarious and engaging video introducing his company. The video was edgy, irreverent, and sarcastic. It did a stunning job of communicating his value proposition in a way that was both easy to understand and could not be ignored.

While Mike's deadpan comedic delivery was effective, the way Dollar Shave Club's process worked for customers was even more compelling. In the video, Mike described his concept for a subscription-based service that mails out low-cost (but high-quality) blades each month to its customers. "Stop forgetting to buy your blades each month, and start deciding where you're going to stack all those dollar bills I'm saving you," Mike taunts in the video. The combination of convenience and cost savings with a fun, humorous approach was an instant hit. One week after the video was launched, over 3 million people around the world had seen it, and Mike had landed over seventeen thousand paying customers. Out of the gate, Mike had launched a $60 million-a-year business, in a mature industry, with a deeply entrenched market leader, at a tiny price point, and with absolutely no product innovation.

The video cost only four thousand dollars to produce, and the company spent zero on advertising.[2] The message was compelling and his model unique; consumers lined up to buy it.

Mike did a number of things to make Dollar Shave Club one of the most successful launches in history. First, he'd sidestepped the manufacturing process by sourcing high-quality, off-brand razors that are easy to produce. From an operational standpoint, this innovative idea was critical: it allowed Mike's company to be much leaner and avoid all the heavy lifting that comes with a factory. Next, he disrupted the supply chain by selling direct to customers over the Internet. He borrowed a low-cost subscription model from Netflix and began offering his monthly razor blade subscription service for as low as one dollar per month. With that process shift, Mike no longer needed a wholesale middle man; he was able to make more money per sale by selling directly.

Naturally you'll probably prefer the Dollar Shave Club's plan that offers better blades for nine dollars each month, driving Mike's average price point higher than a buck. You never run out, blades are shipped right to you, and you save up to three hundred dollars per year. This is crystal-clear value to customers.

Mike's subscription model also meant that he had to sell the customer once, not on a continuous basis the way competitors Gillette and Schick did. Those monthly shipments also afforded him the chance for ongoing communication directly with his customers. He cut costs out of the system at each step of the way, from sourcing to direct selling to advertising, allowing him to deliver higher value to customers while enjoying industry-smashing margins.

Mike sent shock waves through the old-school mature commodity business of razor blades. And he did it with no marketing budget, no salespeople, no distributors, no retail stores, no trade promotion, no supermodels, no TV commercials. His main weapon was market model innovation. His willingness to shatter conventional wisdom allowed him to reinvent a traditional industry from the ground up by doing things in a different way, even with an otherwise identical product.

Innovate Your Operation

How did Toyota surpass GM to become the world's largest car company? How did Dell beat IBM in the computer industry? How could Walmart, a small retailer from Bentonville, Arkansas, not only best rivals Sears and Kmart but go on to become the largest corporation in the world?

It wasn't product innovation, slick advertising, or rock-star executives. It was a commitment to *operational innovation*. The term, coined by Boston-based management consultant Michael Hammer, goes far beyond operational improvement or operational excellence, which refer to making an existing process better (more efficient, less defects, and so on). Operational innovation is the concept of completely overhauling the way a company does business in an effort to create a significant competitive advantage. It in essence rewrites the rules of the game.

Most CEOs don't focus on operational innovation, partly because it lacks the sexiness and glamour of product invention. Marketing, sales, and new products have a sizzle, while operations feel less exciting. This is part of the reason that less than 10 percent of large organizations have made a serious effort at reengineering the way they do business.[3]

It might be less sexy than closing a deal or launching a new product line, but the proof is in the punch. For a classic example, Walmart went from $44 million to $44 billion in revenue over a twenty-year period. One of the drivers of this incredible success was reinventing the way it managed inventory. Traditional retailers took delivery from suppliers, stored the inventory in a warehouse, and then held it in stock until stores needed the goods. In a brilliant act of operational innovation, Walmart invented a concept called cross-docking, where products on trucks from suppliers were loaded directly onto trucks heading for stores, thereby completely eliminating the expense of storing and managing inventory. Lower inventory levels and lower operational costs allowed Walmart to pass the savings on to consumers, driving the giant's incredible success.

Operational innovation works especially well in businesses that are based on commodities such as insurance, mortgages, banking, and office supplies. If you are struggling to innovate the product or service you offer, operational innovation can be your playground for creative expression. Here is a quick and practical five-step process to kick off your operational innovation efforts:

1. *Make the case for change.* It's impossible to let go of something without reason. Be sure to detail both the opportunity and upside that can be seized through a successful change effort and also articulate the true cost of standing still (which is too often underestimated).

2. *Set an audacious goal.* If you seek to improve productivity by 1.2 percent or decrease errors by .6 percent, your mind will lead you to incremental solutions. Challenge yourself and your team to solve bigger problems, and you will uncover bigger innovations. How would you retool your model if you had to improve productivity by 140 percent? Triple sales in twelve months? Reduce costs by 80 percent? The harder your push is, the better ideas you'll generate.

3. *Do a friction audit.* Carefully examine each step of your processes and the way you do business to find all the sticking points. Where are the bottlenecks? What steps could be shortened? Where are costs that could be removed through a better model? Find the pain points, and you'll know where to direct your creativity.

4. *Bypass "who" for "what."* Disruptive changes can be threatening to the established guard. As old ideas are discarded, egos can get

bruised. Set the tone from the start that the mission is all about the "what": finding a better solution and driving the business forward. It isn't about "who": whose idea, who will be upset, or who has the biggest title. Make sure everyone is focused on doing what's in the best interest of the collective good instead of protecting individual fiefdoms.

5. *Borrow ideas from other industries.* Dell borrowed Walmart's cross-docking principle to reduce overhead and produce custom-made computers more quickly and efficiently. If you've ever enjoyed a Subway sandwich, you'll notice how the assembly-line approach applies to the quick service restaurant category. Disrupting your industry probably won't require a lightning bolt from above. Instead, look for creative approaches to similar problems in other industries and explore the idea of applying the same strategy to your own endeavors.

As the founder and CEO of Motown Records, you would expect Berry Gordy to be creative. In addition to having an eye for talent, he was a songwriter and musician, even playing piano on the 1960 hit "Shop Around" by the Miracles. His studio cranked out 163 singles that hit the Top 20 chart, with 28 of them reaching number one between 1961 and 1971. But his real genius transcended the music itself.[4]

Gordy reimagined what a studio could be. While most record labels had studios for recording only, Motown built an entirely new model. He constructed a nine-building campus at the headquarters in Detroit. It was essentially a multistep factory, taking in the raw material of human talent on one end and stamping out hits and stars on the other. It's no surprise that Gordy placed a large sign out front that's still there today, proclaiming the complex as Hitsville, USA.

Artists progressed from one building to the next with assembly-line efficiency. One building was designated for teaching emerging stars about music publishing, and another helped them with record promotion. There were buildings that contained a booking agency, a rehearsal hall, and a training center for teaching artists flashy, crowd-pleasing dance routines. Classes were offered in everything from

costuming to stage production, from media relations to musical eti-
quette. The idea of a full development process to capitalize on raw
talent to produce a string of superstars was unheard of in the day.
Gordy's radical approach to operations helped launch the careers of
Stevie Wonder, the Supremes, Smokey Robinson, the Four Tops,
the Temptations, Aretha Franklin, and dozens more. He expanded
his operational process far beyond recording and promoting existing acts. By systematizing the approach, he built the entertainers up
from scratch through efficiency and scale.

Gordy challenged core beliefs and figured out how to get the
job done in groundbreaking ways. His scrappiness is inspiring. Think
about the way you do business from a perspective like Gordy's, and
you'll be quicker to see the possibilities for fundamental process
innovation.

Flipping some or all of a model upside down has triggered
many operational innovations. These reinventions from within have
propelled companies from pimply-faced adolescence to the status of
Greek gods. For example, Costco doesn't make money by marking up
the products it sells. Instead, it flipped the model most retailers use
to make the majority of profits from membership fees, allowing it to
deliver goods and services at far lower prices than traditional retailers.

Model Inversion

To tinker with your own operational model inversion, follow this basic
formula:

Instead of _____ [the traditional approach, what the
rest of the industry does, what you've been doing to date], let's flip
the model and do this:_____ [often the polar opposite].

At age sixteen, Vanessa Van Petten, a teenager who was often
in trouble, noticed her parents bought a slew of parenting advice
books to deal with her challenges. One day while being grounded
(a frequent occurrence for Vanessa), she browsed through a few of
the books and noticed a problem: the advice was written by parents

with no input from teenagers, and the tips often completely missed the mark of addressing the real issues facing teens. She did her own model inversion by writing a parenting advice book from the perspective of teens: *You're Grounded: How to Stop Fighting and Make the Teenage Years Easier.*[5] Unlike the countless other books on parenting, this one offered the perspective and context that the traditional how-to books lacked. The book was so popular that Vanessa later launched a website, RadicalParenting.com, on which parents can pose questions to a large group of teenagers who are willing to provide advice instead of the other way around. Let's plug Vanessa's approach into our formula:

Instead of <u>out-of-touch parenting advice from parents</u>, let's flip the model and do this: <u>offer valuable advice about teenagers directly from teens</u>.

Long before Van Petten began her divergent thinking, another teenager was inverting models, and for just about everything. This student was in physics class taking a test. The final question on the test was, "Given a barometer, how would you measure the height of this building?" The usual answer for this is to go to the first floor, note the pressure, go to the roof, note the pressure, and run the data through an equation. However, this student took a different approach. His answer: "I'd go ask the building manager."

The student aced the quiz, except for that final question. He went up to the teacher and asked why it was marked incorrectly. Rather than reply, the teacher decided to give him another chance at the question. The student's response this time around was, "I'd trade the barometer for rope, drop the rope off the roof, and measure the distance."

Once again, the teacher marked his answer incorrect. This time when the student approached the teacher, the teacher told him, "You have a barometer for a reason. Use the barometer!" The student replied, "Fine. I'd drop the barometer off the roof, count the time it takes to hit the ground, then use Newton's law of falling bodies to determine the distance."

Despite annoying the teacher, that student ended up becoming one of the greatest inventors of all time, Nikola Tesla. He is credited for inventing alternating current (AC) electricity, and one of his patents led to the invention of the radio.

As you pursue operational reinvention, you'll undoubtedly face the challenge of figuring something out, that is, finding a new or better way of accomplishing a task that has long been solved and now performed by rote memorization. Sure, there are the obvious answers, but often the most elegant and compelling solutions are the least instinctive. Divergent thinking—approaching problems from a radically nontraditional perspective—has led to many of civilization's most important breakthroughs.

The next time you are charged with solving a problem, take a minute to explore unusual approaches before diving in. Could you solve it backward? What is the exact opposite approach to what you're doing today? How would someone from 400 B.C. try to solve it? What about someone from five hundred years in the future?

Never Let Processes Grow Stale

Reinvention is hard work for anyone. It's difficult to reinvent your fifty-person title insurance company or your sixteen-person hair salon. But think how daunting the reinvention challenge is for a company with nearly 400,000 people, $53 billion in revenue, and a one-hundred-year old legacy. Welcome to the executive suite at UPS.[6]

UPS is a story of nearly constant reinvention throughout the company's rise from a bicycle messenger service in Seattle to its position as one of the largest and most powerful corporations in the world. Founder Jim Casey was a maverick entrepreneur who was willing to challenge the most firmly held traditional beliefs about the way business was done. His first leap into uncharted waters was to convince retailers to outsource their individual delivery function to UPS. This was at a time when retailers had their own trucks, and the thought of products being delivered on the same truck as those of competitors was abhorrent. Casey didn't change the product (delivery), but he used sophisticated, shared processes to provide delivery service more efficiently and at a lower cost than retailers could do on their own.

Years later, CEO Jim Kelly continued to embrace the philosophy of process innovation when he took over the helm in 1997. His challenge was especially daunting because the company's extraordinary operational excellence had forged a rigid culture. As an example, the operating manual for drivers was called *340 Methods* and contained instructions for nearly every imaginable behavior, including how to carry one's keys and how many steps per second were required. Kelly had to give his global workforce permission to think on their own and help reinvent the gigantic organization if they were to maintain consistent growth. Mike Eskew, who took over after Kelly retired, described it this way: "He taught us the importance of keeping one eye on the horizon while the other stays focused on the steering wheel."

Kelly delivered a net profit growth rate of 22 percent per year during his five-year tenure. While he certainly expanded the core business, much of the growth came from reimagining how UPS could serve customers in new ways. The expansion began when Kelly and his team restated their mission. They expanded their view of themselves beyond a package delivery company into an organization that enabled global commerce. To do that, they realized it wasn't just about moving goods; it expanded into moving money and information. This insight led to the launch of UPS Logistics, one of the fastest-growing and most profitable divisions. Kelly realized the company had incredible expertise in logistics for its own business, so he decided to offer this as a service to others.

Kelly set forth audacious goals for UPS. Company leadership executed accordingly, making these goals reality. Each of these new divisions reinvented, for the better, the operational force behind UPS.

At its core, UPS delivers stuff. The company's success lies not in the actual service but in the way it has continuously been able to transform the way this service is performed, choreographed, and managed. The executives' artistic masterpiece has been focused on continuously reinventing the way they do their job. With earning over $800 million in net profit in 2012, the company strategy continues to "deliver."[7]

You may think art encompasses only painting, music, or interpretive dance. While those are certainly forms of artistic expression, so too is crafting a gorgeous manufacturing flow or a poetic logistics plan. The *Oxford Dictionary* defines art as "the expression or application of human creative skill and imagination."[8] No matter what title your business card may reflect, you must also embrace an unwritten role as well: business artist. Even if you can barely draw a stick figure, you can use your organization as a canvas for creative expression. The way you do business should be a fluid and constantly changing work of art—one that adapts and evolves with both external and internal change. Here's your chance to leave your fingerprints on the organization. You need not be in the C-suite, marketing group, or R&D department to have the opportunity to create art. Use the proverbial paints at your disposal, and work with conviction to create your masterpiece.

Detroit: Catalyst for Change

When the United States declared war on Japan in December 1941, Americans everywhere seemed willing to step up and do whatever was necessary to win the war. But that patriotic fever grew a bit chilly in the Motor City when, in January 1942, the Office of Price Administration (OPA) informed Detroit factories that they had to stop making cars and retool their operations for military production.[9] The date the OPA mandated for the switchover to be completed was February 1. In other words, the city had just one month to dismantle its chief industry and retool for new work. As the factories retooled their assembly lines, 250,000 autoworkers in Detroit were laid off.[10]

United Auto Workers (UAW) president R. J. Thomas claimed that the UAW had been encouraging the auto industry to begin gradually retooling for war production for some time. But 1941 had been a great year in the auto industry, and many factory owners had been reluctant to do anything that would cut into their production.[11]

Once again, the Ford Motor Company was ahead of the curve. It had begun constructing a bomber plant near the Detroit suburb of Willow Run in April 1941. By the time the OPA's retooling order came down, Ford had already amped up its hiring to fill the facility, but it had some more retooling to do.

With eighty-three acres under one roof, Willow Run had a lot of jobs to fill, but it was also twenty miles outside the Detroit city limits. It wasn't the only Detroit auto manufacturer to move facilities out to the suburbs; Hudson, Chrysler, and other firms had suburban factories too, and none of them were surrounded by ample supplies of affordable housing. With wartime tire and gasoline rationing, no new cars entering the market, and little in the way of available public transportation, these areas were hard-pressed to accommodate workers.[12] At Willow Run, factory workers who commuted from Detroit slept in their cars, pitched tents, or constructed wooden shanties on the grounds—none of which provided a great resting place for the men and women putting in long days building the military's B24 bombers. Eventually the Public Housing Administration stepped in to help solve the problem, constructing a village of dormitories near the factory grounds. By 1943, Willow Run Village housed almost fifteen thousand workers.[13]

The entire nation was called to sacrifice during World War II, but Detroit's contributions to the war effort can't be overstated. Retooling and reinvention in that effort extended well beyond the factory floors. Car dealerships had to either close or rely solely on their repair services (which increased because people had to keep their old cars running), and their salesmen had to pick up a wrench and get under the hood. Women stepped in to fill jobs in factory work, construction, and other previously male-dominated fields. In fact, one of Willow Run's workers, Rose Monroe, brought a human face to the nation's determination to meet any challenge when she was featured in the Rosie the Riveter poster.[14] Sleeves rolled up, she stares fiercely at the viewer over her flexed bicep, under the bold message, "We Can Do It!"

The spirit in that poster is alive and thriving in Detroit, as the city has once again stepped up to the challenge of retooling in the wake of its 2013 bankruptcy filing. We have some weighty issues to wrestle with, but we're gearing up for the fight. Rebuilding our economy, revitalizing our downtown, reinventing our neighborhoods, reshaping our infrastructure—these are just some of the ways Detroit is retooling to build a better future. Whether it involves an entire city or a single operation, retooling is a big task, but it offers big rewards. As history has shown, we Detroiters can do it.

Tools for Transformation: Fire the Cannon

A good way to begin your own process overhaul is to conduct a brainstorming exercise as to your organization's cannonballs.

Assemble a small team, tell the story of the cannonball, and set a timer for ten minutes. The objective is to identify as many cannonballs as possible within the limited time frame. No judging, finger pointing, or criticism of the past is allowed; the exercise is to help move the organization forward, not to cast blame on previous leaders. Simply go for quantity and don't worry at all about fixing these yet. That will come later. Let the group know that there are no wrong answers and that it's great to list any cannonball, big or small.

At the end of this exercise, you will have a list displaying a wide range of areas that can be attacked and improved. Human nature is to get comfortable with the way we work, so this exercise will force you to disrupt your current thinking and raise your awareness of what needs to be fixed.

CHAPTER 5

Create Vivid Experiences

*I've learned that people will forget what you said,
people will forget what you did, but people will never
forget how you made them feel.*

—MAYA ANGELOU

As I walked through the heavy glass doors of the Wynn Las Vegas, I was immediately in a state of sensory delight. Gorgeous, colorful mosaic tile floors shimmered in the perfectly crafted lighting as I breathed in the vanilla-scented air. I could faintly hear sounds of live jazz over the buzz of the slot machines and casino action. This lovely array of sights, sounds, and smells enveloped me. *This* was the good life manifested. I took a seat in a beautifully designed lounge, sank into a luxurious chair, and sipped on the finest martini I've ever had. I sat back and smiled, relishing in the genius of Steve Wynn, the patriarch of modern Vegas.

Billionaire Steve Wynn made his mark not by changing the basics of casino gaming but by reinventing the experience around them. His 1989 launch of the Mirage on the Vegas strip rang in a new era—the age of the experiential casino-hotel. He went on to launch a string of successful properties, including Treasure Island, the Bellagio, the Wynn, and Encore. Each new resort launched at jaw-dropping price tags. Although he's horrible at cost control and lacks operational sternness, Steve Wynn meticulously designs even the tiniest detail as it relates to customer experience. He does this better than anyone else, and it's what has made him an icon in his industry.

While building the Bellagio, Wynn insisted on removing the off-putting security bars around the cashiers who had vast sums of cash and chips before them. He was the first casino owner to implement this change, realizing that although the cage may deter some would-be criminals, it also created an unfriendly barrier to customers. Thousands of similar decisions cascaded together to create one of the most illustrious properties in history. Every decision of building materials, layout, color palate, art, and furnishings was sent through Wynn's mercurial filter. Whenever there was a tough call between saving money and creating an extraordinary customer experience, Wynn opted for the latter, much to the concern of his investors and partners. Despite anxiety-inducing cost overruns, the Bellagio became one of the most profitable casino-hotels in the world, with net non-gaming operating profit exceeding over $1 million per day in 2009.

One month after selling the Bellagio, Mirage, and Treasure Island to MGM, Wynn set out to craft an even richer experience. Wynn Las Vegas opened on April 28, 2005, as the most expensive per-square-foot property of its kind: its whopping price tag was $2.7 billion. The launch included many firsts, including the first on-property car dealership (Ferrari-Maserati), the first room key that also serves as a casino frequent-player card, and a waterfall that combines with an HD projection system to show evocative images on the falling water.

With the opening of his dramatic and bold casinos, Wynn set a new standard, and copycats such as the Venetian, Paris, Mandalay Bay, and Aria followed suit. Wynn changed the ante to play and created billions of dollars of wealth in the process. His reinvention was not of the casino product; his artistry fell squarely in the experiences he imagined. Wynn believes continuous reinvention is a key job of leaders, and says knowledgeably that "what would have drawn a 'wow' fifteen years ago won't draw a yawn today."

The experience you create for customers is a key area for your business to implement reinvention. If your product or service is unchangeable and you've already optimized the way you do business, the experience is another powerful playground for creativity and reinvention. While others are vying for a fancier product package, you can compete in an area that will have dramatic impact on your business.

The Five Senses Test

A good starting point is to experience your offering from your customer's perspective—not just the product or service itself but every touch point surrounding it. Let's say you run a karate studio. The experience you must craft goes far beyond instruction on kicking and punching. To craft an ideal and competitively stronger experience, you need to examine the details of your whole company's interaction with each customer's five senses.

In your karate studio, what do students experience on entering? What does it smell like? Look like? Sound like? Are these elements happening by chance, or have you and your team carefully crafted them? How does the material of the safety mats feel on your customers' bare feet? What temperature will promote the best possible workout? Are the refreshment drinks served cold or tepid? Is paint peeling off haggard walls, or are they covered with inspiring images to motivate and retain your clients?

I highly recommend a five-senses experience audit. Take a look at each possible customer experience and deeply examine the sensory experience you deliver. In the karate example, there are a number of touch points that must be explored: the initial customer inquiry phone call, the sign-up meeting, the first lesson, the first group lesson, the breaks, the ongoing correspondence, the billing process, the after-workout experience, the website, the equipment ordered, and more. Once you establish a similar list of touch points for your own business, do a compare-and-contrast exercise illuminating the differences between your current state and ideal future state.

A quick brainstorming session can yield ideas that cost very little but make a big impact with your customers and help you easily best your competition. What if iced towels were provided at the conclusion of each training session? What if traditional Chinese music played in the background to create a mood and inspire students? What if each session began with a story showcasing an example of how martial arts made an impact in someone's life? Rather than offering ho-hum service, you have an opportunity to dazzle your customers by connecting to their senses and emotions. With business competition fiercer than ever before, creating unique experiences can drive loyalty, retention, referrals, and profits. Only 37 percent of brands received good or excellent customer experience index scores this year, so a few quick, inexpensive changes can immediately catapult you to the top third in your field without much effort or investment.[1]

Make Wishes Come True

Disney is known for creating magic moments. A visit to one of its eleven theme parks will give you a warm, safe, fun, nostalgic experience. You'll smile, be surprised, and of course will happily spend whatever it costs for a bag of Goofy popcorn or a Snow White Slush. And if *you're* enjoying it, your kids are on cloud nine. This is not an accident. Like Steve Wynn, the folks at Disney take great pride in making sure each of the senses is delighted as customers interact with the parks and the Disney brand. As a result, the parks hosted over 120 million guests in 2012, generating over $12.6 billion of revenue.[2] Makes me wish other industries would follow suit.

Doug Dietz is the lead designer of magnetic resonance imaging and computed tomography machines for GE and has been in the field for over twenty years. He's saved countless lives and made a lasting impact on health care, but Dietz was plagued with a problem: despite the life-saving nature of his work, kids were scared to death of these monstrous contraptions. It was unusual for a kid not to break down in tears before entering, and nearly 70 percent required sedation in order to undergo this critical diagnostic procedure.

Dietz struggled to make the machine more open and less scary, but major changes to the machine itself would limit its efficacy. He tried making the opening larger and shortening the cycle time, but

none of these obvious solutions delivered the important medical results that were required. He hit that roadblock we all face.
But then, he decided it was time to think about the problem in a
different way. Rather than changing the machine itself, he decided
to change the experience surrounding the tube. He transformed
the scary situation into one of fun, whimsy, and adventure. For the
frightened kids, Dietz transformed the intimidating machine into
Pirate Island.

The machine and room were redecorated to resemble a pirate
adventure instead of cold, scary hospital equipment. The gurney
became a deck aboard a ship, headed toward the wooden steering
wheel, while the unit floated above waves, under billowing sails, and
across the high seas.

In addition to the design, the hospital staff changed their
approach. Now kids were going on a sailing adventure and were told
to stay very still to hide from the pirates; otherwise, they'd sail by
and tickle them. Crying and screaming ended, sedation stopped, and
Dietz knew he reached his goal when, after the procedure, a seven-
year-old girl tugged on her mom's shirt and asked if she could come
back tomorrow to ride again.

Dietz drove results by leaving the machine (his product) alone.
His breakthrough came by empathizing with his patients and crafting an experience that delighted the senses while distracting his
pediatric clientele from the scary nature of the procedure.

The University of Pittsburgh Children's Hospital took a similar
approach to medicine for children. Inspired by kids' love of superheroes, administrators had the idea to inject some real-life crusaders
into the patient experience. The hospital partnered with its window
cleaning company, which absorbed the minimal additional costs,
to have the window washers dress up as crime-fighting superheroes
when cleaning the windows. Superman, Batman, Spiderman, and
Captain America proudly repelled down the hospital walls with their
window-cleaning gear to the amazement and delight of the young
patients. The program was so successful, that it has now become a
permanent (and much anticipated) routine for the hospital and has
been embraced by other children's hospitals around the country.

When great ideas launch, they tend to spread, explaining why the A. C. Camargo Cancer Center in São Paulo, Brazil, borrowed the superhero concept and included it directly in treatment.[3] At this progressive hospital, the entire pediatric chemotherapy wing became the Hall of Justice. Patients are issued comic books showing their favorite superheroes, such as Wonder Woman and the Green Lantern, who are fighting cancer with their "Super Formula." The IV bags containing the solutions for chemotherapy are placed in colorful capsules that are identical to the ones shown in the comic books. The fresh approach makes the terrifying experience in needles, testing, and overnight stays much more palatable for young patients.

"The treatment, especially in the beginning, is very frightening for both children and family members. The Super Formula project helps to understand the disease and gives children and adolescents more strength to face the pain and overcome the problems associated with the long treatment in order to, at the end of it, get well," Cecilia Lima da Costa, director of the cancer ward, explained.[4]

Kids are not the only ones who benefit greatly from an improved experience. If you were to close your eyes and imagine you are in a hospital, you'd probably describe a nearly universal situation: loud buzzes, sterile decor, disturbing smells. Personally, I'm grossed out by hospitals, unless I'm at the Henry Ford Hospital (HFH) of Detroit suburb West Bloomfield, Michigan. This, in fact, is a hospital like none other.

The first radical departure from the norm as this new regional hospital was being constructed was its leadership. Rather than hiring an old-school physician or hospital administrator, HFH appointed a former executive from the Ritz Carlton Company as CEO. From the ground up, the hospital was designed around a new concept in health care: the intersection of hospitality and wellness. The hospital was the first to enter into uncharted territory on many fronts. There's a gourmet demonstration kitchen for cooking classes that also prepares fresh meals for patients. It has a spa that welcomes not just patients but family and community members. The facility offers yoga classes and lectures on nutrition and wellness, and it has a lovely shopping promenade. The best part of the hospital is that it doesn't look, feel, sound, or smell like a hospital. As you walk in, you feel as if you're in the atrium of a fine hotel or a luxury shopping mall. The smells are pleasant instead of antiseptic. The whole atmosphere is welcoming and warm instead of scary and off-putting. And the staff provide the service and care of a five-star resort.

The facility was built at one of the highest per-square-foot costs of any other hospital. The operating costs are also higher than at most other hospitals. So how does all this high-touch investment pay off? If you had a medical emergency, you'd be transported to the closest hospital. However, if you had to schedule an expensive procedure that didn't require instant attention, would you choose the gorgeous, gushingly friendly one or the typical cold, callous, and smelly one? Most hospital visits, in fact, are scheduled in advance, as opposed to emergency room treatment. Your same, obvious decision is exactly what patients in the Detroit metropolitan area are choosing, which is fueling the Henry Ford Hospital to have served 12,553 patients (in 2011), 11 percent of the overall Henry Ford Health System admissions total.[5] To illustrate, this network had been around for ninety-six years at that point, consisting of a major hospital and other locations like the West Bloomfield campus. The difference maker here is the customer experience, which can be the same difference maker for you.

Avoid the Curse of Inconsistency

Jenna Lyons, president and head of creative for J. Crew, has used customer experiences to move the clothing retailer's brand into rarified territory. In the ten years since joining the company in 2003, she has more than tripled revenue to $2.3 billion.[6] Lyons believes that experiences must connect to one another and create an overall sense for shoppers that transcends any one moment. Her vision for crafting inspiring experience reaches beyond the customer to her internal team. "I don't care if it's an employee handbook or the layout of the dressing room," she insists. Lyons ensures design choices don't clash with themselves and demands that each decision factor into a unified brand message and remarkable experience.

As you craft and refine customer experience, keep in mind that you'll lose a full letter grade for each conflicting message you send to your audience. Think of the experiences you create as an important component to your overall brand, just as Lyons has done for J. Crew. In the same way that Nickelodeon would never show horror films or Ferrari wouldn't start selling discount station wagons, make sure your brand's experiences are cohesive and consistent.

The W Hotel has crafted a hotel experience that is carefully calculated at every step. Enter one of its more than fifty hotels in twenty-four countries, and you'll immediately sense a special experience. Ultrachic, elegant, minimalistic. Candles and ultramodern furniture adorn their lobbies, also known as the "living room." A certain whimsical quality also exists in the playful use of the letter W whenever possible: the pool is named "Wet," for example, and the concierge service is labeled "Wherever Whenever." From the funky bathrooms to the techno music in the elevators to the staff dressed in all black, customers never confuse a W Hotel with a Marriott. The brand experience and W's consistency have made this hotel chain one of the fastest-growing and most creative hotel brands in the world.

Now imagine that you checked into a W Hotel, strolled past the swanky entry, and arrived at your room, only to find a floral quilt and heavy, plaid curtains. Think how you'd feel with the experiential inconsistency. What a buzz-kill. While this a preposterous circumstance will never happen at a W Hotel, mismatches like this occur throughout the business world with stunning regularity: a high-end apparel shop that uses cheap hangers, an American bistro that tries to peddle sushi. As savvy consumers, we have highly developed BS detectors and can identify these inconsistencies in an instant. We internalize each misstep and end up experiencing the entire brand with this confused judgment.

Even if you do 99 percent of things perfectly, it's the 1 percent mismatch that people will most remember. The reality is harsh: poor customer experiences result in an estimated $83 billion loss by US enterprises each year because of defections and abandoned purchases. This staggering figure makes sense only when considering that 64 percent of brands got a rating of "okay," "poor," or "very poor" from their customers.[7]

To avoid this blunder and its grave repercussions, remember to think of your brand as the full 100 percent, not just 99 percent. This crucial 1 percent differentiation, achieved by creating a consistent, positive experience at every stage of customer interaction, plays a big role in your ability to grow and meet emerging competitive threats. Business success is often binary (you win the deal or lose it), and results are determined with increasingly tiny margins of victory. Because of this, one systemic flaw can erode a loyal customer base so quickly you may not even know the shift occurred until it's too late.

The problem we're all facing is that competition has increased tenfold in recent times. Consumers have nearly limitless choices for whatever product or service you happen to be selling, so being prepared 100 percent is crucial. With a few simple fixes and minimal cost, a reinvention of the consumer experience will drive loyalty, goodwill and repeat purchases based on appreciation rather than agony.

Because of this dedication, you put systems in place, you train your employees, and you pride yourself on delivering excellence. However, no matter how hard you try, there will always be errors made: clients will be unhappy, and difficult situations will need to be addressed. As a leader, the way in which you handle these times will have an impact on the loyalty of your customer base and, as a result, your survival.

One special case that deserves extra focus is the predestined screw-up. Knowing that errors are inevitable, you must proactively develop a game plan to make things right. The bad customer experience can be fatal—or it can become a wonderful opportunity for you to deepen relationships, showcase your culture, and delight customers. In fact, you should look at these mess-ups as gifts. It is an opportunity for you to take a customer experience to a whole new level.

A simple approach is to brainstorm the top ten most likely ways you may disappoint your customer. If you operate a rental car company, not having the correct car ready for a weary traveler is an obvious contender. So is a car breakdown, long lines at the counter, and delays when returning the rental. Once you have your top ten list, develop specific "plays" to run in the event of one of these challenges. In the same way professional athletes develop specific, named plays for certain situations, these solutions can become your playbook to transform a negative experience into a positive one and a disgruntled client into a loyal customer.

For example, the "play" for not having the correct car on hand may be to offer an upgraded car immediately for no additional charge. Perhaps there's a special stash of chocolates behind the counter, which could be placed on the seat of the upgraded vehicle as an extra apology and sign of your commitment to the customer. Perhaps in addition to the upgrade, a tank of gas is included on the house on the vehicle's return. Is there a cost here? Absolutely. But let's compare that to the cost of losing a valuable customer who will then use every opportunity to bad-mouth the company. Don't skimp here; the cost of shifting a bad experience into a positive one is an important and necessary part of doing business. It is estimated that the average annual cost of losing a customer relationship to a competitor is $289.[8] Multiply that over a five-year relationship span, and that pissed-off customer just cost you nearly $1,500. Sure would have been worth the $8 in chocolate to keep that person happy from the outset.

Make sure your playbook is generous and ready for deployment on a moment's notice. Also make sure your company takes full responsibility for the situation and uses the opportunity to reinforce how much you value your customers. This will be one of the best return on investments you'll ever make, paying dividends in the form of customer loyalty and word-of-mouth marketing for years to come.

Get Inspired: From Geeks to Dolls

You may be thinking, "This all sounds great, but it can't apply in *my* industry. I sell industrial equipment [or medical supplies, or insurance, or plumbing services]. My field just doesn't have room to reinvent around experiences."

That is precisely how most people felt about the tech support industry back in 1994. In fact, it would have been difficult to imagine a less sexy or more boring business than fixing computers. This was a job for geeks—and that was the inspiration for Robert Stephens to launch his new business, Geek Squad. Stephens set out to create a memorable experience around a dull line of work. He incorporated the nerdy qualities of many tech support workers and used it as the focal point of the business. Service technicians were called special agents. He mandated a special geek uniform: black pants, white short-sleeve dress shirt, skinny black tie, white socks, and black shoes with the Geek Squad logo on the soles.[9] Pocket protectors and black glasses with white tape were encouraged. On arrival at their "mission," agents identified themselves by showing customers their special agent badge. Rusted-out service vans were replaced with a fleet of black and white VW Beetles with the Geek Squad logo prominently displayed, similar to the insignia on a police car.

Training went beyond tech talk and included funny one-liners, playful nuances, and instructions on how to create a memorable experience. The geeks carried their own version of a service manual, called *The Little Orange Book*. It described in detail how to be the best nerd possible, including driving five miles per hour under the speed limit. An agent who committed a major violation in the sense of not playing the part (e.g., in dress, saying certain lines, following procedures) had to wear the Mother Board of Shame, a big circuit board with a painted S that hung from their neck like rapper bling. The booklet explained that this was a natural rite of passage, "similar to the squeaky voice and foul body odor that accompany puberty."

Through engineering a fun experience in a flat-lining industry, Geek Squad immediately became the standout. There were all the other normal, boring service companies—and then there was Geek Squad. Which would you remember? Which would you hire? Geek Squad competed on customer experience, not technical skills, price point, or location. Its incredible customer experience and brand led Best Buy to acquire the company in 2002 and invest heavily in it ever since. By 2012, the company employed over twenty-four thousand geeks and generated over $1.3 billion in revenue.[10] Even under a large parent company and performing many more services (such as home automation installation, and theater design), the company hasn't lost its personality. And the organization chart still has whimsy with titles: counterintelligence agent, deputy of counterintelligence, double agent, special agent, and deputy field marshal.

If this worked for computer nerds, it can absolutely work in your business. Why not have your financial services offices ditch the heavy wood desks and transform into a chic, hip scene with the aroma of freshly brewed espresso? Financial consultants could dress like Steve Jobs instead of Gordon Gekko, techno music instead of classical could be playing, and cool fonts and chic statements could replace computer printouts. Perhaps some traditional customers go to the competition. So what! If you try to be all things to everyone, you end up being nothing to no one. You're better off offending 20 percent of your customers while truly delighting the other 80 percent rather than being just another carbon-copy, flock-following robot.

Here's a pop quiz to anyone who has a daughter, granddaughter, cousin, or niece between five and ten years old: What is the biggest obsession or addiction of these girls?

a. Sugar
b. Music
c. Television
d. American Girl dolls

If you guessed d, you understand the intensity of this iconic brand. With thousands of competitive dolls on the market, it would have been easy to get lost in the pack, which is why American Girl founder Pleasant Rowland set out to change the game by crafting a whole new experience.[11]

American Girl is a phenomenon far beyond a mass-produced toy. Rowland built the brand around the experience the dolls create, not the dolls themselves. The eighteen-inch dolls come in many combinations of hair, eye, and skin color, allowing girls to build one that is just like themselves. Each doll has a story and a set of adoption papers. Clothing for the dolls can be purchased in outfits or by the piece, and most pieces come in both doll size and people size, allowing girls to buy matching outfits alongside their special friend.

The company hit a major growth phase after launching American Girl Place, an experiential retail store in Chicago. In addition to shopping for dolls, clothing, and accessories, the store features a restaurant where girls can take their doll out to lunch or for afternoon tea. Special chairs accommodate the dolls, and menu choices are all centered on a special feast for both the girl and her doll. The store has become a huge tourist attraction, with reservations required several months in advance. This special experience creates a unique connection between the brand, the girl, and her guests (parents, friends, and others). Prices are outrageous for both the meal and the merchandise, but parental cost concerns go out the window when an emotionally charged experience is created for their daughter. In fact, 86 percent of consumers will pay more for a better customer experience.[12] A standard meal and generic dolls are commodities that can be found by thousands of providers at a fraction of the price, but the American Girl experience is both unique and priceless.

As of 2013, the brand boasted twelve stores, with additional ones under construction. There have been seven American Girl movies (one starring Julia Roberts), and the company has enjoyed massive sales growth worldwide. Rowland long ago decided not to compete on price but on experience. It's a much faster path to growth and profitability than saving money by cutting corners or enforcing corporate policies. It's a lot more fun too.

You don't need to create a fully themed business in order to craft memorable experiences. Detroit Metro Airport was consistently ranked the worst airport in the United States for over twenty years, due in part to its low ceilings, bad lighting, and tight walkways. Void of major renovation since the 1950s, it was almost comical how bad the experience was. But in December 2001, all that changed. A new $1.2 billion airport was launched to the joy of all of us who visit regularly. In addition to the obvious changes such as open spaces and comfy chairs, the designers focused on creating rich emotional experiences. There's an indoor fountain, for example, designed by the same folks who built the Bellagio fountain in Las Vegas. Water jets shoot out streams in playful patterns in a well-choreographed routine. Luxurious building materials, an unmanned silent tram, and huge windows punctuate the new airport that was ranked number 3 Best Airport in the country by *Travel and Leisure* magazine.[13]

One of my favorite design elements is the underground tunnel connecting terminal A to terminals B and C. Instead of the standard-issue, boring dark tunnel, architects imagined something totally different. The walls on both sides of the passageway are covered with art glass that has specialty lighting under the surface. Electronic music plays as the lights perform in rhythmic syncopation to the funky melodies. This tunnel has received international praise in the media, blogs, and customer enthusiasm. It sends a message to travelers that Detroit is as unique as the tunnel from which you enter the city. What could have been a utilitarian tunnel was transformed into a delicacy for the senses.

Make 'Em Feel—and Buy!

While customer experience is important in every realm of your company, it's even better for your business when an improved interaction gets consumers to spend more. Of course, driving the bottom line is critical, so if you can kill two birds with one stone, it's more efficient. This two-pronged approach is easily illustrated in your nearest grocery store. Often produce items are in one section and then you need to wander through the entire store to find related items. It's frustrating, and I generally end up forgetting something on my list after all that back-and-forth. That leaves a bad taste in my mouth for when I have to go back.

Not at Whole Foods. This company, aside from its efforts in healthy, organic, ethical food provisions, is an expert in cross-merchandising. When you stand near the fresh vegetables, you'll find a colander and peeler. When certain produce is in season (and featured), the best pairings with it—cheese or sauces, for example—are right there too. When you need to grab a bottle of wine as a hostess gift for that dinner party, Whole Foods is like a mind reader: the gift bags are there, to purchase alongside the bottle itself. At the cheese counter, you'll find a sampler tray and a knowledgeable staff member, but you'll also find crackers, olives, decorative cheese knives, or artisanal beer to go with the cheese.

All of these cross-merchandising efforts appeal to busy shoppers who want to get in and out fast, and it also encourages these customers to spend more. Whereas someone may have just bought wine and carried it to a friend's house without any wrapping, Whole Foods gets this person to spend a few dollars more on the purchase since it's so easy to buy the gift bag too. And I've found that I almost always buy a section of the cheese I just sampled at the cheese counter because it's always too delicious *not* to take some.

Business leaders are often so busy managing resources or reducing costs that they forget about what matters most: delivering value to paying customers. If you're out to build a sustainable organization that gains momentum by delighting customers, you need to go beyond the functional specifics of your product or service and use experiences to create positive feelings. With most of the competitive advantages of the past already commoditized, customer experience is an area that remains largely uncharted and ready for innovation. Only 26 percent of companies have a well-developed strategy in place for improving customer experience, presenting an obvious opportunity to leave 74 percent of your competition in the dust.[14] Make your customers feel your brand, and you'll be on the path to leapfrogging the competition while driving the bottom line.

Think about your own organization and contemplate every experiential element that isn't making your customers say, "Wow." Is it the way you require them to navigate through your automatic messaging system with countless menus when they call? The outdated paperwork you require customers to complete? The dimly lit parking lot? Take a single touch point and reinvent it with purpose. Ask yourself whether people will be talking about the new concept in the same way they talk about a modern airport tunnel, a superheroes window washing crew, or high tea with a doll? Unleash your creativity by crafting a significant overhaul to one area of customer engagement, and the results will speak for themselves.

Detroit: Catalyst for Change

Prior to the advent of the automotive industry, Detroit's population was just under 500,000 people. By 1920, it had doubled to just under 1 million, and it steadily rose from there. The 1950 Census saw the height of Detroit's population, at 1.85 million people. Every year since then, the city's population has steadily decreased. By the 2010 Census, the city had just over 700,000 residents.[15] This dwindling population takes up a radius of approximately 140 square miles. To illustrate the vastness of this sprawl (and dire levels of low density), consider that Boston, Manhattan, and San Francisco combined take up fewer square miles than this one city alone.[16]

As sprawl continued (with the upper middle class moving into the suburbs) and the population continued to decline through the second half of the twentieth century, many of Detroit's neighborhoods were left gutted. Vacant homes lined streets for blocks, without a resident to be found for many homes at a time. Of course, criminal activity occurs in blighted areas, but there's another experiential concern for the residents who are left in these communities. The city's "customer experience" in its municipal services is spread so thin that it isn't effective anywhere. Many neighborhoods have lost streetlights, trash removal, road repair, and snow plowing. Even more of a concern are the emergency response services; police, fire, and emergency medicine personnel are responsible for such large areas that response times are dangerously long.

Pouring salt in a wound, the vast majority of the people who left the city were upper- and middle-class people who could afford to leave for greener pastures in suburbia. This has been unofficially deemed white flight, leaving the city with a lower socioeconomic status and a scathing racial divisiveness between the affluent, mostly white suburbs and the suffering, predominantly African American inner city. In the end, having these two worlds has benefited nobody: the entire region ultimately suffered from a decaying image, though the city itself experienced much more strife than its suburban counterparts.

This population sprawl happened for a variety of reasons (which I cover in later chapters), but the devastating results serve as a powerful warning sign to you and your company. A city government's core responsibility to its customers—its citizens—is to keep communities safe and livable. For decades, Detroit failed to provide a strong customer experience to its clients—the tax base here. As is the concern for you, these people (customers) chose to take their dollars elsewhere. Many people who could afford to do so moved elsewhere to have a better experience as a resident. Your clients are the same: if you're not delighting them, they'll take their business to someone else who will. Learn this painful lesson from Detroit's suffering, and choose to make the choice to reinvent your experience now, before it's too late.

Tools for Transformation: Creating Excellence, Step by Step

Let's explore a seven-step process to help you elevate your customers' experience. Run your own business through this formula, and you'll enjoy a boost in both customer satisfaction and bottom line results:

1. *Identify every touch point.* For a restaurant, for example, these touch points would include pre-dining interactions (TV commercial, print ad, drive-by sign, the phone call for reservations), each step of the dining experience (parking, walk-in, greeting at the maître d's station, menus, seating, servers, ordering, time waiting for food, each course, table clearing, payment, restrooms, leaving restaurant), and postmeal (exiting the parking lot or finding a cab), feeling after leaving, follow-up communication. These are only a few examples of each. A savvy restaurateur would identify every touch point and explore it as an opportunity for customer delight.

2. *Examine the current state.* Take a careful look at each of the touch points and run them against each of the five senses. In our restaurant example, let's start with the menu. How does it look (lettering, cleanliness, wording)? How does it feel (materials used, number of pages, size)? How does it smell, taste, and sound (the menu probably doesn't smell, taste, or sound, of course, but what is happening to these senses as you read the menu)? Make sure you talk to customers and really understand how they experience each step.

3. *Tackle one at a time.* In a systematic fashion, isolate a touch point and brainstorm new ideas to improve it across the five senses. Look for ways to delight customers by creating unique and memorable experiences. Continuing with the previous example, what if the menu was an iPad that greeted the guest by name and included customized specials based on previous dining choices? What if the menu was a leather-bound book? A scroll? An Etch-a-Sketch pad? Don't govern your ideas with cost or

execution concerns; there will be plenty of time to evaluate them later. Just focus on generating as many ideas as possible, and don't be afraid to venture into uncommon territory.

4. *Expand ideas to have an impact on multiple touch points*. You now want to zoom out to see if some of your best individual ideas could be expanded to cover more ground. If you fell in love with the iPad menu, maybe you could expand the idea of using technology throughout the dining experience. The whole restaurant could have apps, screens, social sharing, and perhaps even minirobots. Specialty drinks could be named after tech entrepreneurs (I'll have a Mark Zuckerberg, please. And make it a double!). Remember, this is still wide-open brainstorming.

5. *Develop a specific action plan*. Now that your whiteboard is filled with hundreds of ideas, you need to choose which to implement. Make sure you run the ideas through the filter of your core philosophy: who you are, what you stand for, and why you're in business in the first place. If you run an elegant restaurant, the iPad may be a cool touch, but making the whole building into a tech-theme diner would be going much too far. Take a look at each of your favorite ideas and evaluate them based on cost, anticipated impact, ease of implementation, and expected differentiation. You won't be able to do them all, so take a handful of the best ideas and put them into action immediately.

6. *Surprise and delight*. There's a reason that "icing on the cake" and "the cherry on top" exist as phrases. Customers love that little extra, which is often easy to give and becomes highly effective. To illustrate, a small taste of an unordered item between courses, compliments of the chef, can elevate the restaurant experience to world class, and without much additional food cost. Brainstorm all the little surprises you could deliver to create experiential magic. Those small extras can have an enormous impact on customer loyalty, retention, satisfaction, and word-of-mouth.

7. *Measure, refine, and repeat*. Your customers will likely notice the changes, which will translate into growth and profits. The key lesson here is to live in a constant state of reinvention. You should do this exercise at least once a year, refining the previous changes and looking for new opportunities to improve customer experience, so that you're constantly delighting those who matter the most.

CHAPTER 6

Tell a Memorable Story

It wasn't raining when Noah built the ark.

—HOWARD RUFF

I was accustomed to being second-guessed. Throughout most of my career, when I'd tell people I was from Detroit and that I ran a tech company, I was regularly met with a perplexed look, reminiscent of the way a dog tilts his head when confused. But all that changed in January 2011.

During that year's Super Bowl, a two-minute ad aired that changed Detroit's story forever. Chrysler debuted its "Imported from Detroit" campaign that shifted the way people think about my hometown. Until that point, Detroit had become a punch line of the "worst of the worst," known for its decay and violent crime. But that story changed in 120 seconds. In the ad, Detroit is characterized as the underdog with generations of grit and determination. "The hottest fires forge the hardest steel," the deep voice-over professes. The audience is challenged to think about Detroit in a different way, not the way that "people write about the city that have never even been here." At the end of the commercial, native Detroiter Eminem swaggers into the historic Fox Theater and hops on stage with the powerful Church of God choir. "This is the Motor City. This is what we do," the rapper asserts, as he points into the camera.

There was an instant change in people's perception of Detroit. My interactions with people in different states and countries were no longer met with bewilderment; their response shifted to enthusiasm. "Detroit!" people would exclaim. "I hear what's going on there. A big comeback is under way, right? Tell me all about it." Chrysler's brilliant commercial changed the hearts and minds of millions of people and made it suddenly cool to be from Detroit. In the three years since, that momentum has continued and inspired others to build on this story. Kid Rock, along with my friends at Quicken Loans, recorded a TV spot called "Opportunity Detroit" that ran during the 2012 World Series and continues to hit the airwaves. It aptly describes our city as "a high-tech corridor at the intersection of muscles and brain." These powerful words continue to redefine Detroit's story.

The renewed enthusiasm has generated real results. Thousands of talented people have moved to the region to pursue their careers. The art and music scenes have enjoyed explosive growth. New restaurants and galleries are popping up daily. By the end of 2013, the downtown central business district had a 99.4 percent residential occupancy rate for all rental units.[1] Of course, the activity on the ground supports the enthusiasm, but the new story that's being told is playing a significant role in boosting the reinvention of a great American city.

As you look to your own organization and career, reinventing the way you tell your story, communicate (both internally and externally), and market yourself and your brand can be the difference makers between a highly successful outcome or the unfortunate consolation prize of stinging regret.

The way you position your company, communicate to various audiences, and brand your organization fall into the category of storytelling. Even the best products and services in the world can easily get lost in the shuffle while competitors gain ground not through product innovation but by telling better stories. The average consumer sees over five thousand marketing messages each day.[2] We are flooded with e-mail, social media, texts, articles, and voice-mails from an endless number of sources. Your challenge is to figure out how you stand above that nonstop noise. How do you tell your story in a way that is compelling and unforgettable? How can you reinvent your organization through the use of powerful stories in addition to product or process disruption?

Storytelling is more than slick marketing. Certainly ads can tell great stories, but you should use storytelling in a more profound way. Think of it as crafting the overall narrative of your organization. It's articulating what you stand for. It's capturing how you connect your team, customers, suppliers, and the media to your larger mission. A company with a great overall story can outpunch competitors consistently on many aspects of their business: sales, recruiting, procurement, and even operational excellence.

Reinvent Your Story's Purpose

Luis Duarte and Hector Elizondo's lives are garbage. Literally. In 2009, they founded one of Mexico's first recycling companies, YoReciclo: Get Mexico Recycling. The company, which develops customized recycling solutions for business and consumers, has the potential to be a large and important operation once it reaches scale. It is a bold mission since the country's recycling rate is a mere 3 percent.[3] Providing a valuable service in which good use can be provided for as much as 85 percent of garbage is actually the easy part. Changing long-standing behaviors and, more important, the deeply held beliefs of people throughout Mexico is the bigger challenge. Unlike in the United States, there is low awareness of the importance of recycling, and the people of Mexico have not demonstrated the desire to take extra steps to protect the environment.

To address this issue, Duarte and Elizondo's approach is twofold. In communicating this mission, they put social impact first and economics second. They have to demonstrate in an authentic way that the company is about helping Mexico, not just raking in profits. Duarte says he does this by linking everything the company does to his infant son. "I want to leave a cleaner environment for my son. That is my dream," Duarte beams. By connecting his message to a higher cause that people can relate to, the story now has meaning and relevance, making YoReciclo matter to the community. The second ingredient to launch the company has been to make recycling fun and easy. The recycling bins are brightly colored and convenient to both spot and use. The childlike allure of a fun green or shiny light blue receptacle grabs people's attention and makes it feel good for them to take action. In a brand-new industry with a brand-new concept, the company is making progress. It reached profitability in the first eight months of business and generated over $1 million in revenue by the end of that year. The long-term goal is to bring widespread recycling solutions to all of Mexico and the rest of Latin America. They are well on their way by focusing on how they tell their story and the emotional benefits they create for customers.[4]

Other than baseball and apple pie, few things are as nationally revered as the American farmer. The vast majority of these hard-working men and women produce a generic commodity such as wheat, corn, or apples, and then sell these bulk products to packaging companies for distribution. A potato is a potato. A banana is a banana. But is a clementine only a clementine?

Stewart and Lynda Resnick had something else in mind. With the insight that these small fruits, a hybrid between a mandarin and an orange, are seedless, easy to peel, deliciously sweet, and fun for children, they set out to conquer the industry through creative storytelling. If "Kleenex" could become synonymous with facial tissues, why couldn't they develop a similarly powerful brand for these healthy snacks? At a brainstorming session in 2001, Stewart Resnick held the fruit in his hand and said, "They're just so cute." The name "Cuties" was instantly born and trademarked later that year. In addition to naming the generic fruit, the Resnicks have spent millions telling the story of their new crop, primarily targeting kids and moms. Put succinctly, "Kids love Cuties because Cuties are made for kids": they are sweet, easy to peel, and seedless. Instead of competing with other fruits, Cuties essentially competes with candy bars. The marketing was designed to position this branded, fun treat as a healthy alternative to a bag of M&Ms without giving up any delicious flavor.[5]

The Resnicks' effort created what is now the most profitable cash crop in the United States (well, legal cash crop that is). Per pound, Cuties sell for nearly double the price of the most premium navel oranges. By branding something generic and marketing it in a bold new way, the Cuties brand has enjoyed incredible growth in the same way Duarte's story behind YoReciclo has moved the needle. Their company shipped 75 million boxes of Cuties in 2012, over four times more than their launch in 2005, and the Resnicks' fortune has grown to $2.2 billion, making them one of the richest families in the world.[6] It turns out this wasn't their first effort. They did the same thing with pomegranate juice by marketing it as "POM wonderful," and also creating the billion-dollar brand of Fiji water. Through powerful brand messaging, I'm pretty sure the Resnicks could market topsoil, lumber, or heating oil. Their formula: master storytelling to drive incredible success.

Nick Morgan is a master storyteller who has written memorable and inspiring speeches for elected officials, business executives, and dignitaries for years. He categorizes stories into five types that we are programmed to remember. Without crucial elements that make stories compelling (and memorable), your tale is simply an anecdote, which doesn't do anything for your business. If your storytelling is to leave a mark, you need to reinvent your approach. Match your message up to these classic structures, these frameworks for reality, and your audience will be persuaded. Of course, you want to establish a problem and solution, but you also want to drive your audience to act, using the story as the mechanism to drive this. Let's examine each of Nick Morgan's categories:

• *Quests.* These begin with ordinary people in an ordinary situation. Then a problem arises or an event occurs that forces the hero to leave home or depart from the status quo in some other way, in order to seek some goal or right some terrible wrong, reestablishing the social order. The hero's hunger for the goal is palpable. Even if the journey is long, the hero hangs in there because of the importance of reaching the goal. It's not logical, but we believe it. And that's why it's powerful.

- *A strange land.* These stories are our way of handling things when everything changes and thus work best in turbulent times. In a strange-land story, the heroes suddenly find themselves in a new landscape, one with unknown terrain, language, or rules. We don't know the way. We're lost. Along comes a leader to show us the way. The leader (that's you) offers a new vision, or a new set of rules, or a new way of coping that enables us to survive and eventually thrive in this new landscape. We crave mastery, not bewilderment, and that's the journey our leader takes us on.

- *Love stories.* These are simple: two people meet, fall in love, fall out of love, learn a little more about each other, decide to stick together, and live happily ever after. But their true character is revealed in the nature of the way the two fall out of love and then find each other again—and that's always symptomatic of what's wrong with society today. Is it the difficulties of marriage and property? That's Jane Austen. Or is it the problem of men never growing up, staying immature, and behaving badly in a society that permits them this license? That's Judd Apatow (screenwriter and director of comedies such as *Anchorman, The 40 Year Old Virgin*, and *Bridesmaids*). If you're a leader with an idea about how people need to get along better, love stories are for you.

- *Rags-to-riches stories.* These help us believe that ordinary people still have a chance to succeed in a society that all too often seems stacked against us, in favor of the already rich and powerful. They're about average people who, with a little luck and hard work (but not genius), manage to succeed and achieve material wealth, honor, power, fame. They're good stories for people to tell who are trying to promote economic justice. Chrysler's Imported from Detroit campaign uses this approach.

- *Revenge stories.* We live in a chaotic world, and most people's perception throughout history is that our world is the most chaotic it has ever been, right now, unlike the golden age of X years ago. There is evil in this world, and revenge stories reassert the order that society all too often fails to give us from the start. A good villain and justice served are powerful ways for leaders to persuade their followers that they have the right idea about life.

By applying any of these basic patterns, you can use storytelling effectively in two key ways: functional communication (both internal and external) and marketing and brand messaging. Great storytelling can be the difference maker in winning the client, securing regulatory approval, or getting that big promotion. Let's explore how to tackle each as a mechanism to drive meaningful transformation.

Reinvent Your Communication

As a venture capitalist, I listen to a lot of pitches. Venture capitalists like me raise an investment fund (generally $50 million to $300 million) and then invest that money in start-ups. A pitch in this case is when an eager entrepreneur comes for her big meeting to share her concept and tries to persuade us to invest in her company. It is the business equivalent of *American Idol*, and my job is to play the role of Simon Cowell. The show *Shark Tank* is a simplified and shortened version of the pitch process in action.

Imagine for a moment that you were about to pitch, and this was your big chance to get the funding and support you need to launch your business and secure your future. Just like auditions to get a record deal in the music business, the odds are against you. Only one in three hundred entrepreneurial pitches gets funded, so the competition is steep. It's all on the line, and your fate can be determined in a thirty-minute meeting. With such high stakes, how do you avoid ruining your big pitch?

Unfortunately, we've seen hundreds of flameouts. The botched meetings become painful for the entrepreneur, and even more so for us. After hours of agonizing meetings, we realized there had to be a better way to prepare these would-be start-up leaders to relax and perform better in these critical meetings.

We decided to reinvent the way we communicated. We examined all the areas that drove us nuts and undermined good pitches. Rather than making a strict set of rules, we prepared a set of guidelines, which we now send to every entrepreneur before he or she comes to visit. We use humor to make strong points and to diffuse an otherwise tense situation. Ultimately we wrote eleven points, each touching on a different element of a successful meeting. Check a few of them out for yourself (this is a shortened list):

The Detroit Venture Partners "Meeting Musts"

1. *The talking-to-listening ratio.* We want to hear all about your idea, but we get super bored listening to forty-five-minute monologues where people drone on and on so much that we start to think about paint drying or eating glass. Our meeting should be a dialogue and conversational. Make your points quickly and concisely, and let us ask questions and join the fun. Our suggested ratio is 58.42 percent talking and 41.58 percent listening. Be concise and remember: you are not getting paid by the word.

2. *Keep it nine-year-old simple.* Confession: we ain't that smart. We need you to convey your idea simply enough for my nine-year-old niece to understand. If you can't communicate your idea in two sentences, your customers may not get it either (there is a limited market of brainiac supergeniuses out there). We're more impressed with clear, concise communication than buzzword soup or acronym pie.

3. *Don't take yourself so seriously.* We sure don't! In fact, we'll probably make fun of you the minute you leave. Have fun, laugh, and be yourself. We love renegade, mold-breaking dreamers much more than dull gray suits and power ties. You get bonus points for making us laugh, especially at our own expense!

4. *Defend your assumptions.* It's great that you plan to have 23 million users in month 33, but please make sure you are prepared to tell us how you plan to get there. You should know your numbers cold, understand the key assumptions and moving pieces of your business, and be ready to defend.

5. *Tell us the hard part.* Picking out cool colors for your new digs will be easy. But all businesses have a hard part: getting customers to pay a premium or attracting top talent, for example. We'll have fun together with the easy stuff, but we want to understand from you what the biggest challenges will be. We can plan the holiday party later.

As you can imagine, this is not standard practice in the stuffy venture capital industry. But by reinventing our communication, the quality of meetings has jumped dramatically, which was a win for everyone involved. This new approach to communication left no assumptions to chance for our customers (the hopeful entrepreneurs), and as a result, we significantly improved a key aspect of our business. Multiply a similar improvement across your entire organization, and you've just discovered a meaningful competitive advantage.

Our strategy with these meeting guidelines fell under the category of functional communication. Generally in this form of storytelling, we think of documents—memos, handbooks, and instruction manuals—but your functional communication also encapsulates how your organization responds to the public when things happen—press releases, major announcements, or crisis strategy.

While a response to a bad situation can be difficult to architect, it can hold the biggest payoff for your company if you do it correctly. The way you tell a story of what went wrong, and how you're fixing it, is vital; you have to consider what you're saying as well as the medium in which you choose to deliver that message.

In March 2013, Lululemon, a high-end provider of athletic clothing and gear inspired by yoga, recalled a major line of its product after women worldwide complained that Lululemon pants were see-through. That's a serious problem in the bent-over, contorted positions during which the yoga pants are designed to be used. The recall affected 17 percent of its inventory and cost the company tens of millions of dollars.[7] In crisis mode, the company had to figure out a way to apologize and keep the trust of its loyal following to maintain its position as a truly luxurious, high-performance line of apparel.

At the individual store level (Lululemon has 201 stores), window displays with mannequins set up in various yoga poses were adjusted, and signs and banners in their display windows were added with appropriate messaging. At a store near my home, derrieres were facing outward, with a sign that read, "You saw London. You saw France. We promise no more see-through pants." Others nationwide had similar setups, with taglines such as, "We want to be transparent with you," and, "We've got you covered." This quirky response transformed a corporate problem into an opportunity to deepen their bond with customers by using humor.

The company took this type of story a step further. As the pants were retooled and put back on store shelves in November of that same year, they were branded as the "second chance pant." The tags on each of the items explain that these are a celebration of failure, and they outline the improvements made to keep bottoms covered as they should be. Lululemon could have fixed this problem at the corporate level only, issuing a press release and apology for the situation, but by taking a different, courageous approach and telling this story head-on, it was able to remain ahead of the pack.

Even if you're not a specialist in marketing and communication, there is an easy approach you can follow to reinvent your communication efforts. These powerful principles apply to any form of communication (e.g., written, spoken, online, social media) and for any audience (e.g., internal team, customers, vendors, investors, media). If you follow these six high-impact principles, you'll be well on your way to driving positive change:

1. *Keep it simple.* Translate a concept into a simplified format. Go from "review the cross-functional data to ascertain the appropriate course of action" to "use the info to make smart decisions." With growing complexity in the business world, your task is to make your communications dead-simple for anyone who reads it. Ditch the jargon, and focus on clarity.

2. *Make it clear.* If you've ever assembled a stroller or piece of furniture, you're familiar with the cryptic and confusing language of instruction manuals. In your own writing, do the opposite. Make sure that you expunge vagueness, ambiguity, and imprecision, leaving behind a crystal-clear and easy-to-follow communication.

3. *Speak to your audience, not yourself.* I've been a jazz guitarist for more than thirty years and play frequently in smoky clubs. The other night when the group was taking rhythm changes up minor third, I took the fourth pass. I did a tritone substitution over the bridge, switched to a chromatic minor scale, and riffed

out with a Parker phrase from "Ornithology." As we wrapped the tune, we traded fours and the bass player pedaled on five as we tagged the ending. If you happen to be an experienced jazz musician, this explanation was crystal clear to you. Chances are, however, you have absolutely no idea what I just said. Too often, communication is written in the context of the sender, not the receiver. Make sure you speak in a language that your audience understands, and realize that they don't have the same context and point of references that you do. Start from the beginning and make sure every word will make sense to them, not just you.

4. *Keep it brief.* In our busy lives, we have neither the time nor the attention span to consume superfluous content. Make your message concise. There is an inverse correlation here: the lower your word count, the better your message will be understood and retained.

5. *Make it memorable.* People will remember stories and feelings far more than details and figures. Engage your audience with compelling and unique language, and make sure you're saying something with enough creativity that people can't forget it. Our venture capital meeting musts are memorable because of the humor and our irreverent approach. If a statistics professor wrote the same content in her own style, it probably wouldn't have been as striking.

6. *Activate with action.* Start with the end goal in mind, and make sure your communications all lead to the desired outcome you seek. Lead your audience down a deliberate path with a specific action in mind, and make sure that next step is completely apparent.

Manage Expectations

A sorry pitfall that undermines many customer relationships is the mismanagement of expectations. You would become infuriated if your construction contractor told you a job would be completed in a week for a cost of $2,500 but his crew ends up finishing the work in three weeks at a cost of $3,750. Good intentions and optimism can damage trust, deteriorate your brand, and lead to the collapse of your organization. As a result, expectation management deserves special examination.

In professional services organizations that bill on a fixed-fee basis (software development, landscape contractors, specialized consultants), the insomnia-inducing monster in the closet is known as "feature creep." This is a phenomenon in which the customer contracts for a specific set of deliverables, but that list expands in runaway fashion during the course of the project. It ends up killing margins and driving the team nuts. Clients are often unhappy because deadlines get pushed or errors emerge on new features (that were not part of the original agreement but had since become part of their expectations). This is a bad situation for both clients and providers.

At the fourth company I built, ePrize, we experienced this problem in a big way. We hated to turn down requests, so we ended up taking on more and more work with each engagement, only to burn out team members, reduce quality, hurt margins, and ultimately leave clients unsatisfied.

Our projects began with a high-level (and vague) statement of work, which was open to far too much interpretation. This led, of course, to the dreaded state of feature creep. To eliminate the problem, we began issuing a "receipt" when a new project began. We clearly listed exactly what the customer purchased, and also what the customer didn't purchase. The receipt had to be signed before work began, and since we clarified things at the start, clients didn't object. When the inevitable request for new features came a few weeks later, we could easily refer back to the receipt so the client realized that the new request would be outside the original scope, thus increasing budget and schedule. The simple act of clarifying expectations up front made an enormous improvement for us and can do the same for you.

Sustainable companies and relationships are built by eliminating surprises and delivering on commitments. Landing a deal on shaky terms is not worth it in the long run if you won't be able to deliver. Take a look at each area where the potential to disappoint a customer (or team member) exists. Use your reinvention efforts to eliminate these gaps, and you'll have a lot less aggravation later on.

Communicative transparency is important with any outside contacts, but it's equally vital with the internal stuff at your company. Before the turn of the century (way back in 2000), top-down management practices touted a closed approach: information was on a need-to-know basis, and employees were shielded from bad news and thus didn't really have the full story. The thinking was that they needed protection from the hard facts, and any more information than necessary would be distracting from completing their tasks.

In the same way the Y2K bug was a myth and is now a distant memory, so is this overbearing leadership style. In these challenging times, it is critically important to keep key stakeholders in the loop and give them full transparency. This helps them make better decisions, creates alignment, and builds trust in you as a leader.

Admittedly, I was that closed-off leader back in the 1990s. I was paternalistic and insulated my team from bad news. It was a misguided approach, as if I was trying to get everyone to perform a symphony but failed to share the sheet music. Although I did enjoy some success, it was limited because I was being closed off. I reinvented my own leadership style as I built my next company throughout the 2000s. I made a conscious decision that everyone needed to be aligned to a common vision, and everyone needed to know the score at each step of the way. Here are a few things that worked for me that you're welcome to borrow:

- *Weekly full-company huddles.* From the time we were only a handful of people, the entire company met weekly. We reviewed the previous week's accomplishments, shared our successes, and took our challenges head-on. It was a forum to reinforce our culture and vision and keep everyone completely aligned. The meetings were upbeat and full of practical jokes, skits, funny videos, and laughter. As our company grew quickly to hundreds of people, the rhythm of this all-company huddle kept us united. In addition to the fun, we shared in full transparency our weekly sales numbers, profitability, margin, and goals. This open approach empowered people and provided all employees with a sense of ownership in the outcome. The regular communications allowed us to course-correct quickly and avoid silo thinking.

• *The Jumbotron.* As a basketball fan, I realized the importance of the ever-present Jumbotron while attending a game. It shows real-time key metrics in full transparency for all the players, coaches, and fans to see. Imagine trying to play the game or coach the team if you didn't instantly know critical information: the score, time remaining, and number of penalties, for example. Unfortunately, that's how many companies operate. We decided to install our own version of a Jumbotron. We had dozens of plasma monitors installed throughout the building that reported our key metrics as they happened: daily utilization rates, server uptime, regional sales figures, timely project launches. This clear, up-to-date information gave everyone visibility as to how we were performing at that moment and armed them to make their own adjustments to improve our results. You don't need fancy tech; a whiteboard can do the trick. The key is to share instant information and make sure everyone is focused on a small number of key metrics so they can adapt their behaviors to drive home desired outcomes.

• *The daily dash.* Sales results and adjustments in our forecast were critical to help us plan hiring needs, delivery schedules, and team assignments. As our sales team grew to over one hundred people in six offices around the world, it became increasingly complex to share updates. We decided to automate the process and provide a companywide "Daily Dash"—an e-mail that contained detailed information about our sales momentum. It showed figures broken down by full company, region, and individual team member. Details of pending proposals (weighted based on probability to close), types of expected projects, and projected delivery capacity were all calculated and shared with full transparency. This allowed the whole company to prepare to meet the incoming sales demand, and it also drove our sales team to achieve more (no one wants to be on the bottom of the list). This daily visibility allowed our company to adapt to changing conditions and optimize our performance.

• *Year by the numbers.* Each year, I summarized our results with an annual recap. The team, our investors, and the media received the document, which included all our key statistics and compared them to both the prior year and the current year's original forecast. We shared sales numbers, number of new clients, number of repeat clients, average order size, average revenue per customer, average utilization rates, server uptime, timely launches, worldwide consumer reach, and more. It could be argued that sharing this sensitive information was risky, but I'd argue that not sharing it was far riskier. I wanted to arm people with facts and ensure that we measured what mattered. People needed to be accountable for results, which would be impossible if they couldn't easily see the report card. This transparency drove our performance and allowed us to beat the odds in terms of growth, reach, and profitability.

•   *Project Gold Medal.* It is fun and easy to communicate good news. But what about when you hit a brick wall? In 2006, we grew by over two hundred people in a twelve-month period, and due to this massive growth, our company's solid structure began to crumble. Morale plummeted, profitability tanked, and customers were unhappy. Worse, the team started to lose faith in our senior team's ability to lead the company. This moment had the force to either kill us or define us. We embarked on an all-hands reinvention of every aspect of the company. We looked under every rock and challenged the way we did our work. The communication strategy I used was critical. I called an all-company meeting and shared with everyone in-depth where we stood, how we got there, and the fact that we were in a crisis. I owned it and took full responsibility as the CEO. I then committed to them that I would give everything I had to fixing the problems and that communication was an important part of the process. I named the effort Project Gold Medal, so that everyone knew it was a specific, finite change initiative. I set up a system whereby anonymous feedback could be sent directly to me with no intervention. I took all feedback, paraphrased it to ensure confidentiality, and posted a public response to every suggestion, complaint, and observation. For the next brutal eleven weeks, I sent a highly detailed and fully transparent report, at times as many as eight typed pages, to the entire company. I let everyone know exactly what we were working on at each step of the way. They got to see the process happen, which made them feel part of it. It also went a long way to reestablishing trust in our leadership team and let them know that we were addressing the problems head-on. It was a very painful effort, but we emerged an infinitely stronger company. Honest, direct, transparent communication was a critical element in our successful reinvention, as it likely will be in yours.

Be a Firebrand

As a senior at Pomona College in Claremont, California, Nick Friedman set up a business to make some extra cash. He rented a beat-up old truck and offered to haul junk, provide moving services, and do deliveries. Like the ratty vehicle he was driving, the business was nondescript and blended in with hundreds of similar companies. The business was on a path to end, just like so many other college experiments, until Nick decided to change his company name and launch a memorable brand.

By 2013, College Hunks Hauling Junk had become a thriving business.[8] It is a franchisor of junk removal, moving, and donation pickup services, now boasting thirty-three franchises and a fleet of over fifty trucks. The turning point for Nick was that he used sex appeal in a previously unsexy business. "XYZ Shipping and Freight" is an easily forgettable name, whereas the rhythmic and suggestive name of College Hunks Hauling Junk is instantly recognizable and memorable. His innovation didn't come in the form of a new product or process. The difference maker for Nick was his ability to leap past the nonstop clutter of marketing to seize customer awareness and remain top-of-mind.

We all come across two types of companies (and individuals) in our lives. First are those who blend in with the others, swimming in mediocrity. They don't like to stand out, prefer the safety of the masses, and eke out a profit (or a living). Second are those that dare to stand out and have the courage to tell their story differently.

I really don't care which rental car I drive, paper towel I use, or energy drink I consume. In many industries, the difference between one choice and another is similar to the margin of winning the

Kentucky Derby. It's an arms race of ho-hum blandness in which almost no one stands out.

Of course, this applies to people just like companies. In today's fiercely competitive workforce, each of us is responsible for building our own personal brand. A good degree and the promise of obedience no longer cut it as they did twenty years ago. Going forward, you'll reach your goals and dreams based on your capacity to differentiate yourself, not your ability to blend in.

Whether you're working to drive your company or career, the key to unlocking your full potential is creating a story that is unique, captivating, and irresistible. While your functional communication is important, your marketing and branding is crucial. It's time to make your brand a firebrand. A firebrand is described as "(1) a piece of burning wood or other material and (2) a person who kindles strife or encourages unrest; an agitator; troublemaker."[9] I can't think of a more important recipe for success in today's turbulent times. The ones who make history are burning with passion and creativity. They disrupt, cajole, and thumb their noses at tradition.

You can't help notice a blazing fire, and you can't help notice a white-hot firebrand. There are thousands of coffee shops, and then there's the firebrand of Starbucks. There are dozens of me-too macaroni and cheese options, and then there's the firebrand brilliance of Kraft and its classic blue box. There are endless formulaic video games, but then there's the irresistible firebrand of Call of Duty.

The same thing goes for people. LeBron James, love him or hate him, is a hundred-million-dollar firebrand who stands out over other sports personalities. Mark Zuckerberg's firebrand was so compelling that a major motion picture was made about it. Martin Luther King Jr.'s firebrand changed the trajectory of racial equality forever.

Nobody remembers the also-rans. If you want to drive your company or yourself to new heights, it's time to ignite your firebrand: do something so different that it can't be ignored.

A few years back, an ad really caught my eye. A couple was driving away from the camera in a shiny Porsche Boxster convertible with top down. Their hair was blowing in the wind as they raced along a scenic vista. No ad copy described the mechanics of the car or the horsepower of the engine. There was no toll-free number to call or coupon to redeem—just a simple phrase: "The two-seat Porsche Boxster. The more kids you have, the more practical it becomes."

Let's explore the brilliance of this piece. In two sentences, the ad communicates a six-hundred-page book's worth of information. Any parent who has been frustrated with child rearing or who has just wanted to get away and run free with his or her spouse for a few hours can relate to this ad on a visceral level. It is a siren song of compelling emotion, urging you to live life and savor the reward of hard work. The play on words, that it doesn't include room for your kids, flies in the face of most car advertising ("Our mini-van will hold all your kids and the whole soccer team"), and the use of the word *practical* in a completely different way (for your marriage, well-being, spirit of adventure) made the ad unforgettable. When you are crafting your own brand messages, hold your work up against this Porsche ad. Does yours create the same emotional jolt? Does it have the same grace and simplicity? Is it using uncommon language to accentuate your key point? Is it easy to understand? Concise? If your nine-hundred-word rant describing every product feature doesn't measure up to this elegant standard, it's time to reinvent.

Detroit: Catalyst for Change

For five days in July 1967, Detroit experienced a violent spree of riots. The rioters killed forty-three people, injured thousands of others, and destroyed countless properties. The governor of Michigan at the time declared the city to be in a state of emergency and called in the National Guard to curtail the destruction that the local police units couldn't handle on their own.[10] This situation was devastating. But decades later, this is still, and incorrectly, cited as the sole reason for Detroit's demise. The picture, in reality, is much more complex. Why has this week been so captivating to the world? This jarring series of events and the lore surrounding them have been expressed in a certain way that fits into Nick Morgan's categorical descriptions of stories with longevity. Because of this alignment with our mentality toward storytelling, this isolated incident is perpetuated as the only causation of problems.

By contrast, the issues of racial divisiveness, lowering population density, and resulting crime plagued Detroit before, after, and in spite of the 1967 riots. There was another race riot here in the 1940s, which was nearly as destructive, but it isn't as widely discussed. The oft-mentioned white flight intensified after the riots but began (and gained steam) in the 1940s as well. This outward migration to suburbia was prompted by various building developments and the Housing Act of 1949, which resulted in clusters of affordable, older housing taken up by middle- and working-class African Americans. Upper- and middle-class whites had used this new appropriation of land to move into newer, more upscale housing built in the suburbs. This left clustered neighborhoods occupied by working-poor blacks, whose dissatisfaction and frustration with circumstances and living conditions rose increasingly.[11]

The 1954 decision in *Brown* v. *Board of Education* had been difficult to enforce everywhere, and like many other cities, Detroit's schools remained largely segregated through the late 1950s and 1960s. In 1970, the NAACP filed suit against Michigan officials, including Governor William G. Milliken, arguing that the local schools remained effectively segregated, albeit unofficially, due to policies enacted regionally. The case ultimately reached the US Supreme Court, which determined that the school districts were not obligated to desegregate unless lines drawn for zoning (that were called into question) could be proven to have been drawn with racist intent in the first place. *Milliken* v. *Bradley* became a landmark case, removing pressure from Detroit and other major urban cities nationwide to desegregate.[12]

Although these were all important factors as a collective explanation for the city's struggles, they aren't discussed as broadly as the 1967 riots alone. The question is *why*? This broad historical pattern, woven with complexity, doesn't fit quite so neatly into our mold for mental recall as a week's worth of violent terror does. In similar fashion, people discuss particular elements of the Holocaust—Kristallnacht, the liberation, or a death march, for example—more readily than the massacre in its totality. It's just like the sports fans who are able to highlight a buzzer-beating, game-winning Hail Mary pass in slow-motion, crystal-clear detail, but have a more difficult time giving a summary of the whole game leading up to that. Our brains have gone back to, and focused on, the story that has been told about Detroit since 1967.

For better or worse, people will associate your business and your personal brand with the story you tell. In this case, the story that's in the forefront—and the more complex one left out of the limelight—isn't a positive one. It's the one that's led to decades of ridicule and fearfulness, and it's the one that leaders today are working hard to reinvent. If you can do so preemptively, you can expect the outcome to be much more positive.

Tools for Transformation: Becoming a Firebrand

When crafting your brand itself or developing various marketing messages to support it, use these best practices to break free from the competitive herd:

1. *Make one point at a time.* Marketing a car on the basis that it offers great mileage, slick design, comfort, and safety and is ecofriendly will overwhelm your audience more than preparing a complex tax return. Pick one thing and really own it. Volvo stands for safety. Ferrari stands for speed. Ford pickup trucks stand for utility. The same goes for crafting individual ads, press releases, and other marketing materials. Make a single point in a compelling way instead of trying to jam in every feature and benefit.

2. *Use surprising, uncommon language.* Use words and phrases that others do not, and make sure that any sentence or claim can only be made by you. "Nothing comes between me and my Calvins" didn't happen by accident, nor were they confused with any other jeans. Can you say the same about your product? The more differentiated your language is, the stronger your results will be.

3. *Dumb it down.* Avoid technospeak and industry jargon. Make sure your message is simple, clear, and so easy to understand that a nine-year-old kid or my eighty-eight-year-old grandma can understand it. Simplicity wins.

4. *Connect at an emotional level.* While you may have a PhD, your customers likely do not. The language has to be attractive to them, not you. Work to create an emotionally charged communication with your customer and speak to his or her needs and desires. "High efficiency detergent" is much less compelling than "removes stains quickly so your family can look its best." Building a deeply rooted and highly connected feeling with customers takes a disciplined and coherent effort. In marketing pursuits, one-off ads rarely work. Consistent campaigns that riff off a single theme for months or even years yield far better results.

5. *Use humor to reinforce and exaggerate.* Humor makes marketing and branding memorable. Kulula Airlines in South Africa stands out from competitors by painting mustaches on its planes and other fun designs such as huge arrows signaling "this end up." It's impossible to confuse it for a bland competitor when you look out an airport window. You'll also recognize it in an instant when reviewing its financials. Unlike competitors that have filed for bankruptcy protection, Kulula Airlines has enjoyed year-over-year growth and profitability.

6. *Less beats more.* In the performing arts, the often-repeated wisdom is that you're better off leaving your audience wanting more, not less. The same goes for branding and advertising: use fewer words, make fewer points, and eradicate clutter. Think about the gorgeous simplicity of Apple's ads (and brand)—rich imagery with two words: "Think Different." As to point 2 above, correct grammar would be "think differently," which makes the award-winning ad campaign even better.

7. *Make sure it's aspirin, not vitamins.* If you have a burning headache, you'll do whatever it takes to subdue it. If it's 3:00 a.m. on a cold, snowy night and you are out of painkillers, you'll bundle up, drive to a twenty-four-hour pharmacy, and desperately pay nearly any cost to alleviate your pain. You'd never do the same for a nice-to-have vitamin. As you work to reinvent your communications, ask yourself, "Am I selling aspirin or vitamins?" It's likely the product you or your company sells is somewhere in the middle. The difference is often how you position and market that product. It turns out that selling vitamins is roughly ten times more difficult since you are marketing an optional product. Vitamin purchases lack urgency, are frequently price sensitive, and offer customers the viable alternative of doing absolutely nothing.

CHAPTER 7

Overhaul Your Culture

*I have noticed even people who claim everything
is predestined, and that we can do nothing to change it,
look before they cross the road.*

—STEVEN HAWKING

The East LA neighborhood of Boyle Heights is a rough place, among dozens of other disenfranchised communities ignored by most leaders. Plagued by violent crime and poverty, this rundown area has a history of gangs and prison sentences. In fact, over 65 percent of ex-convicts in California are back in jail within three years.[1] This recidivism represents an enormous cost to society in terms of both prosecution and imprisonment of the perpetrators and also for the toll they take on their victims and the public safety of their communities. The cycle is extremely difficult to break; these communities have few positive role models, are enmeshed in poverty, and a lack of education is pervasive. After inmates complete their sentence (and their debt to society), it is nearly impossible for them to get hired. Even when they apply for jobs such as pizza delivery or garbage collection, employers can legally reject applicants with a felony conviction, and most job applications ask for this information. With few career opportunities and no resources, the cycle continues when ex-cons return to the thing they know for survival: breaking the law. Boyle Heights is hardly the place where you'd think to find a thriving business, especially one with a culture that helps reform its ex-con workers.

Father Gregory Boyle (his name is only a coincidence; the neighborhood wasn't named after him) set out to create radical change. He believed that people with a rough past deserved a second chance and could thrive in the right environment. Boyle realized that these hard-hit individuals needed jobs, not handouts, so he started a company to give them a shot. Homeboy Industries was born in 1992 to employ those who most needed a break. It began as a bakery and has since grown to encompass a wide variety of offerings, including apparel, salsa, and cafés. The story is authentic, and it has driven demand for its products and services. Today the company has over $10 million in revenue and employs four hundred people who might otherwise be back behind bars.

The culture built by this unconventional leader is surprising. Rather than checking workers' pockets, he extends trust. He treats the team with dignity, compassion, and respect, which they give right back to Boyle and the organization as a whole. A deep sense of pride permeates the team members, who will do whatever it takes to contribute to Homeboy's overall success. As new people join the company, those with a longer tenure help assimilate these new arrivals. By giving them a second chance, the company changes its employees' perspectives about their own future, transforming what they do from crime to contribution.

The success of Homeboy Industries illustrates how cultural norms can transform even those who seem most unlikely to change. The impact of behavioral standards plays a huge role in how an organization functions. If the standard at your company is that meetings always start exactly on time, people will be ready to go the minute the meeting is scheduled. But if leaders routinely show up fifteen minutes late, that is the standard to which employees will assimilate. In this case, the Homeboy culture values the whole as greater than each person; every employee is a valuable asset toward this greater good and knows it.

The importance of cultivating an empowered culture and ensuring your team members are fully aligned with your vision cannot be overstated. Organizations are far more than brands, factory equipment, and balance sheets. The raw materials in this knowledge age are people, and these individuals can create either art or havoc. At the core of many corporate reinventions is the need to change roles, people, and philosophies. Transforming anything without a culture of reinvention is like trying to put a new roof on a house with a crumbling foundation; eventually you'll be headed for a disappointing crash.

Companies are the amalgamation of their people, and their people's actions are a result of their culture, for better or for worse. If you take the time to craft a supportive, empowering culture that fosters creativity and the highest standards of performance, that's how the company will perform. But if you ignore your culture, let outdated traditions direct the team as if on autopilot, or allow sinister motives to build an acceptance of deceit, your organization's results will plummet.

Hit the Cultural Reset Button

Changing the rules of engagement is never easy. Many people in your organization may have a vested interest in preserving the past. The problem, as we know, is that successful approaches are not necessarily sustainable. The world is in a state of constant flux, so if your philosophical approaches are stagnant, you run the risk of imploding. Your corporate culture is an excellent platform for reinvention and a critical step to transforming your organization.

Your first step is to diagnose the current state. Do you need a mere cultural refinement or a full-scale overhaul? If a full reset is needed, you must be prepared to stand strong throughout the process to avoid slipping back into established patterns.

Reinvention without a clear purpose is like getting into a car with no destination in mind. Effective cultural transformation must be linked to a higher mission, or the gravitational pull of the status quo will hold back your efforts. Creating what author Jim Collins refers to as a BHAG (big, hairy, audacious goal), on which your team can focus, will serve as an important accelerant in your reinvention efforts.[2]

Apollo Tyres of India used a big, clear vision to launch a successful transformation. By 2005, the company was a small, successful manufacturer of tires in India, but the leaders knew they could build something much bigger. "We found ourselves in the same position that many other companies do," stated managing director Neeraj Kanwar. "We were doing $300 million a year in revenue, constantly fighting fires and spending all our time on things that probably weren't the best use of our time."[3]

Kanwar conducted an executive offsite meeting with the top twenty people in the company to examine the company's assumptions and challenge the group to chart out a path that would lead to its full potential. "For the first time we seriously asked ourselves where we were, where we were headed, and where we wanted to go. Until that point," he says, "what was missing was having a big goal." The meeting concluded with a clearly articulated vision: to grow almost seven-fold to $2 billion of revenue by 2010, which would place the company in the top fifteen tire companies in the world. This big target inspired the team and made them feel their work was contributing to an important cause. It also illustrated the need for change, since there was no way the current game plan would yield such enormous growth. It forced team members at all levels of the organization to reexamine every aspect of the business with an eye on transformative reinvention.

One of the big changes to Apollo Tyre's culture was the creation of an in-house training academy to ensure that team members at all levels of the company were educated on the intricacies of the business and the culture. The company focused on empowering the team with the skills and decision-making framework necessary to win. It focused much more on training team members on the larger goals of the organization and provided a set of guidelines so that individuals could make better decisions. In addition, it became more transparent so everyone knew where they (and the company) stood, thus allowing its leadership personnel to realize their big goal. "Once you've made a commitment to constant growth and you've gotten everyone on board and you've agreed on the principles that will guide your journey, the things that need to be reinvented become obvious," beams Kanwar. "Reinvention isn't something you do once or twice or now and then. It's something you do on a daily basis and leading a business that embraces constant radical change is a lot more fun than listening to a phonograph with a stuck needle."

Despite being a challenging endeavor, reinventing your culture will drive a double win. First, your new streamlined culture will allow you to execute and compete more effectively, driving near-term gain and momentum. Second, by building a culture that supports creativity and innovation, you are releasing an army of artists who will help you continue to reinvent on an ongoing basis.

Reinventing your team and culture can deliver breakthrough results. It is also a path that is filled with obstacles and pitfalls. To ensure a successful outcome, here's are lists of musts and must nots:

Musts

- *Clearly articulate the need for change.* Reinforce why before you get into how or what.
- *Wrap the effort into a tangible, named reform initiative.* "Culture 2.0" or "The New Frontier" are more concrete and motivating than just a series of instructive changes. Add some branding, and have fun with it.
- *Involve others.* Make sure to involve people from all levels of your company as you craft your new approach. This will drive a sense of ownership and avoid feeling that the new ideals are being thrust on the organization.
- *Develop key principles.* Although it isn't easy, you'll need to establish a short list (ideally no more than ten) of key philosophies. These will be your guiding principles and serve as a benchmark for decision making throughout the organization.
- *Be specific.* Vague platitudes like "service matters" won't resonate and will fail to drive change. Zappos' core value, "Deliver WOW through service," is a memorable and embraceable call to action.
- *Align incentives.* Make sure that compensation, status, and job promotions reward the values you've set forth. The quickest way to undermine a cultural reinvention is to say one thing but reward another. If you want to change behaviors, make sure to put compelling incentives in place to encourage adoption.

- *Train and reinforce.* A big rah-rah event may be a great kickoff but won't drive meaningful change. Specific training on each of your core values, along with continuous reinforcement, is necessary to make a true shift in organizational philosophy.

Must Nots

- *Flip-flop.* Choose your cultural values wisely, and then keep them consistent (at least for the time being). Introducing new ideals or removing fresh ones quickly will undermine your effort for change.
- *Establish competing principles.* If you ask your people to excel at two contradictory efforts, the only thing you'll create will be confusion. Make sure each of the values is complementary to the others.
- *Say one thing and do another.* Your team will pay more attention to what you do than what you say. Cultural reinvention will fail quickly if you ask people to embrace a set of ideals that you as a leader fail to do yourself. If you want to change behavior, you need to become the poster child for the desired conduct. Follow-through is crucial, so consistent reinforcement will impact the outcome.
- *Lack follow-through.* Reforming your culture will take time, especially in larger organizations. Consistency in reinforcing the need for change, modeling and rewarding the desired behavior, and holding your team accountable are critical steps during a cultural reinvention.

Few industries are as cutthroat as the restaurant business. Spikes in patronage frustrate and confuse owners who must deal with fluctuating staffing levels, perishable goods, and fickle guests. Long ago, a strange practice became commonplace and legally acceptable in America: restaurateurs have the right to grossly underpay servers, often the lowest legal limit of $2.13 per hour, which is far below minimum wage in any other business. Patrons are then expected to make up the difference in the form of 15 to 25 percent gratuities. The practice is rationalized in that it gives consumers a mechanism to reward great service or punish poor performance. Yet the vast majority of tips fall within the expected range, regardless of the level of service received. The net effect is simply shifting the cost of paying key staff from the business to the consumer. Think how strange it would be if you were expected to tip your doctor or accountant, from whom you'd presumably also want exceptional service.

Restaurant owners have incorporated this strange custom as the universal norm. That's just the way it works in the industry, right? Tell that to Scott Rosenberg, Naomichi Yasuda, and Shige Akimoto, the owners of the acclaimed restaurant Sushi Yasuda in midtown Manhattan. Never one to follow conventional wisdom, they decided to buck the trend and pay servers the way professionals are paid in other industries.[4] Employees of Sushi Yasuda are paid full salaries with benefits, vacation days, sick leave, and health insurance. And as of 2013, tips are strictly forbidden. Printed clearly on each customer receipt is the following statement: "Following the custom in Japan, Sushi Yasuda's service staff are fully compensated by their salary. Therefore gratuities are not accepted."

By reinventing the old-school practice of tipping and offering a comprehensive and rewarding compensation package, the owners have positioned the restaurant as a great cultural option for employment. Ninety percent of restaurant servers in the United States do not get job-related health insurance, and servers' poverty rates are nearly triple the national average.[5] It's a job that is fraught with insecurity, since a slow night or cheap patrons can throw servers into a financial crisis. So if you are in the food service industry, of course you want to work at Sushi Yasuda. The pay structure drives morale, reduces turnover, and improves overall customer service. Yasuda enjoys another win too: customers appreciate the removal of the tipping process and also respect that the establishment cares for its staff. Accordingly, the restaurant stands out in diners' minds, makes the end of the meal easy for them, and mimics the Japanese custom that the Manhattan location emulates.

The net cost to Yasuda? Zero. By factoring appropriate compensation costs directly into the increased prices Rosenberg now charges, he's able to take better care of his workers without incurring additional expense. Patrons don't mind the higher prices, since they don't have to leave a 20 percent tip at the end of each meal. Rosenberg explains he's seen no change in customer volumes since switching to the no-tips policy.[6] The new system is a win for the restaurant, customers, and wait staff. With such a simple and effective improvement, you'd think more restaurants would adopt this wickedly smart practice. Like Yasuda, you can enjoy a tremendous boost in results if you have the courage to disrupt industry norms, stop blindly accepting practices, and rethink the fundamental beliefs of your business.

Learn the Six Rules of Creative Cultures

Creating a culture that empowers creativity at all levels is critical for leaders who have any interest in competing. Creativity has shifted from a nice-to-have to becoming the most powerful (yet often dormant) asset of an organization. The world has become too complex to have team members simply follow an operating manual and expect to succeed. Today team members must thrive in a state of constant change, making judgment calls in the face of ambiguity. The challenge for leaders is to provide a philosophical framework that allows people to express their creativity and have the confidence to innovate.

What are the principles that lead to a reinvention culture? How can you craft a culture that supports responsible risk taking and creative expression? What approaches and techniques can be used to build and sustain a sense of imagination and wonder? Having studied hundreds of high-performance, creative organizations, I find that these are the six common threads of cultural brilliance: fuel passion, hunt and kill assumption, never stand still, embrace oddball ideas, stick it to the man, and fight to win.

Fuel Passion

Passion is the essential ingredient for building a creative culture. Every great invention, every medical breakthrough, and every advance of humankind began with passion: a passion for change—for making the world a better place; a passion to contribute—to make a difference; a passion to discover something new. With a team full of passion, you can accomplish just about anything as long as you are able to focus that raw passion into a collective sense of purpose. Steve Jobs wanted to "put a ding in the universe." Whole Foods Market was founded with the goal of becoming the world's leading natural and organic foods supermarket retailer. Pixar wanted to reinvent the animated film industry. Pfizer is about saving lives. Your specific purpose must be your own, but the bigger and more important your purpose is, the more passion it can create within your team. That passion will allow you to achieve the goal you've outlined, the purpose driving you forward.

Hunt and Kill Assumptions

As organizations and industries progress, assumptions codify and become unwritten rules. Someone may comment, "That's just the way we do it around here," or, "That is how it's done in our industry." Those phrases should be considered fighting words since they blindly follow the past with no regard for current circumstances. The most dynamic organizations challenge their core beliefs on a regular basis and refuse to accept policies, processes, or procedures solely based on tradition. Just because something hadn't been achieved in the past does not in any way forbid it from happening now or in the future. By definition, all great advances in business and society are those that forge new ground.

Never Stand Still

One of the biggest traps in both business and life is imagining that success is a permanent condition. Those who achieve at the highest levels over a sustained period of time realize that reinvention is not a one-time reboot but a continuous process. The truth is that winning is a temporary circumstance. Just after the champagne has been cleared is the time to think about approaching your work with a fresh approach. A championship football team that runs identical plays in the following year may as well hand over its trophy rings before the season begins. But if you build a culture that embraces continuous reinvention, you'll be well on the way to defining an era instead of enjoying a temporary victory.

Embrace Oddball Ideas

The creative leaps that ultimately drive the biggest gains often appear incredibly strange at first glance. Corporate cultures that hold fresh, unique thinking in the highest regard are well positioned to seize innovation instead of letting it slip down the drain. Instead of shunning whacky ideas, make sure you encourage them at every opportunity. Don't forget that divergent thinking is the root of nearly every great invention and scientific breakthrough.

There's a strange phenomenon in our society: if you are in a ten-person meeting and have an idea, the other nine will quickly become the self-appointed creativity termination squad and tell you every reason that your idea will never work. As a leader, you must recognize that early idea sparks are not meant to be fully defensible and ready for prime time, but they are the seeds of future solid ideas. Remove judgment and applaud new ideas. In meetings, what do you suppose the ratio is at your company between these the phrases: "I have an idea" versus "I have a concern"? Obviously you need a balance between control and creativity to run an effective business, but never forget that great companies are always launched and built on the power of fresh ideas. They discover new and compelling ways to solve problems for customers. They play to win rather than not to lose. History recognizes those who broke free from the shackles of conventional wisdom and used their imagination to create something special.

Stick It to the Man

Disruptive cultures have a healthy sense of irreverence—a chip on their shoulders and a disdain for the old guard. A common thread of the most innovative companies is the desire to prove the doubters wrong. When critics emerge, the finger pointing only emboldens the resolve of these renegade troublemakers. If you're not creating a sense of disbelief, you're not dreaming big enough.

Fight to Win

Competition is a powerful mechanism to rally the team around a common cause and then pursue victory with a vengeance. Great sports rivalries, political bouts, and business challenges have led to peak performance and the breaking of previously held records. The most successful people love to win, but they hate to lose even more. Challenging your employees to conquer competitors, ditch dogma, and sink the status quo will unleash their best performance and visceral drive to win.

Change the Guard

In your efforts to reinvent your culture, you may need to make some tough choices with respect to your team. Certainly you want to give everyone the chance to adapt and evolve. Unfortunately not everyone will embrace your new vision and you may have to let the downers go. As a leader, you are better off taking decisive action rather than letting cultural poison spread.

Firing any employee is a difficult, unpleasant task for a leader, but firing a fellow leader is even worse. Over the years, it's fallen on my shoulders to cut ties with a number of executives in order to continue moving my companies forward. While the people being let go have all been very different from one another, their poor leadership traits have been eerily similar. To help you spot those who need to be replaced as you seek buy-in for reinvention, here are the common traits of executives that I've fired:

- *Their personal agendas came first.* The company's goals should be put at the forefront for leaders. When someone thinks, "Me first, greater good second," the team suffers. The logic is inherently flawed because when the company you help lead does well, everyone feels the benefit. Those who put themselves in the way of the company's success risk losing that for the group and themselves.
- *They hid the ball.* Strong leadership requires transparency in communication, for the good, the bad, and especially the ugly. If a leader's mentality implies that bad news should be kept close to the hip, like a football glued to a running back's side, she is doomed to fail in her own silo. Don't hide the ball; instead of keeping things to yourself, show it to coworkers and figure out a way to make a strong play.

- *They treated people differently up and down.* If you brownnose your boss and are rude to your assistant, it shows. Your attitude rubs off on other people. A basic tenet of common courtesy is that people are people, and all of them deserve your utmost respect. Leaders should exhibit kindness and compassion to every person on his team equally, regardless of title. Playing favorites (or playing nice to a supervisor) is obvious and unwelcome.

- *Their blame-to-credit ratio was inverted.* A great leader takes the fall when things don't go as expected and gives credit to her team when the group hits it out of the park. A leader getting fired has done just the opposite. Taking credit when times are good and pointing fingers otherwise is simply being a weenie. Standing tall is part of the job as an executive, so make sure you always take responsibility.

- *They sabotaged projects stemming from a differing opinion.* In private, it's crucial for leaders to discuss future plans with one another, even heatedly. A difference of opinion is healthy, as is back-and-forth debate. But it should stop there, with the door closed. Once a decision is made, the leaders involved in that decision's execution should work on it as if it was their own idea. Regardless of initial support, a unified front in getting the job done is paramount. Anything less is cause for concern—or worse.

- *They were workhorses but exhibited toxic cultural values.* A company's culture is its most important asset, aside from the people within the organization. A leader with a lack of commitment to this cultural tie is detrimental to the entire company. By the same token, sometimes I've had to fire someone who had a great personality but consistently underdelivered; this is definitely a lesser of these two evils and should be done only as a last resort. Culture and attitude come first: skills can be taught and take time to learn. Allow people to grow into positions, fail and learn from that experience, and continually advance themselves (even if it's a bumpy ride at first).

When the writing is on the wall, make the change quickly and decisively. The sense of relief you'll feel afterward, combined with the energy boost you'll give to your organization, will be well worth the few minutes of discomfort in firing the failing leader. Culture is something that must be managed or atrophy will set in. Great culture is not something that gets rolled out and then forgotten; rather, it is a foundation that must be maintained and cared for. Because of this, you need to take action. If you wait, you are tacitly endorsing their behavior, which will simultaneously undermine your company and your own credibility.

Follow the Power of Rituals

Rackspace, the cloud-computing company that was named one of the Top 100 places to work by *Fortune Magazine* in 2012, has a core value of "Fanatical Support," which includes responsiveness, owner-ship, resourcefulness, expertise, and transparency.[7] Fanatical support goes beyond customers and also applies to internal support, as well as supporting external audiences. Employees, known as Rackers, are simply fanatical about being fanatical. There's an employee-led blog (Rackertalent.com) where team members can post their thoughts and observations about the culture to the world with full transpar-ency. The blog celebrates the Rackspace ideals and encourages every-one to contribute. The headline graphic shouts, "FANATICAL. Kiss any hope of leading a normal life goodbye." This isn't a warning sign, but a unifying message for those who are passionately commit-ted to the work. The highest level of recognition that an employee can receive is his or her very own Fanatical Jacket, a straitjacket that symbolizes achievement in delivering fanatical support. This quirky ritual reinforces the playfulness of the company's culture, as well as its core belief about service. If you were a new team member and witnessed someone running down the hall in a Fanatical Jacket, you'd quickly understand what the company values and rewards. Accordingly, the ritual drives the desired behavior.

One of the most powerful tools in your arsenal as a leader working to reinvent your culture is ritual. Organization rituals are a mechanism for reinforcing core values when you take them off some dusty sign in the lobby and put them into action. According to Paolo Guenzi, a researcher and professor at Bocconi University in Italy, "Rituals create a sense of shared identity, activate team members' external networks, stimulate emotions while reducing anxiety, and reinforce desired behaviors."[8]

Whether you know it or not, your company has rituals. Some are meticulously designed and crafted, while others may have evolved on their own over time. They can become one of the most effective tools to change cultural norms and beliefs if you manage them with purpose. A good way to put rituals to work for you is to first envision the desired cultural value you are hoping to reinforce and then reverse-engineer a ritual to support it. For example, leaders trying to enforce health in their employees bring in a weekly trainer and keep nutritious snacks on hand for everyone. Rituals can be fun or painful, brief or extended, serious or filled with whimsy. Just make sure that the rituals you establish are authentic and create alignment rather than confusion. Here are a few examples of thoughtful rituals that have been established to drive home core values.

Daily Huddle

At Fathead, a company that makes large wall graphics of sports heroes, cartoon characters, and other images, CEO Pat McInnis gathers his team at the same time each day for their "morning stand-up" meeting. The meeting has the identical format each day. First, the team reviews the previous day's results (e.g., sales, returns, website traffic, top-selling items) and discusses its goal for the next day. Next, members of the team are encouraged to share a story or lesson that will help the rest of the team for the upcoming day. The whole meeting takes less than ten minutes and is primarily led by team members, not senior management. This rhythmic approach keeps everyone focused, holds the collective group accountable for daily results, and is a mechanism to reinforce their culture beliefs.

Innovation Days

The Australian-based software company Atlassian holds several innovation days throughout the year for the purpose of allowing their developers to "go rogue." They encourage team members to tinker and explore new ideas. The only requirement is that individuals or teams must deliver something at the end of these twenty-four-hour creativity bursts. The output could be a prototype, a PowerPoint presentation, or even a rap song. They just have to ship and deliver something to demonstrate the results of their efforts. These days of imagination are called FedEx Days, which reminds people that they have to actually deliver something in a day or less, just as the shipping giant does. This idea has caught on, and now many other companies throughout the world are doing their own version in an effort to engage their teams and reinforce the cultural value of innovation.

The Lineup

Ritz-Carlton Hotels didn't become the gold standard of excellence inadvertently. Rituals play a key role in driving consistent superior performance. In this case, the company borrowed a practice that French chefs commonly use. Just as many of them gather everyone in the restaurant together before dinner service so everyone is on the same page, the hotels in the Ritz network have a "lineup." For a few minutes every day, at every shift and every property worldwide, the same message is communicated, and that consistency is unwavering. Employees, referred to as "ladies and gentlemen," describe something incredible that someone has done for a hotel guest to enforce the importance of the "wow" factor.

Even the naming convention of employees, "ladies and gentlemen," has an impact. Their motto is, "We are ladies and gentlemen serving ladies and gentlemen." These are the little things that drive organizational performance by reinforcing their core values.[9]

Acknowledging Family

At ePrize, one of our values was "family first." We realized that each team member had loved ones who were affected by both the rewards and sacrifices of the job. With that in mind, I created a few rituals that extended beyond the employee and into their family. When we hired a new person, we sent a gift, such as flowers or a bottle of wine, to his or her spouse with a note thanking that person for letting us borrow his or her loved one. We'd do the same if a team member was stuck on an extended project and had to spend extra time away from family. We also created an over-the-top annual Halloween party called eeeeek-Prize. We transformed our entire building into a haunted house and invited team members' kids, cousins, nieces and nephews, neighbors, friends, or anyone else they wanted to bring. Kids ran around the decorated space to trick-or-treat for candy and participate in carnival games and costume contests. We'd regularly attract up to a thousand guests, and this ritual became a highly anticipated event. It was designed to extend our company's relationship into team members' families and give a little love beyond the individual employee. This clear demonstration of our values had a lasting effect, and kids better understood their mom or dad's obsession with their job.

Lead Without Title

At a visit to a New York City jazz club, I witnessed a near disaster averted only by a selfless act. The vocalist (the leader in this instance) instructed the musicians to begin a classic jazz standard in a specific key. Once she began to sing, however, the highly trained musicians cringed with fearful anticipation. The singer had selected a key too high for her range, and it would clearly botch the song's big finish.

The musicians had been hired by the vocalist to be "sidemen," that is, to do what they were told. If the singer crashed, it wouldn't be their fault. They were just playing what they were supposed to. But this time one of the sidemen made the decision to lead.

Realizing the gaff, the guitarist quickly got the attention of the other musicians. He held up three fingers, which is a musician code to change to the key of E-flat. The other musicians gave a quiet nod and waited for the guitarist's cue. Next, he discretely signaled his plan to the singer as a look of relief and joy swept across her face. At just the right time after a drum solo (so the key change wouldn't sound awkward to the audience), our guitar hero gave the subtle nod and the band changed key with precision. The number ended with a stunning vocal finale and was met with loud cheers from the crowd. Our understated sideman had saved the day.

In *The Leader Who Had No Title*, Robin Sharma shares the importance of fostering leadership skills and embracing new thinking from your entire organization, not just the top brass.[10] He encourages all people, regardless of their job title or position, to seize the opportunity to lead on a daily basis. Don't wait for a new promotion; start leading now, and you will end up with the title you seek.

Whether you're the CEO or an intern, there are always opportunities to leave your creative fingerprint and advance your organization. Sometimes little improvements don't get noticed right away, but if you continue to lead, you'll become indispensable. Opportunities to make a difference are abundant. The real question is whether you will seize them. The pass-the-buck, not-my-job, just-doing-what-I'm-told mentality helps no one. But those who don't wait for the authority to make a difference will always benefit.

The unassuming guitarist gave a small, all-knowing smile as the singer took credit for her big finish. He knew he'd contributed to the whole beyond his own individual requirements. He took pride knowing they won as a team. He also knew exactly which person that singer would call the next time she needed to hire a guitar player.

As you craft your own cultural reinvention, make sure you champion leadership initiatives throughout your organization, regardless of job title, rank, or serial number. The most fluid organizations, those that are adept at continuous innovation and deliver sustainable results, encourage leadership at every level. To win over the long haul, you need to tap into the leadership skills of your people no matter what their business card title may happen to currently display.

Detroit: Catalyst for Change

Kwame Kilpatrick was inaugurated as the mayor of Detroit in 2002. Having grown up in the city, he promised change for the better from someone who understood what it meant to be a Detroiter.[11] In fact, he's been a shining example of toxic culture, demonstrating what happens to the whole bowl of ice cream when one drop of poison is added.

During his first term, he racked up $210,000 in charges on his city-issued credit card, spent on personal extravagances. From the beginning, he put himself before the citizens he served instead of being a servant leader.[12] In 2003, two former Detroit Police Department officers, deputy police chief Gary Brown and Kilpatrick's ex-bodyguard Harold Nelthrope, filed a lawsuit against the mayor, claiming they were fired after investigating his personal actions, which went against a whistle-blowing law. The pair had probed into a rumored party at the Manoogian Mansion, the city-owned mayoral residence (the mayor was accused of having a Gatsby-like bash with strippers, booze, illicit affairs, and overall chaos at the mayoral mansion that was funded by taxpayer dollars); the mayor's dubious affair with his chief of staff, Christine Beatty; and the murder of Tamara Greene. Known as "Strawberry," Greene was an exotic dancer who supposedly performed at the event and was shot to death months later while sitting in her car, killed with the same model and caliber gun then used by the Detroit Police Department.[13]

While the party and Greene's unsolved murder were never proved and remain urban legend, the affair would prove to be true. After miraculously winning a reelection campaign, Kilpatrick took the stand in this whistle-blower trial, denying his involvement with Beatty, as did she. The plaintiffs received a multimillion dollar reward in 2007, and their lawyer then came forward with evidence Kilpatrick and Beatty had perjured themselves and tried to cover it up. As a result, the county prosecutor charged both with obstruction of justice, conspiracy, misconduct in office, and perjury.[14] In September 2008, Kilpatrick pled guilty to multiple felony charges, agreeing to pay the city $1 million in restitution, along with his resignation and four months of jail time. Midway through his time served, Kilpatrick missed required restitution payments, claiming poverty (even with a lavish home and cars), which violated his probation, and he was sentenced to more time in prison.[15]

Later that year, Kilpatrick was again indicted, this time with thirty-eight charges of corruption, centered on contracts with kickbacks—all with the city's money. Others indicted alongside him were Kilpatrick's father, aide, close contractor, and water department chief. In October 2013, Kilpatrick was sentenced to twenty-eight years in federal prison.[16] From the day he stepped into the mayor's office, Kwame Kilpatrick was a destructive, sinister force that crumbled nearly ten years' worth of citywide morale. With a blatant disregard for honesty, he put himself and his direct contacts' needs first, above those of the group—in this case, the electorate that voted him into office. For a city already struggling, Kilpatrick's toxicity became the final element to crumble our foundation entirely. His actions spread throughout city hall, leaving a path of greed, dishonesty, and finger pointing behind him.

In your organization, a bad egg is just as problematic, so you must be vigilant to constantly support a positive culture while pushing these negative forces out. Even if a person isn't a felon like Kilpatrick, his or her bad attitude, poor work ethic, or lack of acceptance of new ideas will spread to others. You risk more by not tending to your organization's culture. The poisonous effect varies, of course. In the case of Detroit, this poison drained the city of millions of dollars, ruined citizens' trust in local government, moved the city into the national spotlight as a punch line, and prevented the efficacy of the remaining municipalities from doing their jobs. Detroit couldn't afford to pay this price, and regardless of outcome, neither can you. Culture matters, so remember to keep it front and center as an integral part of what you do.

Tools for Transformation: The Hot Seat

As you work to improve and reinvent your corporate culture, transparency, vulnerability, and trust are all crucial elements. To work on these values, the gift of feedback is the ideal method. A helpful, albeit challenging, exercise to give and receive direct feedback is called "the hot seat." It's most effective with a maximum of eight people, so think of this as one leader with his or her direct reports. The people you work closely with will be the best source of feedback and are the most important people to deliver it.

If you left lunch with your best friend and had spinach in your teeth, you'd want her to tell you; so too should you want your closest colleagues to give you straight-between-the-eyes feedback in a candid way so you can improve as a leader.

Here are the steps for giving feedback using the hot seat:

Step 1: Assign a scribe. Make sure someone is taking notes at all times.

Step 2: Everyone sits in a circle or simply around a large conference room table. The first volunteer identifies himself as being "in the hot seat."

Step 3: Everyone around the room then has to tell that person two things, with blunt honesty. First is the one thing each most admires, respects, or appreciates about that person and the way he conducts himself. Second is one critical piece of feedback that she wishes he'd improve. Throughout the process, the person in the hot seat is not allowed to say anything except to ask a clarifying question. In this way, you can't be overly appreciative of the nice things people say, but you also can't get defensive from the feedback. Receiving feedback is just as difficult as giving it, but is equally important.

Step 4: Everyone goes around the room and gives the first person his or her individual feedback, as the scribe continues to take notes. When everyone has said their optimal and critical pieces, the scribe tears off the note sheet and hands it to the person who just stepped down from the hot seat. This way, the person walks away with a strong sense of what to improve and what's already a strength.

Step 5: Repeat the process for everyone in the room so each person takes a turn in the hot seat.

While this exercise can be incredibly difficult at first and even a bit uncomfortable, it needs to happen to further your team's growth and connectedness. Without feeling vulnerable, how can you be expected to be empathetic? Without being trusting of your team, how can you feel comfortable with them leading a project effectively? Without a sense of transparency, how do you know that what you see is what you get? You'd want to know you have food stuck in your teeth, so providing this forum for your employees to do the same helps promote a deep connection, only bolstering your culture.

CHAPTER 8

Reimagine Your Customer

*They always say time changes things, but you actually
have to change them yourself.*

—ANDY WARHOL

Harley-Davidson, the iconic American motorcycle brand, nearly
suffered a fatal crash. From 1973 to 1983, the company's market share fell from 78 percent to only 23 percent as Japanese competitors produced higher-quality, lower-cost alternatives. Foreign-made
better bikes, combined with gigantic advertising budgets, tamed
Harley's roar. The company was days away from bankruptcy when
a group of twelve passionate employees facilitated a management
buyout of the company and took matters into their own hands.[1]

Realizing there was no way to compete on price, these maver-
icks decided to play to the company's strength: emotion. As Japanese
manufacturers used low-cost plastic, Harley doubled down on heavy
steel. "The real power of Harley-Davidson is the power to market
to consumers who love the product," says Harley-Davidson's former president and CEO, Richard Teerlink. The bike represented to
America, he continued, "the adventurous pioneer spirit, the Wild
West, having your own horse, and going where you want to go—the
motorcycle takes on some attributes of the iron horse. It suggests
personal freedom and independence." So in an era where price was a
big deciding factor, Harley *raised* its prices.

As the company reinvented its manufacturing processes to improve quality, it also reinvented its customer base. Throughout the company's rebirth, the profile of Harley riders changed dramatically.[2] The allure of the open road and the freedom that Harley symbolized began to appeal to white-collar professionals too. Doctors, lawyers, accountants, and bankers fell in love with Harley-Davidsons, and having a "hog" became a status symbol. Groups such as the Rolex Riders and the Rich Urban Bikers began to form, driving up demand and price. By 1990, 60 percent of the company's customers were college graduates, and professionals around the world were drawn to the unique roar of a Harley.[3]

The company also reinvented its relationship with existing customers. The new employee-owners loved their bikes and wanted to cultivate that same crazed sense of passion among their customer base. The Harley Owners Group (HOG) was launched in 1983 to connect Harley owners to their passion of the open road. What started as a way to unite customers around the brand has evolved into a cult-like fervor. By 2007, the HOG had more than 1 million members, who typically spent 30 percent more on clothing, events, and accessories than other owners.[4] A whole subculture of devotees has emerged.

Don't let the beards, long hair, and leather chaps fool you. The leaders at Harley-Davidson are among the smartest and most insightful disruptors in business. They saved a troubled brand by finding a large, new set of customers and emotionally charging their existing core.

Accept the Death of One Size Fits All

Mass-appeal marketers have been losing ground for years to savvy businesses that attack specific segments. Since the digital age allows content creators to speak to a very niche audience, this approach has never been more important. The three TV networks have given way to hundreds of cable channels and millions of on-demand choices. Broad-based magazines are losing ground to specialty publications for everything under the sun. While there will always be Super Bowl ads that try to appeal to millions of people at once, smart companies are seizing new windows of opportunity by tightening the aperture of their lenses and hunting down specific audience niches.

We've covered many ways to reinvent your organization so far in this book, from product and processes to experience and branding. Transforming your customer is another way for you to drive your organization forward and seize new opportunity. Look around corners and under proverbial rocks to find new places to sell your products and services. The irony is that many organizations remain deadlocked in a futile battle over a specific audience, with costs and collateral damage spinning out of control. All the while, there may be customers who are in anxious need of what you have to offer if you simply branch out and provide something special to fit their needs.

There are literally millions of permutations of various customer segments: advanced-beginner female skiers in the Northwest between the ages of eighteen and twenty-four; Hispanic vegetarian seniors with advanced degrees who enjoy Caribbean cruises for leisure travel; jazz guitarists from the Midwest who are also authors, entrepreneurs, and venture capitalists (if you come up with any products or services geared to this segment, e-mail me immediately). A multidimensional grid with nearly unlimited squares, there is boundless opportunity for you to discover fertile new ground. Let's explore how to slice and dice the population of potential customers into a variety of segments that are easy to target in your effort to transform your organization.

Adam or Eve?

As a guest at the Bella Sky Hotel in Copenhagen, you may feel as if you have ventured into an alternative universe if you entered a room on the seventeenth floor. These rooms have warm tones, fresh flowers, fashion magazines, and fruit smoothies. You've arrived at Bella Donna, Europe's first hotel floor designed by and dedicated exclusively to women.[5] The hotel's CEO, Arne Bang Mikkelsen, explains: "Men's and women's preferences are very different. When men come into a hotel room, the first thing they do is check the view, turn on the TV, plug in their computer, and check out the minibar. Women on the other hand go straight for the bathroom. Does it smell nice? Is it clean? Does it have a nice bathtub and shower?"[6]

Every assumption was challenged as management crafted a new style of room. The bathrooms are stocked with exclusive products, including day and night moisturizers. High-powered hair dryers, full-length mirrors, and healthy room service options are among the options customized for their intended guests. As you might expect, women traveling for business to Copenhagen have kept Bella Donna constantly booked to capacity and have given a big boost in exposure to the entire hotel property.

Bella Donna's success has spurred a string of other hotels hoping to capitalize on the idea of specialized offerings for women. The Orchid Floor in the Georgian Court Hotel in Vancouver, British Columbia, has been so successful that the hotel is adding a second women-only floor. The London Dukes Hotel's Duchess Rooms have enjoyed a 25 percent surge in bookings. These thoughtful hoteliers are riding the trend of a rise in women traveling for business. According to a research report by Cornell University, nearly half of all business travelers in the United States are women, up from 25 percent in 1991 and less than 5 percent forty years ago. These forward-looking proprietors realized that specifically targeting a female audience is a powerful way to beat the competitive pack.[7]

Gary and Diane Heavin took the same approach when launching Curves, the largest women's-only gym in the world, with thousands of locations across ninety countries.[8] The founders realized that women wanted a workout but didn't want to be on display to men trying to catch a glance. By the same token, they observed that some women didn't feel confident if they were beginners. The Curves program includes a time-saving circuit that gets busy women in and out in thirty minutes while specifically targeting their needs. The Heavins took an existing commodity business (gyms) and used a specific customer segment (women) to create their point of differentiation. The bottom line is that if you try to be all things to everyone, you end up with a value proposition that is so diffuse it loses its potency.

Kathy Tolleson recognized this specificity all too close to home. Having loved motorcycles since she was a little girl, she wanted to be involved with her passion in a deeper way. After forty years as a hobbyist, this grandmother of thirteen founded Roar Motorcycles for Women in 2008. In the same way Harley-Davidson increased its business by focusing on specific customer segments, Tolleson saw her opening to enter the industry she understood personally: women. What if she started a motorcycle company that specifically catered to the underserved female market? As an enthusiast herself, she learned that women accounted for 12 percent of motorcycle ownership that year, up from 9.6 percent in 2003. Although the segment was growing, few businesses catered to these women.[9]

Roar Motorcycles for Women customizes existing bikes for women riders and creates unique custom-made bikes from scratch. The staff members study the behavior and tastes of women with an aim of adding some female flair in a traditionally male-dominated sport. The team adapted their entire approach to serve this specific audience—from the colors of the bikes they produce, to the design of their website, to the layout of their shop. They take into consideration every detail for their customers. From lowering seat heights to offering woman-only gear, Tolleson and her team have fully differentiated themselves from all the other standard bike shops.

Taking the polar opposite approach can also yield big wins. While hotels are typically geared toward men, carbon-copy hair salons are generally built to serve women. This duplicity presented the exact opening that Chad Johnson needed to launch Lady Jane's Haircuts for Men in 2004. Johnson explains, "We set out each day to make the Lady Jane's experience better for each and every guy. That's what sets us apart, that's what makes us the best—no, *only* place for guys to get a great haircut in an environment designed specifically for them."[10]

There's no confusing a Lady Jane's with a traditional female-focused salon. As a guest, you'll notice the leather recliners in the lobby, the dozen HD plasma TVs throughout the salon, sports memorabilia adorning the walls, and plenty of guy-focused decor and accessories throughout. In an industry with thin margins and brutal competition, Lady Jane's has grown to more than forty locations across seven states by 2013 and is poised for explosive national expansion.[11]

Take a look at your own product or service, and imagine how it could be tailored to a specific gender focus. The Victoria Law Firm (located in Detroit) caters exclusively to women in divorce matters. Anthony Logistics for Men is the leading men's skin care and grooming line, simply because founder Tony Sosnick saw an opportunity to serve an unmet demand for men's products in a women-dominated industry. Even if your immediate instinct is that gender customization won't work in your field, you may be surprised if you give yourself permission to explore the possibilities.

Forever Young?

Lady Jane's used gender to reimagine the beauty salon. Using the same approach, Curious Chef customized the cooking experience using age as the point of differentiation. This company sells functional kitchen tools that are safe for kids to use. Normally we think of cooking as something that only adults do, but this company tailors everything they do to kids and their parents who want them in the kitchen. By broadening into a different clientele to approach healthy eating, the company is on a growth tear in an all-kid market.

In similar fashion, seniors represent an enormous market for customized solutions. As baby boomers age, the market for specialized products and services continues to expand. Other explosive customer segments are Gen X, Gen Y, and millennials. Each age bracket has a specific set of tastes and desires, so catering your offering directly to their needs can create just the opening you need.

From Coast to Coast

The hit TV series *Hardcore Pawn* features "the biggest and baddest pawn shop in Detroit," American Jewelry and Loan. The owners have been propelled to celebrity status: over 3 million weekly viewers tune in to see the insides of this rough-and-tumble business. Owner Les Gold (perfect name, right?) realized that this hugely successful business could serve customers beyond its twenty-mile radius. He took his newly hot brand and years of experience and opened a second store in Pontiac, Michigan, to widen his geographic reach. As he contemplates further expansion to other major cities throughout the United States, the business is also online at PawnDetroit.com. Gold seized the opportunity to capture a wider customer base by expanding his geographic reach.

Whereas the Gold family thought broadly about geography, my partners and I looked narrowly at a map when founding Detroit Venture Partners. Conventional wisdom suggests that tech start-ups *must* be in Silicon Valley, Boston, or New York. That's where all the action is, the theory goes. Predictably that's also where all the competition exists. Instead of following the herd and getting lost in the shuffle, we decided to disrupt by launching a tech venture fund in the least likely place of all: smack dab in the heart of downtown Detroit. As critics pointed fingers and gave looks of confusion, we proudly marched into virgin waters.

Our belief was that taking a nontraditional route and serving an unlikely geographic region would create an enormous advantage. And that's exactly how it has played out. Rather than tripping over other venture capitalists for deals, talent, and service providers, we enjoy almost no competition. Less than thirty miles from the University of Michigan, a top research university, we have incredible access to ideas and talent. Our cost basis to launch start-ups is a fraction of what's needed on either coast, and we are able to stand out as the dominant firm in our region. It made no sense to us why someone would want to cast their line into an already saturated fishing hole, especially when the alternative is so enticing: finding bountiful rewards without becoming entangled by competitors.

While geographic expansion (or narrowness) is obvious, finding new ways to reach potential customers can be a creative challenge. Nemo's Bar in Detroit cuts into competitors located within walking distance of Comerica Park (home of the Detroit Tigers) by offering free busing. Instead of dealing with crowds and overpriced parking, Nemo's provides sport fans a smarter alternative: park for free, enjoy great food and drink, and then let the Nemo's game shuttle give round-trip transportation to the game. The addition of a bus expanded the bar's competitive battlefield and allows it to serve a previously inaccessible market.

This same global mind-set can be applied to your industry by targeting ethnic groups specifically or by bringing elements of a global palate to the broader public. Examine the growing popularity (and expanded merchandising) of the international food aisle at generic grocery chains. Even five years ago, this aisle included marinara sauce, refried beans, and soy sauce. Today the options are endless, even in mainstream stores.

An Apple a Day

Health conditions may be a less obvious customer segmenting strategy, but can be incredibly powerful as you tailor your wares. Nearly every symptom and condition represents a new group of customers who may be eager to work with you based on your specific expertise or solution set. Even if you are not part of the $3 trillion health care industry in the United States, you may be able to customize your products or services to fit the needs of one of these groups. PositiveSingles.com is a dating website for people who have sexually transmitted diseases. The site claims over 60,000 dating success stories and has over 15,000 members per day using the service, accounting for over 120,000 daily conversations.[12] It helps an underserved community and provides a valuable service while simultaneously growing a great business. If the founders had launched another generic dating site in 2001, they'd probably be long out of business after getting crushed by industry giants such as Match.com and eHarmony. Instead, they targeted their service to an audience that was unified by a health concern and have enjoyed tremendous success as a result.

From obesity to anorexia, sleep apnea to narcolepsy, diabetes to Alzheimer's, each condition represents a customer segment that has a deep connection to its health situation and will pay attention to specific offerings that are marketed toward their needs.

It doesn't have to be all doom and gloom. Olympic athletes, marathon runners, and personal trainers are also deeply connected to their own health conditions, which in these cases are positive ones. Helmets for women cyclists, fashionable yet functional apparel for weight trainers, or board games for vegans are all hypothetical ideas to bring products to various segments united by health. GU Energy Gel is specifically designed to keep athletes fueled during exercise. The company manufactures small packets of gel that can be consumed while jogging or biking. GU is made for those who participate in endurance sports and need a nutritional boost to keep going strong. Started in 1991, the company is now the leader in this niche industry and has enjoyed incredible success on a global scale. Because it targeted its product to a narrow audience (endurance athletes), it was able to avoid competition and quickly win the hearts and minds of consumers.

Choose Your Coffee Table and Your Magazine

Websites, blogs, newspapers, TV channels, and magazines exist for nearly every subgroup imaginable. You can find content specifically designed around southern vegetarian cooking, private aviation, bikram yoga, or home school Jewish education. Fox News has unabashedly delivered a conservative, right-wing slant on political news, while the *Huffington Post* covers the other end of the spectrum. In each case, catering to a specific audience and speaking in an authentic and relevant voice created wealth. If you are a consumer of luxury goods, fine jewelry, and Italian sports cars, reading *Budget Living* magazine won't cut it. If you meet that description, you probably prefer the *Robb Report*, which caters to the affluent lifestyle. By that same logic, if you're a gym rat and love to pump iron, *Muscle and Fitness* may be your main read.

Think of your own business and imagine you're standing in front of an enormous magazine rack. As you scan the various titles, ask yourself which of these segments could be an area for you to serve. Let's use an example: financial planners, who are as prevalent as mobile phones and generally as exciting as waiting in traffic. If that's your business, stop trying to be everything to everyone in your dark gray suit. If instead you built your practice around a very specific lifestyle, you'd not only stand out; you'd leap forward. What about a financial services firm that caters to a gay and lesbian clientele? While you may alienate some customers, you could quickly become the leader in your category while gaining loyal and supportive customers. If you happen to love the arts, you could gear your practice to artists, musicians, actors, and those who are directly involved with or support this segment. Your beige office would give way to stunning art works, which you could likely secure for free by asking your customers to showcase their work on a rotating, monthly basis. You could host art showings, complete with live jazz and wine tastings to attract both patrons and performers. Would you lose some of your customers who run grocery stores? Perhaps. But would you become the toast of the town in the arts world? Absolutely.

Slicing and dicing customer segments to discover new opportunity provides limitless possibilities. Segments can be formed based on historical experiences such as law graduates from Yale, women born in East LA, or Marines who served in the Gulf War. You can also find new customer segments in specific industries or titles. Plant managers in advanced manufacturing facilities, registered nurses in intensive care units, or chief technology officers of Fortune 500 companies are all valid customer segments to pursue.

Disrupt Distribution

Finding new segments is one way to reinvent your customer, but finding new ways to reach them is another. After a bitter divorce in 1942, Brownie Wise had to find a job to survive. She ended up selling cleaning aids and equipment to housewives for Stanley Home Products to keep a roof over her head. She managed to eke out a living, but Wise wasn't satisfied. An insight in the early 1950s led to reinventing herself and developing an entire distribution channel at the same time: she noticed a new product sold in stores but thought of a different solution. Wise invented the Tupperware party concept, in which a female sales representative hosts a tea party for other women in the area. During the party, Tupperware products were demonstrated, discussed, and sold. The new distribution format provided jobs and self-esteem to sales associates, convenience and entertainment to customers, and a huge boost in sales to manufacturers. Revenues exploded as in-home sales parties became all the rage. Annual events, known as Jubilees, were held to celebrate Tupperware saleswomen and share new products and techniques. Wise became a legend and is now known as the founder of in-home, multilevel marketing. Her techniques are still used today to sell cosmetics (Mary Kay, Avon), candles (Pink Zebra), kitchen gadgets (Pampered Chef), jewelry (Stella & Dot), and other household products (Amway).[13]

Discover New Routes

Delivering your products and services through nontraditional means can open up rich opportunities. Your software could be preinstalled on Android devices instead of marketed online. Your restaurant could offer food truck service to boost your lunch business in busy urban areas. Your law practice could deliver legal work over the Internet. Not buying it? Check out LegalZoom.com. Cofounded by legal celebrity Robert Shapiro, the service offers "personalized, affordable legal protection." The company set out to deliver fast, low-cost, template legal solutions at a fraction of traditional pricing. They traded wood-paneled offices for an online storefront to support the most common legal procedures: wills and trusts, business formation, trademark filing, and real estate purchases. The company has become a "category killer," with over 2 million customers while enraging old-school lawyers. Rather than changing its product (legal services), the company reinvented a new distribution model (sell templates over the Internet). This innovation broke down traditional cost barriers while expanding customer reach. This new model helped the business score $66 million in venture capital funding from top firms in 2011 as it prepared for its initial public offering.[14]

Reach Up

You may be thinking, "Sounds great but my industry doesn't work that way. We are a mature industry that's highly competitive and not as open for reinvention." That was the prevailing wisdom of the hair care industry in 1980 when John Paul DeJoria and Paul Mitchell launched John Paul Mitchell Systems. Realizing they didn't stand a chance competing with giant brands in grocery stores and pharmacies, Paul Mitchell began by selling only through elite salons. DeJoria and Mitchell launched a high-end, four-product system that stylists embraced as a better alternative to conventional shampoo and conditioner. Because they sold only through salons, competition was limited and the brand's cachet soared. As of 2013, the company sold its large line of products in eighty-five countries and brought in over $1 billion in annual revenue.[15] While the company has innovated many times along the way, including launching its own chain of beauty schools, the founders launched a successful operation based on their choice to sell in a less crowded, more elite environment.

Reach Down

Typical furniture stores offer limited selection and then deliver fully assembled pieces to local customers. The word *Ikea* is actually an abbreviation of the founder's name, but it might as well mean "opposite" in the company's native Swedish language. This rule-breaking powerhouse has built a $34 billion enterprise and become the world's largest furniture retailer by bucking tradition.[16] Look at how they used an opposite approach to win:

Traditional Furniture Store	Ikea
Open layout, sectioned by room type	One-way design, "districts"
Fully assembled	Build yourself
Delivered	Customer pickup
Big margins	Small margins
Constant discounting	Everyday low prices
Sell many manufacturers' products	Sell only Ikea products
Goal: sell expensive items	Goal: sell low-cost products
No food or drink allowed	In-store restaurants

Ikea reinvented the entire shopping and distribution system. By catering to budget-conscious shoppers who are willing to pick up and assemble their own furniture, the company has achieved rock-star status among consumers.

Plug into Other Industries

The solar industry has been heating up in a big way over the past few years, and so has the competition. Technology advances have created high demand from home owners, since a solar installation can reduce energy bills by up to 35 percent. Simultaneously, there's a market for commercial installers to secure roof placement of panels and then sell excess energy back to the utility companies. Although these are exciting developments, friction existed on both sides of the equation. Enter GridBid, a start-up that offers the "world's first roof-top auction." Founder Thomas Kineshanko explains, "After speaking with over 100 players in the solar market, we found that solar installers were paying way too much in business development costs (sometimes up to 20 percent of total project cost) while building and home owners were struggling to find and select high quality, affordable solar installers. We came up with Gridbid to solve both problems."[17]

Gridbid allows homeowners to place their roofs up for auction. Installers bid on not only the installation project itself but also the shared revenue from excess energy produced, which can be sold back to utility companies. The homeowner gets a lower-cost, higher-quality solar installation, along with a new revenue stream from their own rooftop. The installer gets low-cost placement of solar panels that can be turned for a profit as they generate power. Gridbid auctioned more than $300,000 in rooftop solar panels during its first *week* online. The company has reinvented the distribution process for both audiences. By finding a better way for both homeowners and installers to secure rooftop panels, Gridbid stands to capitalize on the $100 billion solar energy market. Its innovation came by changing the way the sales process works for all parties involved, not by creating a new type of panel, price point, or experience.

Reinventing the Buying Process

Here's a list of questions to ask yourself as you reinvent the way your customers buy from you:

- How do customers buy my type of product or service today? What are our existing distribution models and standard industry practices?
- What would it look like if I did the opposite?
- What friction exists in the current model? Are there steps that I could take to reduce it and offer a better customer solution?
- Is there something I could remove from the current model to create significant differentiation (the way Ikea removed assembly, for example)? Is there something I could add to it?
- Could I change the billing process, financial structure, or even economic model to stand out from competitors? For example, a doctor could charge a flat monthly "wellness" fee rather than a fee for each appointment.
- What trends are driving consumer behavior that could affect the way you sell? How could you incorporate these trends to increase revenue?
- Could you combine your current offering with something else to drive performance for both? For example, Dunkin' Donuts and Baskin-Robbins now have stores that offer both doughnuts and ice cream. The combined offering has driven sales for each brand. There are many doughnut shops and many ice cream joints, but the combination has been embraced by consumers and allowed sales of the combined company to reach over $8.8 billion.
- In a perfect world, what alternative ways could your customer buy your product? Think: location, packaging, price point, complementary offerings, wait time, and customer experience.

Hold the Postage

Fast Company's Most Innovative Food Company of 2013 wasn't Kraft, General Mills, or Coca-Cola. It was Israeli-based SodaStream, the largest producer of home carbonation. The company has sky-rocketed in popularity by offering consumers the opportunity to save money and help the environment when drinking soda. Instead of purchasing cans or bottles of cola, consumers use their

SodaStream machine to make their own concoction using tap-water and the company's flavoring packs. The company changed the distribution model by eliminating bottlers and avoiding the high shipping cost of heavy liquid. When consumers provide their own water, costs go down for everyone and a brand-new consumer experience stands out from the competitive herd. SodaStream is carried by sixty thousand retailers in forty-five countries and sold 2.5 billion flavor cans in 2012.[18] These renegades took on one of the most mature and competitive industries, soft drinks, and used a disruptive innovation around distribution to seize an enormous opportunity.

Add the Postage

While attending Harvard Business School, Hayley Barna often received makeup samples from a friend who worked in the fashion media industry. Hayley's friends in Boston couldn't wait to see what came next, and these samples became highly coveted merchandise in Barna's circle of peers, especially Katia Beauchamp. She became obsessed with the surprise and discovery process. This insight led to a breakthrough business idea that Barna and Beauchamp launched in fall 2010: Birchbox.[19] The newly formed company offered a sub-scription service, costing ten dollars a month, where customers would receive a monthly sample kit of upscale lipsticks, shampoos, skin care products, and other cosmetics. This idea created a revolu-tion: it was the first time a mailed subscription involved discover-ing new products without ordering specific items. Consumers loved opening their monthly shipments to discover new, surprising, fun products. At the same time, manufacturers loved the concept as a mechanism to get samples into the hands of eager buyers. Boom! The discovery commerce industry was born.

Birchbox expanded to offer discovery boxes for both men and women. It also sells products directly on its highly trafficked site and even produces a magazine for customers to become better edu-cated on beauty products. The company has expanded into France, the United Kingdom, and Spain and boasts over 100,000 subscribers.[20]

Barna and Beauchamp touched a nerve with consumers. In an age where limitless choices can become overwhelming, the idea of having a trusted company pick products for you and ship them on a regular schedule took off; other industries quickly followed suit. BarkBox is a monthly box of dog goodies; it's the same model, but for pets. NatureBox provides healthy snacks delivered to you on a monthly subscription basis. TrunkClub promise that customers will become the "best dressed guy in the room."[21] The model has been adapted to men's fashion and offers a monthly subscription that sends shipments of clothing from button-downs to T-shirts to sport coats. In this case, customers are not charged until they inspect the merchandise, decide what they want to keep, and then mail back what they don't like (free of charge, of course).

As a venture capitalist, I can tell you that eager entrepreneurs are leaping toward this model. I've seen dozens of start-ups claiming to be the "Birchbox of . . ." Garden seeds, perfume, gluten-free foods, art supplies, and even tech gear have become "Birchboxed." In Detroit, a new start-up, MyBrownBox, is riding this trend by offering "the #1 subscription service for women of color delivering beauty, lifestyle, and luxury monthly." The founders borrowed the business model of Birchbox and applied it to a niche—in this case, African American women.

In the same way Birchbox reinvented a mature industry using a unique distribution model, you can find fresh opportunity in your field if you're willing to let go of traditional thinking and let your imagination soar.

Innovate Now, Before It's Too Late

If you feel stuck, it's time to discover new customers and explore fresh ways to sell to them. Imagine that your customer base completely dried up and your distribution practices became illegal. What new customers would you serve? Where would you find them? How could you sell and deliver in a new way? This exercise is exactly what your competitors are doing right now, so it's your job to beat them to the punch. Even if you're at the top of your game, you must realize that customer segments and tastes are fickle and always changing. Twenty-something entrepreneurs racing with rabid fervor to dislodge your leadership position can disrupt distribution models overnight. Cost cutting, legal wrangling, lobbying, or following won't deliver the results you need. The only way to drive sustainable competitive advantage and seize your full potential is to embrace continuous reinvention as an ongoing discipline. It's time to create something fresh and compelling before your competition beats you to it.

Detroit: Catalyst for Change

With its population loss, declining quality of city services and public education, racial tension, an incapacitated governmental body, and resulting poverty and crime, Detroit plummeted into despair. Because of this, the city got to a point where its sales model to its citizens completely shattered: in 2011, more than half of property owners citywide did not pay taxes.[22] Things reached a breaking point, and in March 2013, Michigan state officials appointed Kevyn Orr as Detroit's emergency financial manager. He took the helm, and sweeping authority (trumping that of elected city officials), tasked with bringing the city's finances back from collapse. Orr, who had worked successfully on Chrysler's bankruptcy case four years earlier, assessed the grim situation.[23]

He (and other state officials) decided that enough was enough: after plunging $18 billion into debt, Detroit needed to file for bankruptcy, which it did later that year. To date, this had been the largest municipality to request bankruptcy protection in history.[24] I cannot overstate the enormity of this action and what it means to this city, along with cities nationwide. Tens of thousands of people lost their pensions, the city's support and infrastructure temporarily bottomed out, and the future challenges seemed undefeatable.

As a multigenerational Detroiter and someone who is passionate about rebuilding our beloved city, you might think this news would have been devastating to me. In fact, I feel just the opposite. The announcement in July 2013 represented long-awaited decisive action and a commitment to ensuring a bright future for our city.

While the news made headlines at the time, the problems were created long ago. It was not a setback, but an important and positive step forward in Detroit's rebirth.

Orr made the courageous decision to finally draw a line in the sand. For a half-century, government fat cats, reckless city politicians, and power-hungry unions avoided blame, resting on their laurels. That formula led to decay from within, one day at a time, for literally decades. While the media thrust the spotlight on our city during bankruptcy proceedings, these long-standing issues—stifling bureaucracies, corruption, and scattered blame without solutions—didn't swell overnight. So although we experienced pain in the near term, we will feel these challenges for a finite period of time. From there, we'll be able to move beyond this heavy moment with a truly fresh start, emerging with a spirit of reinvention.

I applaud both Kevyn Orr and Governor Rick Snyder for their action; they made the right choice, even if it was not the easy one to have made. In his statement about the filing, the governor explained, "By filing for bankruptcy, Detroit can get back on the right path." For this, I stood strong with Snyder, as did the vibrant business community within the city's central business district. We're in a time of thriving resiliency and couldn't be more excited for what's to come.

Our city followed a specific legal course to reorganize, Chapter 9 bankruptcy. However, our city is not bankrupt, and we're certainly not done fighting. Chapter 9 of the municipal code is a legal mechanism to reorganize and dig out from an unmanageable debt load, much like a Chapter 11 bankruptcy in the business world. General Motors, Pacific Gas and Energy, and United Airlines are all examples of organizations that filed bankruptcy to shed previous debt, but today are strong and profitable entities. In Detroit's case, the bankruptcy is not the end of a city but rather a new beginning. What's at stake is whatever rests just on the other side of this Chapter 9 filing, in a proverbial "Chapter 10." To what new beginnings can we look toward? To what new heights can we strive to reach?

I'm a firm believer that when I look back in decades, that five-year period when the city filed will be the stint that I tell my grandkids about. This will be remembered as the period when Detroit got its mojo back, and the bankruptcy announcement sets the public sector on a course to do just that. I chose to view this moment as a chance to recalibrate, reinvent, and revitalize. Many of my colleagues in the private sector shared the same confidence in our ability to move beyond this, standing with the city during that difficult time.

Ultimately I believe that Detroit will be studied for decades to come as the greatest turnaround—*and* reinvention—story in American history. Bankruptcy marked an important step in that journey, as we Detroiters march confidently toward a brighter future.

Tools for Transformation: Disrupting a New Customer Segment

To enjoy success, it's important to build a specific plan of attack around each customer segment. Just claiming that your bank branch is now serving Hispanic females between eighteen and twenty-four years of age won't do much to attract new customers. You need to map out both a product and a communication plan to enter a new segment. What will your new offering provide, and how is it different from that of your competitor in the market? Will your bank offer Spanish-language ATMs and Spanish-speaking tellers? How do you plan to reach the new audience? Will you offer budgeting and savings lectures at local Hispanic community centers? If you plan to make a serious run at eleven new niche markets, make sure you have eleven distinct plans. Each plan should spell out your strategy of attack and have a way to track your progress.

Reinventing your customers can lead to new areas of growth and can also help you cut out unprofitable client segments. Using a step-by-step process will help you identify new opportunities in a logical and productive way:

Step 1: Get clarity on what you offer. Make sure you understand and can clearly articulate your existing value proposition. Don't just list product features and benefits. Instead, illustrate the specific problem you solve for customers and how you do it in a unique and compelling way.

Step 2: Expand out. Imagine at least three alternative concepts that you could provide by tweaking your product or service. For example, if you have a really cool breakfast and lunch restaurant, your value proposition is that you provide customers with an energizing and inspiring experience. An alternative idea would be to open in the evenings for live music and poetry readings. It's the same value proposition and an adapted product offering.

Step 4: Explore new customer segments. Brainstorm at least ten new customer segments that could benefit from your original value proposition or one of the new concepts. In our restaurant example, if you typically serve a business crowd for power lunches, a younger, more urban audience may be attracted to the late-night music scene.

Step 5: Examine each segment and see which trends lead to opportunity. Explore changes (growth or contraction) in each segment, as well as the strength of competitors trying to serve the same audience. If there are eight other music clubs going after your newly targeted young audience on the same block, hip music may not be the way to go. Maybe offering live classical performances would differentiate you and appeal to an entirely different crowd.

Step 6: Brainstorm and prototype. Select the three most attractive new segments, and then brainstorm how you could tailor your existing product, process, message, and experience to them. No matter what idea you determine, don't bet the farm before testing it out. For your restaurant, do an experiment by holding a few "special evening events" and gauge demand for the new offering.

Step 7: Connect with real customers. The best business moves come to life by deeply connecting with actual customers, not through financial modeling in a boardroom. Go out and talk to people in these new segments to get feedback and see what resonates. If you are down to three potential segments to pursue for your new late-night experience, spend a couple of weeks talking to as many people in each segment as possible before making your final decisions. The real-world feedback will be invaluable.

Step 8: Select thoughtfully. Score each idea on a variety of factors such as capital required, execution risk, opportunity cost, competition, link to your overall mission, timing, sustainability, and upside. It's easy to just go with your gut, but taking a measured approach and applying a numerical ranking can help you avoid the trap that traumatizes so many businesspeople: getting seduced by instinct. Ultimately it will be a judgment call, but make sure to lay all the factors on the table before making your final decision.

CHAPTER 9

Transform Your Career

Your time is limited, so don't waste it living someone else's life.
—STEVE JOBS

Carlo Sweeney's biological parents experimented heavily with drugs and suffered from a host of challenging circumstances. By the time he was about six weeks old, they gave him up to an older couple in the neighborhood that could better handle the responsibilities of child rearing. His adoptive family lived in a house in one of Detroit's roughest neighborhoods and was plagued by poverty. Despite these challenges, they did everything in their power to raise him right, including boxing lessons from another family member as a form of discipline. As he says, that might have worked, but that family "mentor" wasn't actually around consistently in his life so he felt that the world was against him. He'd take that chip with him to school: by the time he was in the third grade, he still couldn't read or write. To avoid the embarrassment of illiteracy, he'd cause trouble and get kicked out of class, then manipulate his parents to take his side when he got in trouble.

To his detriment, apathetic teachers passed him to the next grade every year, even though he wasn't qualified, until he finally dropped out in the tenth grade. With time on his hands, Sweeney found himself completely immersed in the street life and affiliated with gangs. As he explains, he had wasted much of his life by the time he reached the age of twenty. He would have remained on this destructive path, had it not been for his brother making an offhand comment about a photo of Carlo and two close friends. His brother explained, "All of your friends are either dead or in jail." Sweeney started doing the math and realized his brother was right; this wake-up call would change his course of destiny on a path toward reinvention.

As his family fell on hard times—no gas, no lights, no running water—he knew enough was enough. Slowly but surely, he made the arduous transition to become a responsible adult, taking care of his family by working construction and security. In his spare time, he started teaching his own kids and some of his colleagues the art of boxing, returning to his own childhood training over the years. This led to training other kids in the neighborhood in similar circumstances who could relate to him, his story, and his dedication to the sport. These kids weren't educated, which would lead to poverty, which would lead to crime. If the cycle could be stopped, they'd be on a path to a brighter future.

With that, Sweeney, now known as Coach Khali, opened the Downtown Youth Boxing Gym. This nonprofit program is an academic one that uses boxing as the hook to get kids excited. The free after-school program keeps academics at the heart: kids meet with tutors daily, working on their studies as the core focus. They also give back and do community service, and through it all, they receive boxing training from Khali and other trainers. Some have gone on to be national champions and Olympic contenders, which speaks to the impact Coach Khali has made. More important, the main asset to celebrate here is that the program boasts a 100 percent graduation rate, more than double the rate of the rest of the neighborhood. Khali knew he had to change his career and in the process found a way to give back to his community in a special way. When you have a burning desire for change and add creative vision and relentless determination, as he has, an explosive reinvention formula comes to life.[1]

We've covered many approaches to reinventing your organization; now it's time to focus on you. No matter how stuck you may feel, there is almost always a way to discover new possibilities. From those who were homeless to those living with debilitating diseases, many of the most successful individuals came from less-than-ideal circumstances. You may be in a tough spot or, like millions of others, you may be doing just fine but feel unfulfilled professionally. In the same way that it's your responsibility as a leader to help your company innovate before it's too late, the same logic applies to your own career. Even if you've enjoyed success to date, your calling is much bigger than being a one-hit wonder. Any one of us can cling to past wins and ultimately fizzle out, losing relevancy and becoming forgotten. Or we can commit to using our own creativity to put ourselves out of business with revived vigor. In this chapter, I've decoded the most common approaches to reinventing your career in an effort to help you both win and contribute more.

I've reinvented myself—a few times in big ways and dozens of times in smaller ones. While at the top of my game playing jazz music, I decided that a career in business would allow me to make a bigger impact on the world. So back in 1990, I used the money I saved from playing jazz gigs to launch my first business. After selling my third company, GlobalLink New Media, to a large publicly traded firm, I could have stayed there and built a safe career as a corporate executive. Instead, I decided to reinvent again and launch my fourth start-up, ePrize. After spending eleven years as the CEO there, I could have continued to stay in my role and ride the waves of success; however, I felt compelled to do something new, something bold. In 2010, I did a double-reinvention when I left ePrize and pursued two new career choices. First, I became an author, writing *Disciplined Dreaming: A Proven System to Drive Breakthrough Creativity*. With the book's success, I've been able to affect tens of thousands of people around the world through writing and public speaking. Second, I launched Detroit Venture Partners (DVP), the Detroit-based venture fund that invests in tech start-ups. With DVP, I have the privilege to help rebuild my hometown while helping entrepreneurs seize their dreams.

I was in a position of strength at each transition. I wasn't forced out and could have continued down those paths with comfort and ease. But at each of these inflection points, I realized that my calling had diverged from my current route and decided to forge a bold new path instead of hiding in the safety of what I already knew. These transitions contained risk, but I believed that staying in a role just for perceived security was far riskier. Although each shift was a bit scary, they all opened up a new world of opportunity and allowed me to grow personally and professionally.

You are here for a reason, and it isn't to hide in a cubicle forever. Your real job is to leverage your strengths and creativity in order to realize your full potential. It's time to reinvent your career, and put the you of six months ago out of business. It's time for You, Version 2.0.

Getting to the next level in your career means something different to each of us. For you, it could be launching a start-up, landing a big promotion, improving your work/life balance, or making a bigger impact in your community. The thing all of us have in common, even the best of the best, is the opportunity to break through to a higher level of performance and achievement.

Working on yourself is an excellent starting point. There's an ancient Chinese proverb, "When the student is ready, the teacher will appear." This implies that a person must prepare and be in the right condition in order to recognize the opportunity they desire. The same applies to personal transformation. Working on yourself and developing fresh ideas while nurturing your strengths is the kindling to light your blazing fire of positive change.

Create Plan Z

Chances are that no matter what career you pursued, your parents instructed you to have plan B. We all are familiar with the widespread concept: a fallback plan in the event that things go very wrong. The notion is so widespread that it's even the name of a morning-after contraceptive pill. Most people focus first on their careers, which are often fairly risk averse to begin with. Next, they spend time carefully plotting out their plan B so they have a safety net in case of a fall from grace. While it's practical to wear both a belt and suspenders, I think we're missing something far more important: a plan Z.

The "Z" can stand for zoom, zap, or zigzag. It is the opposite of a plan B; it is the dream plan—the plan that you had in mind before you learned all the things that could go wrong, the plan that you'd pursue if you knew you couldn't fail. Plan Z is your road map for things going incredibly right instead of horribly wrong. It is the intersection of our passion, heart, and soul. It's your calling. It's what you're meant to do.

Imagining Your Own Plan Z

Reflect for a moment on what you would do if you had $250 million in the bank but weren't allowed to retire. Would you still suck up to your overbearing boss? Would you hold your best thinking back for fear of looking foolish? Would you write cover-your-ass memos? Or would you pursue your art?

If you are going to build an alternative plan, ditch the plan B and go all-in on plan Z. The very act of crafting it will be both inspiring and liberating, and each step toward it will be cathartic. What have you always wanted to do? How could you make your biggest impact on the world? How do you want your grandkids to remember you? These are the guideposts of your real plan, not how many sick days your employer offers.

Sophia Amoruso had her own plan Z. She left home at age 17 to "dumpster dive." She held a number of low-level jobs to survive and floated up and down the West Coast. In 2006, she dropped out of photography school to start a small online business selling vintage clothes out of her boyfriend's apartment. She had an eye for fashion and sold her finds from garage sales and the Salvation Army on eBay and from her MySpace page. Her approach to fashion had a sexy edge and she targeted a moderate price point, generally fifty to seventy dollars. Her company, NastyGal, was born and has been on a tear ever since.[2]

By 2013, NastyGal racked up over $240 million in revenue and continues to expand. Amoruso did things her own way at every step, bucking conventional wisdom. Instead of hiring anorexic six-foot models, she hired normal people to model her clothes, often for as low as twenty dollars per day. She wanted her approach to feel inclusive, the exact opposite of the elitist, exclusionary feel perpetuated by most fashion lines. She also didn't advertise, instead promoting her wares primarily through social media. The company has nearly 1 million Facebook and Instagram followers each, and over 550,000 shoppers browse her site every day. Her raw, sexy edge, combined with affordable prices and a close connection to customers, has created an extremely loyal customer base that continues to expand. The company explains that half of its sales are driven by 20 percent of their overall customer base. "I've accepted what I have, and I feel like I've completely done it on my own terms," says Amoruso.[3]

A high school dropout with no formal training built a multi-hundred-million-dollar business with no help, capital, or additional education. Amoruso spent every waking moment crafting and executing her plan Z, the plan that matched her dream, carving her own exhilarating path.

Draw Up Your Personal Reinvention Plan

No matter what your circumstances, age, upbringing, education level, geographic location, or previous career path, it is never too late to reinvent yourself. Just like organizational transformation, personal reinvention can be achieved by taking a systematic approach with your career.

1. *Set a clear vision.* Imagine trying to assemble a thousand-piece puzzle without looking at the box cover that displays an image of the finished project. It would be nearly impossible to decide where to put each piece. Having a crystal-clear vision (your equivalent of the puzzle box cover) is critical in driving a successful reinvention. You should map out your desired end state with incredible detail. I recommend creating a vision board, which could be a giant poster board, a private board on Pinterest, a written manifesto, or any other medium you choose. Assemble images of what the desired state will be like for you, how you'll feel, and what your surroundings will look like. Keep these images handy and refer to them often.

They will be a powerful weapon to keep you focused and help you fight back adversity along the way.

2.   *Do a gap assessment.* As you build your reinvention plan, identify the soft spots. What areas do you need to change, improve, or supplement in order to achieve your desired outcome? For example, if you plan to become a motivational speaker but have stage fright, conquering this phobia would be at the top of your list. Since most professional speakers are published authors, writing a commercially successful book would be on your list as well. Your gap assessment should list all the differences from your starting point to your destination, so it ends up becoming a critical path to-do list as you pursue your plan. In his classic *The Seven Habits of Highly Successful People*, Steven Covey encourages you to always start with the end in mind.[4] Rather than planning from your current point toward your goal, try working backward, reverse-engineering the steps you need to take in order to achieve your vision. When building a step-by-step plan of attack, ask this question at every milestone: "What would I need to have just done in order for this to occur?"

3.   *Identify costs and sacrifices.* There's an old saying, "Everyone wants to go to heaven, but few people are willing to die to get there." Since winning the lottery or inheriting a gigantic trust fund may not be a realistic game plan for you, it's important to take an honest look at what costs and sacrifices will be necessary to bring your vision to life. If your dream is to become a rock star, keep in mind that you'll likely be on the road two hundred days a year away from your family. If you plan to rise to the top of Wall Street, you should plan on spending $100,000 (or more) on your MBA and working ninety hours a week for several years as you climb the ladder. Make sure you approach your journey with an eyes-wide-open strategy so you don't get hit with unexpected surprises. All things worth doing require sacrifice and commitment. Make sure you know these parameters going in.

4.   *Find mentors.* Getting inspired by others, through a connection with a mentor or two, can be the difference maker in your reinvention efforts. If your vision is to become a world-renowned pediatric oncologist, reach out to those who are already in that position and respectfully request their help. You may have to ask thirty people to

get one to say yes, but an experienced mentor in your corner can be priceless. Mentors can help steer you in the right direction, hold you accountable, and offer insight into the new arena you crave. While it may feel intimidating to ask, successful people are often willing to give back and really enjoy the process of helping others.

5.   *Conduct a premortem.* A postmortem is an analysis or discussion of an event after it is over; a premortem is doing the same thing before the event.[5] From your current jumping-off point, think about all the ways your reinvention could fall off the tracks. What are the threats that could hinder your efforts? What distractions may pop up to lure you away from your goal? Rather than waiting until the end, do this examination up front and use the insights as guardrails throughout your transformation.

6.   *Build accountability markers.* Putting a system of penalties and rewards in place will boost your ability to achieve. Blowing a deadline or skipping important steps with no consequences will not help you achieve your ultimate mission. The best plans include both rewards and penalties for specific actions. For example, if you're charting daily progress and miss more than two targets in a week, you could make it mandatory that you donate one hundred dollars to charity or spend two hours volunteering (perhaps a deterrent to you but makes the world better simultaneously). If you achieve all of your weekly goals, a reward could be treating yourself to a massage or enjoying a movie. For optimal results, have someone else help hold you accountable. You may be able to rationalize behaviors to yourself, but having someone else track your steps and administer rewards and penalties will keep you moving ahead. This is the same reason athletes collaborate with a coach or workout buddy, using external accountability to drive performance.

7.   *Track, measure, refine.* Management guru Peter Drucker once proclaimed, "What gets measured gets done." Tracking weekly performance in specific areas will allow you to keep yourself focused and on track. Keep a close eye on your key metrics, and use this information to refine and adapt your plan along the way. Measure often to avoid getting too far off your path and to detect problem areas early. This way, you can adjust your actions without losing ground.

Explore the Many Flavors of Reinvention

From stories of garbage collectors becoming millionaires to successful executives becoming teachers, personal career reinvention comes in many variations. Determining your own route is an individualized decision with many influencing factors, including your stage of life, passions, skills, and resources. As you consider the approaches, think about each concept as if you're trying on a new outfit at a department store. Some will feel strange and unnatural—essentially not your style. Certainly every form of personal reinvention won't be right for you, so simply let those models go, in the same way you don't buy every clothing item you've tried on for size. But one of the frameworks may hit home and represent the right path for you to pursue. If the outfit fits, that's the one you'll take to the proverbial cash register and wear around town right away.

You'll find the various "flavors" of reinvention—The Miles Davis, The Butterfly, The Bill Gates, The Curve Jump, The Passion Leap, and The Adventure—both memorable and instructive. Each contains actual examples of how individuals have embraced the reinvention philosophy.

The Miles Davis

Recognized as one of the key figures in jazz and one of the most influential musicians in American history, Miles Davis is an iconic figure. His legendary status—his genius—is celebrated due to Davis's ability to constantly reinvent himself and his music. There are many people who reach a level of success at one point in their career and then spend the rest of their lives living in past glory. Not Miles. More than any other musician of the twentieth century, Davis continued to push the boundaries and was a constant source of disruptive change. He led transformative breakthroughs as the pioneer of five distinct musical movements: bebop, cool, blue, hard bop, and electric fusion. Each style was a complete departure from previous genres, as if he was uncomfortable standing still. Miles had an incredible gift for mastering a challenge, completely discarding it, and then moving on into the wide unknown. He is known for constantly forging new ground and reinventing his craft every few years rather than milking his previous successes.

Davis's brand of reinvention kept his core industry, career, and skill set consistent. In other words, he didn't leave the trumpet to become a carpenter or auto mechanic. In his type of reinvention, Davis maintained his same primary career choice (musician, composer, trumpet player), but reinvented his work regularly rather than becoming stagnant.

The style of reinvention that I've affectionately named for Miles, a personal hero of mine, involves a careful examination of your existing field and skills. If you're a lawyer, how could you reinvent your approach to the law, marketing, brief writing, jury selection, or closing arguments such that you forge new ground? If you run a landscaping company, how could you change your leadership behavior in order to expand your business, better serve your customers, differentiate from the competition, or use new technologies? In the same way we systematically explored many areas within organizations such as product, process, customer experience, and communication, apply the same careful examination to your own career. By reinventing yourself, you'll transform the results you generate and your impact on the world around you.

Louis CK, one of my favorite comedians, takes this same approach. Each year he throws away all his previous material and refuses to ever perform it again. He begins anew, challenging himself to create a fresh, new body of work. In this way, he remains relevant and in high demand instead of being known for just a handful of punch lines, like so many in his competitive field.

The Butterfly

We all learned by second grade that caterpillars are born to do more than creep. They start out in one state and naturally progress to a more advanced condition. You can think of this as the ultimate personal reinvention and one that serves as a good approach for you as you work to take your career to the next level.

Charles Best, a history teacher at a Bronx high school, evolved into his own style of butterfly. After shelling out his own money to offer projects for his students, he realized that underfunded teacher projects were a universal problem. Best had the idea to launch a website where teachers could post classroom project requests and donors could contribute to help kids in specific schools and classes. His idea was that anyone with five dollars could become a philanthropist and make an impact on kids' lives. He rallied his fellow teachers to post requests, and Best anonymously funded them all himself to show that the concept worked. Word spread and DonorsChoose.org took off like an Olympic sprinter.

As momentum continued, Oprah Winfrey heard about the site and featured it on her show. Donations of $250,000 were received immediately, and DonorsChoose.org was launched into the public spotlight. With other big-name supporters such as Stephen Colbert, the site now posts projects from all fifty states and over half of all public schools in the United States. In 2012, the site generated over $30 million of donations and is now fully self-sustaining, with more than 75 percent of donors choosing to also give to the site itself. Their big goal is to "inspire one million people to give $100 million to classroom projects from 100% of our country's high-poverty public schools" each year.[6] Best stayed within his field of education but evolved into making a much bigger impact than he could have done by teaching history in one school.

Luke Holden is another example of someone who cracked the code of reinvention while evolving in his field—or maybe I should say cracked the claws. Holden is a multigenerational lobster fisherman who learned the tricks of the trade from his father's forty years of experience in the Maine lobster business. Throughout Maine, simple seafood shacks that sell fresh lobster rolls are meaningful competitors to fast food burger joints. Luke noticed, however, that this delicious concept only appeared in his home state. His butterfly moment came in 2009 when he launched Luke's Lobster, a simple carryout establishment offering fresh lobster rolls at low prices. What started as a tiny store in the East Village has since expanded to eleven locations in New York, Philadelphia, and Washington, DC. His company now employs nearly 150 people, and he's expanding at a dizzying pace. By keeping costs low and volume high, Luke is on a mission to dominate the fresh and fast seafood category. His success has come from building on his industry experience and transforming himself from an average lobsterman to an extraordinary restaurateur.

Mona Bijoor is another butterfly, albeit an especially fashionable one. As a wholesale fashion buyer for Ann Taylor and A Pea in the Pod, she realized inefficiencies in the buying process. In an era where you can buy just about anything online with ease, fashion buying was still being conducted via old-school telephone calls, pen, and paper. Bijoor's butterfly moment came when she launched Joor, an online marketplace to connect fashion designers and retailers in a controlled, wholesale environment. Since launching in 2010, she's signed up 580 brands as clients and over thirty thousand retailers that use the service.[7] By catering to the specific needs of her industry and using her own experience to guide the way, the company processed nearly $400 million in orders in 2013. This is one butterfly that has taken a remarkable flight.

This butterfly form of career reinvention is readily accessible. A law clerk becomes a lawyer and then becomes a judge. A dancer becomes a singer and then becomes an actor and finally a director. A software engineer becomes a team leader, then the chief information officer, and eventually writes her own code and launches a start-up. Take a look at your current position, and explore what the next logical step would be in your evolution. Once you have your eye squarely on the target, you can begin the necessary steps to seize your desired outcome.

The Bill Gates

Arguably one of the most ruthless and driven business leaders of the twentieth century, Bill Gates has dominated the rankings of the "world's richest man" for two decades. His current $72.7 billion fortune is astronomical, but it would be even higher had he not donated over $28 billion to charity so far. Throughout his career, Gates was criticized for being an exacting and callous leader who put profits above people. Yet today he is recognized as the greatest philanthropist the world has ever known.

After stepping down from his position at Microsoft, Gates brought his same intensity and drive to the world of philanthropy in one of the most significant reinventions in modern history. In addition to donating billions of his own wealth and pledging to give away more than half of his riches at or before his death, Gates has used his influence to transform the field of philanthropy. He has recruited Warren Buffett and dozens of other billionaires to join the Giving Pledge, a commitment to give at least half of their wealth to charity at or before their death. In addition to raising the pool of available capital, he's managing charitable giving with the same attention to detail he used to manage Microsoft. Instead of forking over huge sums to poorly managed charities, the Gates Foundation demands detailed business plans of how each nonprofit will deploy funds. Charitable entities are given limited funds and measured with the same scrutiny as a public company executive. Organizations that can demonstrate meaningful impact and efficient use of donations will receive additional funding. If they underperform, they run the risk of being cut.

By holding purpose-based organizations to a higher standard and demanding accountability, Gates ensures those huge amounts of money are put to their most productive use. In inflation-adjusted dollars, Gates's impact will surpass previous philanthropic greats such as Carnegie and Vanderbilt by a long shot. He simultaneously reinvented himself and the world of philanthropic giving. Because of the incredible impact Gates has made (and continues to make) on the world, I've named this type of reinvention the Bill Gates: changing to a completely different career with the specific goal of helping the world instead of enriching your bank account.

Jessica Alba followed a similar path as she morphed from movie star to social entrepreneur. Pregnant with her first child in 2008, she became concerned that her daughter would be exposed to toxic chemicals after reading Christopher Gavigan's book, *Healthy Child*

Healthy World. Since toxic-free options weren't readily available for certain types of baby products such as diapers, wipes, and lotions, she launched a start-up called the Honest Company to fill the void. The company offers a monthly delivery service that ships nontoxic diapers and cleaning products directly to customers.[8] She also set out to add some flair, producing fun and colorful products, instead of the typical ecofriendly neutral or brown. Alba entered the start-up arena not to chase money but to improve the lives of parents and children. Like Gates, she reinvented herself out of her sense of service to others. Ironically, her social mission has also provided a boost to her balance sheet. When the company scored a $27 million venture capital investment in 2012, Alba's shares in the company became valued at over $50 million, which is more than she earned as an A-list actress throughout her entire career.[9]

There is no shortage of important causes, and connecting with the ones that resonate the most with you can be a jumping-off point for your own personal reinvention. Take a look within and explore how your passions and skills could help the world. In my case, I love jazz music and believe it is one of the greatest American art forms—a national treasure that must be preserved. I'm also deeply committed to Detroit and believe that education is the pathway out of poverty. With these building blocks, a natural reinvention could be starting a program that teaches jazz to at-risk kids in the city of Detroit. The musical instruction would not only serve as an art form, but a powerful tool to teach discipline, focus, persistence, goal setting, and teamwork. I could start by establishing a ten-week curriculum and seeking volunteers to help. Based on carefully tracked results, I could then expand and seek donations or grants to continue to build the program. In my case, it could become a whole new chapter that allows me to do what I love and make a difference. Maybe such a program just might be popping up in Detroit's future—my own flavor of Coach Khali's boxing gym.

If cause-based reinvention appeals to you, take an inventory of your core beliefs and explore how you could drive meaningful social change along with your own personal fulfillment. Bill Gates would be proud.

The Curve Jump

If making a change feels challenging to you, think how it must have felt for Ruth Fertel back in 1965. At only five feet two inches tall and 110 pounds, her petite stature wasn't the only thing that made her feel small. Growing up in a poor family, she certainly didn't have the inside track on business or a long list of connections. She was recently divorced and unable to support herself and her two children as a lab technician at Tulane University. She was determined to make a better life for herself and her family, yet the only resource she had was her own conviction.

Responding to a classified ad, she decided to make a bold move. A local restaurant was for sale: a sixty-seat steakhouse in her home of New Orleans. Fertel mortgaged her home, her only possession, to buy the restaurant and reinvent her career. With no restaurant or business experience, she had to teach herself everything. She learned how to butcher a steak, close the books, and serve hungry customers. She staffed the restaurant with single mothers like herself, saying they were hard working and reliable.[10] One customer at a time, one steak at a time, she gave it everything she had. Six months after buying the restaurant, a risk that was highly discouraged by everyone she knew, she had doubled her annual salary. Fertel expanded the operation by selling franchises and opening more locations of her own. Today there are 120 Ruth's Chris Steakhouses in eight countries, plus another twenty restaurants under the Mitchell's and Cameron's brands. The now publicly traded Ruth's Hospitality Group has a market valuation of over $500 million.

As a broke, divorced single parent with no industry experience, Ruth had no business jumping into a totally new line of work. It turned out that her curve jump is exactly what made her so successful. Sometimes, a straight and logical path just won't carry the day. Many of the world's biggest success stories are of those who leaped from one line of work to a radically different field in order to seize enormous prosperity. As someone who went from jazz music to entrepreneurship to writing to investing, I can tell you that curve jumping can yield tremendous results.

Wayne Huizenga is the ultimate curve jumper. Starting with a single garbage truck in 1968, he grew his company, Waste Management, into the largest waste disposal company in the United States. When it came time for Huizenga to reinvent his career, you'd think he would have stayed in the garbage business. Instead, he opened Blockbuster Video in 1985, which by 1994 was the country's largest video rental chain. At its peak in 2004, the company had sixty thousand employees. So Huizenga's next reinvention would surely be in the video business, right? Of course not. In 1996, he formed AutoNation, which has become the largest automotive dealer, with revenues of $16 billion.[11] Huizenga became the dominant leader in three completely different industries, creating large public companies—and tremendous personal wealth—in each. Rather than staying within a specific field, he hunted down new industries where he could apply his experience of building national operations and dominating growing markets. He followed an opportunity theme rather than a specific craft, and this college dropout curve-jumped all the way to becoming a multibillionaire. In 2013 he was the 222nd wealthiest person in the United States according to *Forbes* magazine, with a net worth of $2.5 billion.[12]

The Passion Leap

Q: What do you do next when you sell your sunglasses company for $2.1 billion?
A: Completely disrupt the film business. Duh.

In his twenties, Jim Jannard's passion was motorcycles. Rather than pursuing a career at a giant corporation, he decided to manufacture motorcycle goggles and founded his company, Oakley, in 1975. Jannard built the goggles with a cool look, largely because he represented his own target market and knew what fellow bikers would want. As his motorcycle goggles caught on, he launched ski goggles (as you can guess, skiing was another of his passions). With this gaining brand power and popularity, sunglasses came next and the company's growth became unstoppable. The company went public in 1995 and was sold to Luxottica in 2007 for $2.1 billion.[13]

Over the years, Jannard ventured beyond motorcycles and skiing to find a new muse. As a result, he became a photography nut. His personal collection includes over 1,000 cameras, and he became obsessed with digital photography. His inner desire, not a business opportunity, drove him to launch his next company, Red. He was driven to pioneer the new standard for cinema-quality, digital video cameras and stick it to the complacent old-school camera makers at the same time.

Jannard's idea was bold: to create a small, manageable camera that could shoot the same (or better) quality as film but for a fraction of the price. At the time of his launch, the prevailing technology of the day needed a 100X improvement to meet the standards of Hollywood's A-list directors. When the Red camera was launched, skeptics quickly tuned into fans and Hollywood went digital. More than one hundred movies have now been filmed with Red cameras, including some of the most recent blockbusters. The private company currently has over five hundred employees and has sold more than ten thousand cameras to date.

Jannard's career was born from his passions: first motorcycles and skiing, then photography. His path wasn't dictated by a financial calculation, demands from his parents, or society's dogma. As you explore your own reinvention, consider taking the passion leap with Jannard as your role model. When you are on fire with passion and excitement, you'll be more creative and give more of yourself to your work. As you evaluate new opportunities, think about the areas of life that fuel your energy the most. If you pursue what you love, the challenges will feel smaller and the upside exponentially greater.

While many of the examples have involved launching a new company, you don't need to create a start-up to reinvent your career. If you are a claims specialist at an insurance company but are passionate about books, perhaps exploring opportunities in the publishing field is a route to explore. If you're an accountant who loves cars, becoming an auto dealer, mechanic, or sales agent may be a fresh new path. Doctors become studio engineers to follow their love of music, while attorneys have become private chefs or judo instructors. Ditch the "ought to" and "I'd better just" and follow your heart instead. You'll end up happier and more fulfilled, and will likely outearn your current situation as a by-product.

The Adventure

As someone who fought forest fires in Alaska at age seventeen, Tom Lix knows a thing or two about both adventure and reinvention. A lifelong rebel, Lix was teargased for protesting the Vietnam War, yet later enlisted in the Navy for six-year stint. After flunking out of Penn State on his first try at college, he went on to receive a PhD in business administration from Boston University years later. He served as the president of a marketing research firm and had a successful run as an entrepreneur, creating a software company that ultimately was sold to National Public Radio (NPR).

After a successful exit, Lix had a big idea. He founded Bulldozer Camp, a retreat for white-collar executives who would play with heavy machinery during the days and relax with steaks and whiskey at night. It was to be the ultimate man's man vacation destination, catering to an upscale crowd in the Pacific Northwest. He raised capital and was ready to see his vision come to life. Then, as if part of a dramatic novel, the economy crashed and his dream evaporated before his eyes. His investors lost their money while Lix lost his land and his pride.

Always one to explore new possibilities, Lix was reflecting on his beautiful land before he handed it back to the bank. He began wondering if he could produce alcohol on it and his mind wandered to the similarities of the damp and cool climate in Scotland. After losing it all and at his lowest point, Lix had the idea to explore a new adventure in a completely unfamiliar area: whiskey. At that moment, any logical person would have advised Lix to run for financial safety in some soulless desk job. Taking a leap into a new field, coming right off a colossal failure, and attacking a mature, highly competitive industry sounded like certifiable craziness. That's exactly what fired him up and gave him the motivation to prove the critics wrong.

As Lix began to learn more about making bourbon, he realized that time was not on his side. Unlike the burgeoning craft beer market where product can come to market immediately, whiskey generally requires a decade or two of aging in order to compete. After initial production, the liquor needs to be stored in oak barrels, charred on the inside, for an average of ten years before being ready for primetime. Since he had no intention of waiting around, Lix had to innovate. Although he had no background in chemistry, he flipped the aging method upside down and devised a concept to dramatically speed up the process. "The basic concept is relatively simple," he explains. "Instead of putting the alcohol inside the barrel, we put the barrel inside the alcohol."[14] To accomplish this, small and uniform pieces of charred barrel are placed in a stainless steel, 120-gallon pressure vat, along with the alcohol. Since the wood is porous like a sponge, it soaks up the liquid when pressure is applied. When the pressure is released, the alcohol flows out of the wood and retains its flavor and color. By adding and releasing pressure, Lix is able to bring a high-quality product to market in a week instead of a decade. His brazen approach goes beyond innovative production techniques and also applies to packaging and marketing. Made in Cleveland, Ohio, the filled bottles proudly boast the name "Cleveland Whiskey" in an effort to defy conventional wisdom that great whiskey must come from Kentucky. Made quickly and as a newcomer, you may imagine the product would boast a low price point. No way. Lix entered the market at a premium, charging thirty-five dollars a bottle, which is more expensive than industry leader Maker's Mark.

Lix's bold, adventurous approach to personal reinvention can serve as a model for your own transformation. He followed a dream and had the courage to tackle an opportunity for which he was clearly unqualified. Rather than just entering a new field and learning the ropes, he sought to disrupt the status quo from the start. He refused to get lost in the shuffle and immediately differentiated from the competitors in all aspects, from production to packaging to price point.

Think of the adventure flavor of reinvention as a siren song calling you into the wild. Rather than tapping into your inner child, you must harness your inner Louis and Clark. Maybe your adventure is a foray into politics, having never been involved in public service before. Or it could be moving to a different country to seize a fresh opportunity while exploring uncharted waters. Even if you fall flat on your face, the insight and experience you'll gain from trying something bold will be priceless. Do you want to tell your grandkids about your experiences sitting at the same office for thirty years, or do you want to share stories of daring exploration? The familiar may feel safe today, but the pain of regret will harshly burn in the future if you can't muster the courage to follow your imagination.

Face Down Inevitable Obstacles

"I could never do that."

"This is impossible."

"There are a million obstacles."

When facing a serious challenge on our road to reinvention, it's easy to amplify the hurdles in our minds, which in turn makes these roadblocks seem overwhelming. Our fearful inner voice has a way of exaggerating the barriers and then talking us out of even trying. The things we want most in life—business success, great relationships, and vibrant communities—can feel unreachable and overwhelming.

The old parable instructs us how to eat an elephant: one bite at a time. The same is true when scaling the brick walls that guard your biggest goals. When you fixate on the magnitude of the challenge, it's easy to get discouraged. But a funny thing happens when you carefully examine these fears and bring them into the light. The scary monster quickly loses its bite, as these big boundaries shrink faster than you dreamed them up in the first place.

In the same way you'd unpack your suitcase after a long trip, start unpacking the things that are holding you back or getting in your way. Take the individual components out, one at a time, and evaluate them on their own merit. What was once frightening can quickly dissolve into something that becomes both tame and manageable.

Let's take that "million obstacles" comment. No question we can feel this way and can easily be dissuaded from achievement.

Instead of walking away, make a list of them. My guess is that you'll end up with fewer than ten real obstacles, which is not even close to your original estimate.

From there, you can proactively map out a specific strategy to overcome each obstacle. As you tackle them one by one, you'll feel charged up with energy and your resolve will strengthen. One of the saddest things in life is squandering opportunity because you never had the courage to try. Next time you're up against a challenge, problem, issue, or even an opportunity that feels overwhelming, unpack it. Once you break it down, the fear will dissipate and your personal power will skyrocket. It's time to drag those scary challenges out of the shadows and into the bright sunlight. One component at a time, you'll conquer and overcome. And, yes, you'll savor that big elephant of opportunity, one bite at a time.

Joanne "J. K." Rowling is one of the most powerful examples of reinvention by overcoming obstacles. Rowling worked as a researcher and secretary for Amnesty International before her life took a decided turn for the worse. Over a seven-year period, she lost her job, got divorced, lost her mother after a ten-year fight with multiple sclerosis, and became impoverished. Struggling as a single parent and needing to accept welfare, she described herself as the "biggest failure I knew."[15] At the same time, she acknowledged that this failure was liberating:

> Failure meant a stripping away of the inessential. I stopped pretending to myself that I was anything other than what I was, and began to direct all my energy to finishing the only work that mattered to me. Had I really succeeded at anything else, I might never have found the determination to succeed in the one area where I truly belonged. I was set free, because my greatest fear had been realized, and I was still alive, and I still had a daughter whom I adored, and I had an old typewriter, and a big idea. And so rock bottom became a solid foundation on which I rebuilt my life.

Rowling finished her first manuscript, for *Harry Potter and the Sorcerer's Stone*, in 1995. She submitted the work to twelve different publishers, all of whom rejected it. After unwavering persistence, she persuaded Bloomsbury Publishing in London to go forward with the project. Offering Rowling only a three thousand dollar advance, editor Barry Cunningham advised Rowling to get a day job since she had little chance of making any money by writing children's books. What started with an initial print run of only one thousand copies in 1997 has since become a multibillion-dollar franchise. The Harry Potter series has become the best-selling book series in history,[16] and the series of accompanying films has become the highest-grossing film series in history.[17]

As one of the wealthiest women in the world with a net worth of over $1 billion, Rowling is now a long way from poverty.[18] Her incredible transformation was fraught with adversity, but she focused on her art instead of her fears. She pursued her vision as if her life depended on it, which to a large degree it did (and does for all of us). Rowling made history and affected millions of people worldwide with her work, which was launched out of a burning desire for personal reinvention. *Harry Potter* became her catalyst for change. It was her platform for creative expression and enabled her to create the life she envisioned. You have your own version waiting to be unleashed. It may be a book or invention, a service or idea, a commitment to social justice or the desire to serve others. Look within, discover your own unique opportunity, and embrace it as a responsibility—to yourself and others—to manifest that vision. Your own sorcerer's stone awaits. Now grab it.

Detroit: Catalyst for Change

As the city's governmental infrastructure crumbled amid financial emergency and bankruptcy, local business leaders realized one point of causation. Singularity of industry and a long-standing fear of diversification beyond manufacturing destroyed our city's economy from within. The new guard knew better.

Compuware moved its four-thousand-employee headquarters to downtown Detroit in 2003, into a new, fifteen-story building. By 2010, Quicken Loans had followed suit. In eighteen months, it had doubled its staff, and in three years, the original amount had tripled, to more than eleven thousand employees working in the heart of the city. Chairman Dan Gilbert credits this explosive growth partly to the advantages of being in an urban core. Alongside such technology giants are the technology start-ups, many of which are in the Detroit Venture Partners portfolio. The burgeoning start-up scene here has made it clear that manufacturing jobs in the new era are software engineers and developers.

Beyond the scope of these big business leaders, the diversity of industry has more fully extended. Artisan food purveyors have popped up all over town, and art galleries are full of critically acclaimed works. Whole Foods opened in Detroit in 2013, becoming the first national grocery chain to do so in years. The store has since exceeded the company's own expectations for success.[19] Shinola, a manufacturer of watches, bicycles, and leather goods, opened up shop in a historic building, previously used by GM as its design epicenter. The company immediately exploded in popularity and its product line became a hot commodity at Neiman Marcus, Barneys New York, and its own flagship store. When the city became less heavily reliant on the automotive industry alone, it flourished once again.

During the second half of the twentieth century, Detroit public and private sector leaders' reinvention efforts languished. They chose to coast on past success. Their revelry in the status quo and accompanying stagnation resulted in our own demise.

Your destiny is nobody's fault or source of pride but your own. Detroiters have that burden to bear, but they also stand to leave a different, more exciting mark through this newly found reinvention effort, in its totality.

Tools for Transformation: Six Habits for Reinvention

If you are committed to reaching your next level of achievement, the following habits should be practiced with rhythmic consistency:

1. *Weekly planning.* Most people spend more time planning their summer vacations than they do architecting their lives. Take twenty minutes (ideally Sunday nights) to plot out how to make the upcoming week most successful. Refine your calendar, make time to be proactive instead of

firefighting, and make sure you are controlling your schedule instead of it controlling you. We all are limited to twenty-four hours each day, but you get to decide how to make the most of them.

2. *Reflection.* It may feel strange at first, but schedule at least thirty minutes of reflection time each week. This is time without e-mail, calls, or distraction. It is time to reflect on your goals and progress and put your efforts in context of your larger vision. Connect with your dreams in vivid color, and let your mind explore the possibilities. You'll quickly find this to be one of your most productive weekly activities.

3. *Learning.* The world is changing faster than any other time in history, and it's only speeding up. If you are not growing, you'll soon be falling behind. The most successful people are lifelong learners and are constantly absorbing new ideas. Spend at least an hour each week reading, watching lectures, listening to books on tape, or exploring new content online. These new insights will not so coincidentally become just the thing you are looking for to solve problems and unlock potential.

4. *Gratitude.* Looking for a cure to anxiety and stress? Each week, take a few minutes and write a "gratitude list." List the things in your life, big and small, you are thankful for. Personally I'm appreciative for health, business success, and my little puppy, daVinci. Set a timer for ten minutes, and see how long you can make the list each week. After this short exercise, you will feel completely energized and ready to perform.

5. *Adventure.* Adding some adventure to your week can open new doors to reinvention. You don't have to skydive or swim the English Channel in order to venture into new arenas and break old patterns. Visit a new neighborhood, attend a live performance of any kind, try a new food, or even take a different route to work. Shaking things up will drive renewed energy and creative thinking. It may even help forge new relationships with people you would have ordinarily never met. Plan weekly miniadventures to help discover new areas for growth.

6. *Trend spotting.* Staying on top of the latest trends and advances will keep you sharp and help you stay relevant. There are dozens of trend-spotting websites, blogs, and periodicals. Staying up to speed on pop culture, technology, and new business approaches will open your mind to fresh possibilities. Regularly practicing this technique can yield the inspired breakthroughs you seek.

Human achievement is nearly limitless, from invention to art to social change. Practice these habits, and you'll be well on your way to unlocking your full potential.

CHAPTER 10

Forge Your Legacy

*Certain things catch your eye, but pursue
only those that capture the heart.*

—ANCIENT INDIAN PROVERB

By the mid-1990s, Andre Agassi had reached the highest levels of society's standards of achievement. He had fame, money, power, and trophies galore. But the more he "succeeded," the more miserable he became: he was unhappy and unfulfilled, and while he wouldn't admit it to anyone, he hated tennis. From a young age, his father had pushed him so hard that the game of tennis devolved into his prison. The more he excelled, the more he lost in the rest of his life. Although he made the grade by all external standards, he was deeply depressed; his unparalleled career success didn't equate to happiness.

Agassi hit the bottom in 1997 when his internal pain became unbearable. He fell out of the top one hundred, got addicted to drugs, and watched his life unravel in a tailspin. At his lowest point, introspection and help from friends gave him the courage to reinvent himself. He decided to embrace a new scorecard, where money and rankings gave way to his new key metrics: compassion, humility, generosity, and thoughtfulness.[1] He connected with a new purpose in life: "to make others feel safe." Rather than chasing fleeting external markers, this new mission gave him stability and determination. Ironically, he realized that tennis would be the vehicle that would allow him to maximize his impact on the world. Reaching the highest levels in the sport would give him the capital and exposure to make the biggest difference.

With a renewed sense of purpose, Agassi took a fresh approach. He rebuilt his life with a clean lifestyle, relentless conditioning, and a steely sense of conviction. By 1999, he was ranked the number one tennis player in the world. His character reinvention not only made him a happier, better person, but it enabled him to reach previously unattainable heights in his career. This commercial success allowed him to follow his true passion: he's raised over $60 million for the Andre Agassi Foundation for Education and now devotes much of his life to helping at-risk children.

As you develop your overall reinvention plan, focusing on yourself can be the most challenging yet rewarding effort of all. Becoming a better person and a stronger leader will likely drive greater financial success, and, more important, it will fill you with a much deeper and lasting sense of accomplishment. We've studied how to rebuild your company; now it's time to rebuild your character. The two are not mutually exclusive competing forces, but rather symbiotic in achieving sustainable success. Interestingly enough, the more you help the world, the more commercial success you'll likely gain. Becoming a more caring, giving, purposeful person will actually drive the economic gain you seek. It's an and, not an or.

Choose: Giver or Taker?

Gandhi was a giver. So were Mother Teresa, Dr. Martin Luther King Jr., and Thomas Edison. They profoundly contributed to the world, leaving our home better than they found it. Because they gave so much, they are revered and hold a special place in history.

Bernie Madoff is a different story. The same is true for the Enron guys, Osama bin Laden, and Jeffrey Dahmer. Their malicious souls never contributed to the greater good or elevated civilization.

Things get a little dicier in the fifty-seven shades of gray that nearly all of us possess. We all embody strong and weak attributes, and we play the roles of both giver and taker. Through the years, I've noticed that people tend to overestimate their own ratio of give to take. Those who leave a negative impact often believe they are the heroes in their own play. They justify their hurtful actions and become desensitized to the fact that they are part of the problem instead of the solution. The bureaucrat who inhibits progress probably believes she is helping to maintain rule and order. The lawyer who greedily launches frivolous lawsuits likely justifies his actions through the notion that he's helping his client. The petty thief rationalizes her crime because she herself has been victimized throughout her life.

Throughout this book, I've referred to reinvention primarily for the sake of economic gain. As we know, that is not the only yardstick by which we can measure success. There are many people who are labeled a success by traditional measures such as wealth, fame, and power but are miserable and leave a destructive wake. There are others who haven't achieved as much in economic standards but enjoy tremendous success helping others, raising children, and making the world a better place. True success comes from the ability to do well *and* do good. How you win is as important as winning itself. Getting to the top of your field while helping others along the way is far more rewarding than the emptiness felt from achievement at the expense of those around you.

It's time to take an honest look in the mirror and examine your true give-to-take quotient. When you cut through the cloudiness, you'll clearly see your our own true colors. You may be enjoying a great financial ride, but at what cost to others?

Assessing Your Impact

- Do you liberate or restrict?
- Do you enact solutions or complain about problems?
- Do you energize or drain?
- Do you elevate others or set them back?

- Do your actions help or harm?
- Do you bring out the best in people or the worst?
- Do you do the right thing or the easy thing?
- Do you have the courage to stand up for your beliefs, or do you bow to conventional wisdom?
- Do you add more value than you extract?
- Is the world better off as a result of your efforts, or do others have to compensate for your mischief?

Now more than ever before, we each need to amplify our own positive impact. If each of us improves our ratio of give to take by only 15 percent, our community improves dramatically. We all know the truism: the more you give, the more you get. Let's rally together to accelerate positive change in all shapes, sizes, and forms. Let's all take personal responsibility for giving more than we take, and we will reach new heights. We all have the ability to be heroes. It's time to seize it.

Be → Do → Have

Many of us chase success, only to find it to be an elusive tease. We say to ourselves if "I could HAVE what I want [money, fame, power, clothes, spouse, car, house], then I could DO the things I want, which would allow me to BE who I truly am."

We think have → do → be. Unfortunately, that's backward.

When you study the most successful and happy people, they run the reverse model. They first focus on who they are (philosophy, character, values) and are uncompromising on BEING true to those beliefs. This allows them to DO the things they want. Because they are authentic and follow their destiny, they end up HAVING what they need. The HAVING is simply a by-product of first BEING, and then DOING.

If you really want to maximize your true potential, turn the conventional approach upside down. BE true to your core beliefs, DO the things you care about, and the HAVE will take care of itself.

In terms of being, a good starting point is to write your own eulogy. When it's all said and done, how do you want to be remembered? As a selfish, workaholic jerk? A fear-laden rule follower? A liar? Most of us want to exude strong character, contribute to humanity, and express our creativity. You don't need a new Porsche or a five-bedroom house to begin being an admirable person.

When you think about doing, forget about what you think you ought to do. Instead, follow a path that is both inspired and inspiring. Step away from what you perceive as safe since you have only so many years to make your mark. Start by asking yourself these seven questions:

1. What do you love to do the most?
2. What gives you the most satisfaction and joy?
3. When do you feel like you are making the biggest impact?
4. What activities most energize you?
5. What would you do if there was no possibility you could fail?
6. What are you doing when you lose track of time?
7. If you could be remembered for one thing, what would it be?

If you've identified a path that is different from your current gig, it's time to seriously consider pursuing your true calling instead. If you don't, who will?

As for the have, it will take care of itself. If you follow your passion and purpose, you'll get all the stuff you need. By focusing on being the person you are meant to be and doing what you are meant to do, the having will end up being a whole lot less important anyway.

Decide How You Want to Be Remembered

The best place to start your personal transformation is at the end. Ten years after you've passed, what will people still say about you? Were you the frazzled executive who cut corners, berated your staff, and ignored your family just to buy another trophy (car, house, trip)? Were you highly successful in your career but failed to build meaningful relationships and never took the time to help others? Did you take the safe route, squandering your potential and avoiding risk of any kind such that you were quickly forgotten?

Having a deep connection to the ultimate legacy you want to leave behind is the most powerful guidepost you can have. In the same way your company has its mission statement posted in the lobby, it's important that you develop your own personal statement to help you make the best decisions throughout your journey. As a reference, here's mine:

> To seize my full potential while making the biggest possible impact in the world. To challenge myself and others to achieve at the highest levels and to harness the gift of creativity that we all share. To leave everyone and everything I touch better than I found it.

You'll notice my personal mission statement includes no reference to net worth, toys, or far-reaching fame. The best statements are geared toward a higher purpose, a calling. Discovering your calling can provide overwhelming inspiration and help you navigate even the most challenging circumstances. Once you connect with that calling, even the most mundane actions become filled with meaning, since they are merely stepping-stones for what matters most.

I was reflecting on this topic at a recent dinner with friends when a waiter I can best describe as "radiant" approached us. As he told us about the specials, he didn't simply drone on with emotionless facts. Instead, with the animation and passion of an opera singer, he told us about the Kobe beef "experience" and the incredible "intensity" of the dry-aged steaks. This guy was doing much more than his job. Perhaps he was connecting his work to a deeper meaning.

In *The Happiness Hypothesis*, author Jonathan Haidt talks about the differences among a job, a career, and a calling:

- If you see your work as a *job*, you do it only for the money. You look at the clock frequently while dreaming about the weekend ahead, and you probably pursue hobbies, which satisfy you more thoroughly than does your work.
- If you see your work as a *career*, you have larger goals of advancement, promotion, and prestige.
- If you see your work as a *calling*, however, you find your work intrinsically fulfilling; you are not doing it to achieve something

else. You see your work as contributing to the greater good or as playing a role in some larger enterprise. You have frequent experiences of flow during the work day, and you neither look forward to "quitting time" nor feel the desire to shout, "Thank God it's Friday!" You would continue to work, perhaps even without pay, if you suddenly became very wealthy.[2]

Maybe my enthusiastic waiter plans to own a chain of restaurants someday and is working his way toward that vision. Perhaps he views his role as delighting others and bringing people together with the highest-quality food and service. You don't have to be saving lives or writing the next Great American Novel to find deep meaning in your work.

I have the privilege of pursuing my own calling (and living out my mission statement) by backing passionate entrepreneurs in an effort to rebuild the city of Detroit. I also spread ideas on creativity and innovation throughout the world. This is my calling, and I do these things to contribute, not just to receive. With a background as a jazz guitarist instead of a Harvard MBA, I could have easily talked myself out of this pursuit and landed in some dead-end job. But when you sprint toward your authentic calling with reckless abandon, obstacles melt away and your vision comes to life.

If you are sick and tired of being sick and tired, examine what you are most passionate about. It may not happen overnight, but setting yourself on a path toward your calling will liberate you. Your income will likely increase, but that will become a by-product rather than a focal point.

Whether you are a waiter, student, executive, or playwright, now is the time to launch yourself on a trajectory aimed squarely at your best and highest purpose. While the path less traveled may feel risky, it will surely beat the regret you'll feel for not trying in the first place.

Expand Your Scorecard

"What gets measured gets improved" is a universal truism in business. Your business scorecard likely contains key metrics around revenue, costs, profits, operating leverage, utilization, customer satisfaction, retention, billable hours, morale, and competitive standing. You may also have a personal scorecard, which in most cases includes income level, title, sphere of influence, net worth, retirement age, savings, size of your house, number of vacations, or months until your next promotion. There's nothing wrong with these, but I want to challenge you to expand your personal scorecard to include intrinsic measures in addition to the extrinsic markers of success.

I recently attended a surprise party honoring my close friend David Farbman's fortieth birthday. Naturally the several-hundred-person bash was fun, but I got a lot more out of it than a Saturday morning hangover.

David is a successful entrepreneur, author, speaker, and investor, but I realized he was far wealthier than his balance sheet would suggest. As dozens of friends and family fought back tears, they gave speeches that lavished love and appreciation onto the man who touched their lives so deeply. It got me thinking about the current incomplete measures of success and wondering what would happen if we added some new metrics.

In the United States, we measure success by things like money, power, fame, good looks, possessions, toys, trophies, and degrees. In the digital age, we also strive for likes, followers, a high Klout score (measuring the size and impact of your voice on social media), and a giant LinkedIn network. At the same time, big-picture numbers like unemployment, divorce rates, environmental quality, educational results, trade deficits, and even overall happiness continue to plummet faster than a teen idol whose fifteen minutes of fame have expired. Today someone can have a lot of cash and power and be an overbearing jerk with no points deducted. Narcissistic celebrities are allowed to act like thumb-sucking infants, amid a temper tantrum vying for attention. A great-looking, well-dressed guy can be a total jackass, yet his cup still runneth over with praise and admiration.

It's time to add some new metrics to our scorecards. What if you measured the number of times you bring joy to others each day? Or any of these:

- The number of people you have a positive impact on or teach per week
- The amount of sadness or fear you helped a loved one overcome after receiving a devastating personal setback
- The number of times you said no to life's temptations and allowed character instead of impulse to carry the day
- The things you created
- The compassion you extended
- The responsible risks you took
- The people you helped
- The lives you changed
- The impact you made

My friend David showed me that when you make a difference and build relationships, the success comes as a by-product. In today's complex and competitive world, being a cold-hearted Scrooge no longer gets you to the Promised Land. In order to win today, a new set of metrics is needed to measure not just near-term material gain but long-term societal impact. The more you drive the latter, the bigger the former will become.

As you work to reinvent yourself, there are limitless facets for personal growth and improvement, ranging from reducing bad cholesterol to anger management. There are thousands of self-help books covering every area of individual improvement. In our case, we'll focus on the seven areas of personal, intrinsic reinvention that will make the biggest difference and simultaneously boost your business success. Think of each of these categories as important muscles that you must build and maintain for optimal performance and well-being:

1. Empathy
2. Compassion
3. Courage
4. Positivity
5. Discipline
6. Creativity
7. Grit

Empathy

Driven leaders often bulldoze over the emotional well-being of those around them. At the same time, business decisions are regularly made without truly understanding the impact they will have on customers, employees, or the community. As you seek to reinvent yourself and elevate your business, empathy has become the new killer app. Empathy is best understood by feeling for yourself the dissonance of being around those who can't relate. And as anyone who's been on the other end knows, it stings—another soul-crushing reprimand from a boss, parent, or spouse; that nauseous feeling when you feel unappreciated, misunderstood, and blamed. We've all been there, and in that knee-wobbling state we are far from playing at our best.

Now remember how you felt after receiving a big boost of positive reinforcement. A "great job," "thank you," or "I love you" injected a thousand kilowatts of energy into your step. You felt invincible, awake, in the groove. I find it ironic that while each of us knows both feelings so well, many people fail to think about how their own behavior affects others. They don't realize that their harsh words can smash someone they care about like a mallet to overripe cantaloupe.

Naturally there's a better way. The best business leaders carefully manage the emotional state of those around them. They realize that people perform at their very best while feeling supported and appreciated. In our competitive world, you'll seize your full potential only by supporting the imagination, confidence, and sense of purpose in others.

I'm not suggesting that leaders should just be feel-good softies or hand out daisies instead of holding their teams accountable. Whether you're engaged in business, art, medicine, community development, or politics, you still need to manage to specific outcomes. I'm suggesting that with the speed and complexity of the times, being acutely mindful of the emotional impact of your actions will drive the bottom line far better than simply cracking the whip again.

The same applies outside the business world. In any human relationship, you will perform far better if the other person has your back. Knowing this to be true, it's time to connect with the perspective of those around you. If you think taking someone down a peg is "teaching them a lesson," you're about as accurate as Zena the midtown tarot card reader.

When you change your approach to thinking about how your words and actions will affect others, you will transform those around you. Relationships will come to life, imagination will flourish, and to top it off, people will return the favor and start treating you with the respect that both of you deserve. If your go-to move makes others feel the burn, it's time to take a radically new approach. It's time to be more user friendly.

A website is considered user friendly if it is simple and painless to explore. Ergonomics engineers study human-machine interactions to ensure that cars and other manufactured products provide an enjoyable experience in addition to their core function. *Consumer Reports* ranks dishwashers and flat-screen TVs alike based on their level of user friendliness.

Twenty years ago, this concept was an afterthought. Computer geeks used DOS, which required memorizing a series of bizarre tech commands. Carmakers focused on function and style, giving far less thought to consumer experience. And there was no such thing as a user-friendly VCR—only that infamous blinking 12:00 clock that we never knew how to set. The same was true with leadership: tough bosses barked orders, issued harsh criticism, and seldom gave thought to their impact on others.

Today websites that lack impeccably designed usability will fail to attract users, and prickly leaders who beat down their employees will fail altogether. User friendliness is now a requirement for high-performing leaders. Competency in this category is the ante to play, and excellence can become a significant competitive advantage.

What hoops do people have to leap through to interact with you? Each layer of difficulty you craft has an inverse effect on the productivity and creativity of those around you. The best leaders today are accessible, open-minded, and supportive. That's the formula for stimulating passion and seizing potential. When you choose encouragement over abrasiveness, opportunity opens up like a new checkout lane at a crowded grocery store. You'll attract talented people, new customers, and media exposure. Great leaders who govern by inspiration instead of intimidation are the ones who end up with the feast instead of the scraps.

Never confuse kindness for weakness. The opposite is true for leaders seeking to extract the most value from their teams. Give yourself a thorough examination and quickly rectify the jagged edges to improve performance. You will enjoy the direct correlation between improving your user friendliness and driving the results you seek.

Compassion

Bosses, parents, teachers, clergy, and government officials are well trained to catch you doing something wrong. There are elaborate systems for checks and balances, controls and consequences. It's apparently very important to catch the mischievous child or the wayward employee in the act of disobedience. With so much effort spent catching people doing something wrong, it's time to start catching each other doing something right.

In our society, widespread labeling is a devious force that robs individuals of achieving their true potential. When a parent tells a child he is average, slow, or stupid, these sharp words become a self-fulfilling prophecy as the child internalizes the erroneous labels. When a boss repeatedly lashes out at a team member, pointing out her every flaw, her confidence shatters and her performance plummets.

When a kid is slow to pick up violin or painting, teachers and parents routinely label her as "not creative." And business leaders are quick to pick favorites while admonishing the laggards. These labels seep into our souls, and we end up becoming their personification. Label someone a troublemaker, and trouble he will make. The good news is that labeling can work the other way too. Catch a team member in the act of delivering great work, and you'll inject her with confidence and energy. Label a colleague a rock star, and he'll kick out the work version of a Grammy.

Most of us have self-talk that's so negative we'd be institutional-ized if we said it out loud. In addition to exhibiting compassion to others, go ahead and catch yourself in the act of doing good more often and celebrate those wins auspiciously. Let's all flip the poison of negative labeling and catch each other and ourselves in the act of doing things right. These new, positive labels will tip the scales in favor of results, momentum, and overall achievement.

Steve Jobs was flawed. Serena Williams has soft spots in her tennis game. Even Brad Pitt has bad hair days. No matter how successful, powerful, or good looking, all of the people we admire have at least some deficiencies.

If we can accept that industry titans and Olympic athletes have flaws, why is it so difficult to accept our own? Our knees buckle from the unyielding pressure to be perfect at everything, and then we hide in shame when we can't live up to these wildly unrealistic expectations.

You may be a math whiz and a great conversationalist but stink at painting. Or perhaps you are a brilliant sales rep and a giving parent but can't hit a golf ball farther than six feet. Instead of beating yourself up for all the things you stink at, acknowledge these shortcomings and then get on with the far more important work of nurturing your strengths.

In fact, the most successful people focus relentlessly on their strengths. They readily admit their shortcomings and devote their time to improving what they're best at instead of trying to "correct" other areas of their lives.

Here in Detroit, we have suffered overwhelming setbacks over the past four decades. As a one-industry town, Detroit saw its economy crumble when the automotive sector took a nosedive. Population dwindled, the tax base dried up, crime increased, and our community was spinning with hopelessness and despair. We've been apologizing for years like a guilty child sentenced to sit in time-out.

But today Detroit's pulse has returned, and we are coming out of intensive care. To be sure, there are still many challenges and obstacles to conquer, but this city is rising from the ashes and focusing on a bright future. The economy is diversifying, and the swing of hammers restoring our buildings can be heard for miles.

Why the turnaround? Many factors are driving our reinvention, including passionate business leaders who have the courage to invest ahead of the curve. But I've seen something special from a front-row seat. I've noticed a renewed sense of pride and optimism: a self-reliance and scrappiness that's true to our heritage, a deep compassion for our fellow citizens, and a commitment transforming our situation into something we'll be proud to leave to our kids and grandkids.

Core to this new vibe is that we've stopped apologizing for what we're not and started rejoicing in what we are. We've had enough of comparing ourselves to others and began the hard work of rebuilding both our confidence and our city. All the while, this resilience is being driven in a most unapologetic fashion.

Our city will once again become a beacon of opportunity by deeply connecting with our inherent strengths. The same can happen for you. No more crying in your soup about your soft spots. It's time to double down every ounce of energy on your strengths and leap into action. No more cowering in the corner. Show compassion for yourself and others, and you'll be well on your way to making sustainable change.

Courage

Think about how much time you spend fretting about what might happen. Those stressful moments are not only agonizing but they are profoundly unproductive. With each minute you spend in a state of worry, you're robbing yourself of the opportunity to contribute to your own success and the world around you.

The funny thing about worrying is that the vast majority of our internal concerns never materialize. Stewing about what might happen if a client changes her mind was wasted time when, in the end, the client does no such thing. Worrying about a disease that never emerges or being scolded by a boss who ends up giving a compliment is absolutely wasteful.

Only a small percentage of most people's concerns actually come true. The majority of worry time could be deployed into something—anything—far more effective. You'll stress less and end up having more resources available when a setback actually occurs. Let's look at the math.

If a typical person worries for a total of 3 hours per week, this adds up to 156 hours per year of immobilizing anxiety. Now let's say 5 percent of the worries actually come true. That means that 148 hours were utterly wasted worrying about stuff that never ends up happening.

What if you recaptured the entire 156 hours and spent your days full of energy and free of concern? In addition to enjoying life more, you can use that time to create art, learn a new language, get in shape, read a book, play with your kids, counsel a friend, or help your community. Instead of the depleting act of wallowing in fear, you can be making an impact and advancing your life.

But what about the negative things that do end up happening? Even if you carve out 30 hours to deal with the fallout of setbacks once they occur (instead of biting your nails in advance), you still end up with a gift of over 120 hours to pursue your calling.

It's time to let go of the worry demon and embrace the new abundance of time and energy that will come as a result of developing courage. Break free from useless anxiety and sprint toward the activities that will drive the most progress in your life. You get to choose what you think about, so you might as well instruct your mind to think positively and release those unproductive concerns. Crunch the numbers, and you'll be well on your way to seizing your full potential. This kind of math sure beats long division, no?

Positivity

I'm short. And impatient. I stink at details, I am a horrible dancer, and I am a lousy athlete. Like you, I have dozens of imperfections and spend a lot of time focusing on them. *How completely unproductive.* Worse yet, I spend far too much time focused on the shortcomings of others. The driver in front of me going ten miles per hour under the speed limit. The salesperson who talks far too much. The entrepreneur pitching me for capital with a sloppy game plan. Unless you are serving on a jury, being judgmental of yourself and others yields just about the same benefit as eating nine glazed doughnuts in a row. Not only is this tendency a total waste of time and energy, it depletes us. It robs our mojo when directed internally and fuels anger and resentment when directed at others. Seriously, why bother?

Why do we spend so much time finding our faults instead of celebrating our strengths?

What would happen if we took all the time we spend beating ourselves and criticizing others and repurposed it into something positive? Think about how different your days would be if you replaced blame with gratitude. Think about how your confidence would skyrocket if your internal dialogue shifted from resentment to praise. Think about how you could spend all of that newly found energy directed at pursuing your full potential instead of tearing yourself (and others) apart.

Perhaps it is the wiring in our brains designed to protect us from the fundamental dangers of a million years ago. No matter how it got there, it serves no useful purpose today. Working to inject others and ourselves with positive reinforcement will drive humanity forward, whereas exacerbating weaknesses is nothing but a pointless and destructive act.

Positivity can be contagious. The sneeze of your aisle mate on an airplane sends a bolt of disgust through your mind. "Now I'm going to catch what this bozo has!" From popping endless vitamins to dousing with hand sanitizer, we go to great lengths to protect against germs. We just don't want to catch what someone else has. Or do we?

Emotions and ideas can also be highly contagious. When you spend an hour with someone who is full of energy and has a positive outlook, you leave the meeting feeling pumped up and ready to take on the world. This is how motivational speakers make a living. If you have a thought-provoking, intellectual conversation with a group of friends, you leave with fresh ways to tackle your own challenges.

But if you are berated by a boss or screamed at by a customer, you will unconsciously need to purge that negativity. Your anger becomes contagious as you unload on your spouse or kids. In the same way positive thoughts and ideas are contagious, so are the sinister ones. Fear, hatred, bigotry, and jealously are all easily transmittable afflictions. Most of us don't realize the impact of our own perspective on others. We fail to see that we have the power to energize or deplete, inspire or enrage. When you are curt, grumpy, and dismissive, you are performing the emotional equivalent of coughing in someone's face. And when you are encouraging, positive, and compassionate, you are giving a vaccine instead of spreading disease.

Knowing that each of us can be the carrier of both helpful and hurtful emotional bacteria, let's make the choice to infect those around us with energy, laughter, and hope. Negative outbursts and soul-crushing criticism have no place in our companies, communities, or families. If these are your feelings, we all prefer that you keep them in quarantine. If you're going to spread something, why not unleash a positive, helpful, encouraging virus? Hopefully it will spread faster than a cat video on YouTube, and we'll all be better off as a result. Your prescription comes with unlimited refills and no side effects, and it is fully covered by all insurance. Take ample doses, several times a day. Doctor's orders.

Discipline

While envisioning the change you want is an important first step, the necessary follow-through and persistence needed to accomplish your desired breakthrough can pose your greatest challenge. To build discipline throughout the various aspects of your life, you need to start with a training regimen.

There's an old saying in the boxing world: "Champions don't become champions in the ring; they are merely recognized there." The implication, of course, is that the hard work of winning happens during an intense training schedule. The blood, sweat, and tears on the gym floor; the relentless planning for every possible scenario; the sacrifice and careful preparation: this is the stuff that ultimately enables victory.

Professional athletes achieve at the highest levels by spending 90 percent of their time training and 10 percent of their time performing. In most areas of life, however, we do the exact opposite. In fact, most business leaders, parents, and professionals spend closer to 0 percent of their time in thoughtful study of their craft or training for improvement. Instead, we labor through the days in full-exertion mode and then wonder why we fail to reach our full potential.

Imagine a star tennis player who never trained and stepped foot on the court only during major tournaments—or a professional football player who never bothered with conditioning, learning the plays, or running drills with his teammates. Predictably these athletes would unravel in spectacular fashion, which is exactly what we do when we fail to commit the time and energy to our own personal development. While you probably don't have the luxury of devoting 90 percent of your days to training, carving out just 5 to 10 percent of your time for focused improvement will quickly advance your performance. If you are in sales, spend a few hours each week in role-playing sessions, carefully practicing your pitch. If you write code, spend time studying others' work, attending hackathons, and solving complex problems.

Simply put, a training regimen will drive your character and career to the next level. In addition to the skills you perfect, you'll build and fortify your "discipline muscle," which will have positive implications in all aspects of your reinvention efforts. Just like professional athletes who develop a written training program with specific maneuvers and goals, you should be taking the same approach for your own career. Reading books, attending lectures (or watching them online), running drills, solving practice problems, doing simulations with colleagues, and even trying to decode your competitor's approach are all helpful exercises to include in your training plan. If you have the discipline to improve yourself without the prodding of others, you will quickly fly past those who lack the ambition to push themselves to becoming world class. The time to get started is now. Your championship awaits.

Creativity

As I wrote about extensively in my first book, *Disciplined Dreaming*, creativity has become the most powerful tool in reaching world-class levels of performance in both business and life.[3] It's the one thing that cannot be outsourced. It's your most important source of sustainable competitive advantage, the core building block of all reinvention.

Luckily we are all immensely creative as human beings. Even if you've let your creativity muscles atrophy, you can reignite your imagination and unleash it with a small amount of focus and practice. Those sparks of creativity—little twists on what already exists in favor of something new—can lead to inspiring results.

Too often we accept defeat when challenges seem insurmountable. We concede quickly, bowing to the pressures of the day by rationalizing that nothing can be done. While some shrug their shoulders and accept the unacceptable, others are busy getting creative and generating meaningful results. They develop a new ingredient—a *twist*—that becomes the difference maker. When you study the many incredible stories of against-all-odds success, the ones who break through the barriers don't relent. Instead, they look for fresh approaches to tackling the most difficult hurdles.

To see this in action, let's look at one of the toughest problems of all: education in the city of Detroit.

Like most schools in other urban areas, Detroit schools are facing serious challenges. Lack of funding, community apathy, and school violence are just a few of the issues plaguing teachers and administrators. The result is abysmal: by 2007, the city's school district had a pathetic 25 percent high school graduation rate (the worst in the nation at the time), which brings forth outrage and disbelief.[4] With such an uphill battle, could creative twists really make an impact?

Twist 1: Individual focus. Beyond Basics, a nonprofit organization dedicated to "changing destiny through education," attacks the problem at its root. Going into the most troubled schools and working with the highest-risk kids, its volunteers offer intensive one-on-one literacy coaching combined with positive energy and respect. Instead of the typical thirty-to-one ratio, the tutors work on each child's individual challenges. The result is that nearly all students reach grade-level literacy skills within six weeks, even those who were years behind. This program is breaking the cycle and has helped thousands of students over the past ten years.

Twist 2: Music. The Sphinx Orchestra offers classical music programs to children in Detroit schools. These kids learn discipline, creativity, and teamwork under the direction of the inspirational Aaron Dworkin. Besides delivering some amazing concerts, Dworkin's program delivers something even greater: participants enjoy a 100 percent high-school graduation rate.

Twist 3: Working world. Detroit's new Cristo Rey High School pondered this question: College students can put themselves through school, so why not high school students? The program includes corporate mentors who hire students to work one day a week on site at their company. The pay they earn goes back to the school to help fund better programming and staff. These teenagers get real-world experience, connect with role models, and develop a strong work ethic. As a result, 100 percent of the school's first graduating class was accepted at college.

If creative twists can deliver such dramatic results in the highly challenged Detroit schools, think what they can do in your own reinvention.

Grit

Having been around hundreds of start-up leaders, I can tell you that the highest correlation of a founder's characteristics to success isn't intelligence, contacts, degrees, or charisma. The most important attribute I've seen for entrepreneurial success is grit.

Why do some companies consistently outperform their competition? Why do some people become champions while others fall short? What skills do you need to improve to reach your highest potential? It turns out that good old-fashioned grit has been statistically linked to being the number one indicator of high performance.[5]

In a joint study from the University of Pennsylvania, University of Michigan, and the US Military Academy at West Point, researchers define *grit* as the combination of perseverance and passion for long-term goals. They found that as a trait, grit had better predict-ability for success than IQ. The study lists these attributes as the building blocks of grit:

- A clear goal
- Determination despite others' doubts
- Self-confidence about figuring it out
- Humility about knowing it doesn't come easy
- Persistence despite fear
- Patience for the small stuff that obscures the path
- A code of ethics they live by
- Flexibility in the face of roadblocks
- A capacity for human connection and collaboration
- A recognition that accepting help does not equate to weakness
- A focus and appreciation of each step in the journey
- An appreciation of other people's grit
- A loyalty that never sacrifices connections along the way
- An inner strength that brings them to their goal

More important than a go-get-'em-tiger pep talk, grit can be developed and harnessed. The good news is that grit comes from within, and none of us is precluded from building this attribute. It doesn't matter if you're rich or poor, come from a good neighborhood, have an impressive degree, or are dressed for success. We all have nearly limitless potential, and the opportunity to seize it is waiting for you.

Trouncing Your Obstacles

If it were easy, everyone would enjoy perfect health, a billion dollars, and an untarnished character. Of course, the world is filled with challenges to test your commitment and make the taste of success that much sweeter. Now that we've covered the seven building blocks of reinventing yourself, we need to tackle the most common challenges: caving to the naysayers, letting setbacks derail your advancement, and falling to temptation.

Never Embolden the Naysayers

At some point on the journey, every great contributor to the world was met with resistance. The ones who made the biggest impact in business, politics, invention, education, and even humanitarian and civil rights were attacked as much as they were cherished. Innovation is routinely met by fear from those the advances disrupt. Bold thought leaders are attacked by parasitic naysayers who would rather criticize than create. For every courageous doer, there are dozens of detractors, eager to toss a wet blanket on progress.

In your own efforts to drive your career forward, build your organization to the next level, or reinvent yourself from the ground up, you will undoubtedly be met with negativity. It's as if a gravitational force has been established to hold you back from seizing your full potential. This resistance exists for a single purpose: to test your resolve. And while it may not feel that way in the moment, you have complete and total control over your response and the eventual outcome.

The first thing for you to do is put up two filters. One is intrinsic: ask yourself if this feedback is pointing out a true red flag, as something out of character for yourself. If so, respond graciously, and adjust your behavior accordingly. Second, assess if the person is providing truly constructive criticism with your best interests at heart. When this is the case, feedback is a gift. Absorb as much as you can, and use the advice to move the needle. However, if the commentator doesn't meet either of these points, the person is simply throwing sand on your ideas, hampering your creativity.

When you feel the assault of abrasive critics whose real intention is to destroy instead of contribute, your instinct may be to cave, to give a little ground, to settle, to allow your most potent ideas to become watered down. The problem is that by giving even an inch, you embolden the naysayers. Your effort to diffuse the situation has the opposite effect: it strengthens your adversaries. If you feed this monster, it will grow and end up eating you. Instead, you must starve it. You must fight back with the force of a thousand armies. You conquer the detractors only by determination, not by compromise.

Like any schoolyard bully, the amoral rivals will eventually back down when they realize their fight is unwinnable.

These debilitating forces can appear in many forms. They may show up as a soul-crushing boss, a ruthless competitor, or an emotionally abusive partner. You may be dealing with a broken political structure, a frivolous lawsuit, or a neighborhood stuck in the past. Each of us has our own opponents, but conquering them is achieved with a singular approach: tenacity.

Let's all stand firm as business leaders and community rebuilders. Never back down. Never waiver. Never empower your critics. Never cede your values and beliefs. Never cave to your detractors. Never embolden the naysayers.

Learn from Setbacks

You probably know it well—that sinking feeling in your gut when you feel as if you were just punched: heart-pounding, head-throbbing, room-spinning agony. We've all been there. Perhaps it was losing a huge client, a key team member jumping ship, or a major technology glitch. Or maybe it was a sharp comment by a spouse, an unexpected job loss, or that big setback you've been dreading. These are the moments we fear, the ones that nightmares are made of. You're not alone: every great leader, hero, and champion has had them too.

The real question isn't whether you'll experience this acute terror. Assuming you are pursuing anything worth doing, you will. The question becomes, How will you react? Some of us cave to the pressure. We roll on our backs like helpless animals exposing their vulnerable bellies. We allow ourselves to become victimized by the event and relinquish our power to the callous circumstances. We let things happen *to* us. Luckily you need not suffer this hapless fate. Instead, you can regain your power and use the setback as a teachable moment. Rather than getting overwhelmed by it, you can look at it as information that is helping you grow as a person or organization.

Throughout my own career building start-ups for more than twenty years, I've had my fair share of these moments. But now, looking back, most of these painful setbacks turned out to be a blessing. In fact, many of my biggest breakthroughs came just after events that appeared to be devastating losses. Often our biggest moments of growth come from our darkest moments of adversity. Life has a funny way of teaching us, and sometimes those painful wake-up calls can be just the jolt we need to effectuate change. In these moments, you have a choice: you can cower in the corner like a guilty child or use the sting as an opportunity to strengthen your determination. You can own it, take personal responsibility, and leap into action with unwavering commitment.

The most successful people have bad days too. We all stumble, but the champions don't let that derail them. Instead, they extract every valuable lesson that can be gained. And you can too. That dreaded setback will likely crop up when you least expect it. The next time it does, don't run from it. Seize it, even when it's tough. It's an opportunity for you to shine and grow.

Tackle Your Temptations

Temptation, the dark side, comes in all forms. It is shiny, juicy, and tempting. It comes perfectly packaged and marketed directly to our soft spots: that delicious candy bar or cheeseburger that poisons your body, expands your waistline, and steals your vitality; the expensive handbag that you just *have* to have, but drives you deeper into debt after momentary pleasure; that relationship that's all surface and no substance. In fact, the dark side looks anything but dark: it is appealing in every way. It's much harder to say no to temptations that by their nature are enticing.

I once sat with a friend who was down on his luck. His situation, which had been worsening for years, felt hopeless. Like so many others, he was in a state of despair and couldn't get unstuck. When I asked him what he was doing to improve things, he rattled off a long list of obstacles. He had obviously spent many thoughtful hours contemplating all the things that were holding him back, all the reasons he couldn't change direction.

To be sure, he was facing many real roadblocks, many of the same issues that plague individuals throughout society. But he really didn't answer my question. He was solely focused on the problem and refused to let his mind explore possible solutions. I decided to press him: "Okay. I get that you have many, many tough obstacles. How about this: tell me one thing you could do to improve things. Just one. Doesn't have to be game changing. Just *one* small positive action."

When the pressure of solving the world's problems was off, the conversation took a sharp turn for the better. "Well, I could go to the library and start learning more about my industry to become better at my job."

"Great! Go on," I prodded.

"I could start going for walks a few times a week to drop some extra weight. I could also cut out fried foods. Oh, and I could spend more evenings engaging with the kids instead of hitting the couch." The guy who had been tightly closed transformed before my eyes. His energy skyrocketed. His list of small ideas compounded into a solid plan of attack to turn his life around.

While it's overwhelming to try to solve all your problems at once, the act of putting just one small change in place can create the momentum you need. Find one thing you can do to improve your condition, and do it consistently for a week. It will jump-start your situation. In a time of adversity, my friend's one small step allowed him to pivot and begin walking down a more positive and productive path.

It often comes down to small choices. Should you watch trash reality TV or read something inspiring? Should you hit the bar or hit the gym? Should you perpetuate a relationship that provides nothing more than momentary indulgences or seek a partner who helps you reach the next level? At nearly every turn, you'll face scrumptious temptations. The good news is that you get to make each choice along the way: momentary pleasure or sustainable fulfillment, the easy thing or the right thing, darkness or light. If you think about it, your life becomes simply the product of all the choices you make.

If you prioritize true fulfillment, you'll have to make some tough choices along your journey. You'll need to have the strength to say no to overwhelming temptation in order to say yes to your real calling. Your weapons are purpose, passion, and commitment. You'll win the fight with inner focus rather than outer strength. The dark side is only getting more alluring, which means your commitment to excellence is needed more than ever before.

Detroit: Catalyst for Change

Detroit has been the cradle of both world-changing innovation and soul-crushing stagnation. In the past sixty years or so, it has missed multiple opportunities to throw off the shackles of "what we've always done," embrace new ideas, and prepare to move into the new century as a dynamic, healthy city, teeming with the same spirit of possibility that produced the automotive age. But no matter how many lost opportunities have darkened Detroit's history, I see many more shining possibilities in its future. This city's legacy is still being written, and I suspect that some of the most exciting chapters are yet to come.

We've entered a new phase in Detroit that is squarely focused on the future. I am incredibly fortunate to have a front-row seat to what may be the greatest reinvention in American history. My venture capital firm, Detroit Venture Partners, has a mission to help rebuild Detroit through entrepreneurial fire. We believe that by backing passionate entrepreneurs, we'll create jobs, urban density, and hope. By providing capital, coaching, and access to tech start-ups, we can reestablish Detroit as a beacon of innovation once again. We can reconnect to our rich history of entrepreneurship and build a vibrant new city that our grandkids will be proud of. We are using the platform of tech start-ups to help reinvent our troubled city.

We aren't alone in our efforts. A growing posse of unlikely characters is banding together to improve our city from within. Business titans like Dan Gilbert (chairman of Quicken Loans), Roger Penske (chairman of Penske Racing and Penske Corporation), and Mike Ilitch (founder of Little Caesar's Pizza) are collaborating with artists, retailers, educators, and philanthropists. The federal government and local elected officials are working together. Previously hostile factions are laying down their arms and uniting in a singular mission: to reinvent. Together we are boldly sharing our own vision and inviting others to come and share theirs with us. With a national ad campaign and a matching website and presence, Opportunity Detroit is actively marketing to young entrepreneurs, targeting them to bring their ideas here.

When you're championing a cause and making a difference that goes beyond personal gain, your results will be better and more widespread. That's just one part of the legacy of ongoing reinvention. Ted Serbinski, one of my partners, moved to Detroit from San Francisco. People often ask him why he came here, to which he always replies, "Ten years from now, San Francisco will be just as good as it is today. But in ten years, Detroit will be a roaring city once again, defining a new technology hub. Where do you want to be in ten years? Status quo? Or one of the heroes that rebuilt a city?" Couldn't have said it better myself. Clearly in Detroit we've had decades of struggles, so positive changes are always welcome, especially for people who play with heart and soul.

As you begin crafting your own legacy of ongoing innovation, it may seem as if you're alone in your corner. Once people recognize your greatness, they'll get on their soapboxes on your behalf. Until then, spread your message yourself. More than anything else, remember to play the game of reinvention as if you've got nothing to lose. As an underdog, you have to put it all out on the line. You've got bills to pay, mouths to feed, and nowhere to go but up. You'll have to fight with the ferocity of a streetfighter if you hope to achieve at the highest levels. When you talk to visionaries in Detroit, they'll tell you there's no question of what's to become of this area. For you, greatness can't be a debate either: it's your destiny. Believe in it wholeheartedly so you see the full vision clearly. With this well-defined result in mind, it's simply a matter of continually moving forward toward the realization of that bold vision. Keep your dreams big and ever-evolving, not bound by the confines of the past. Remember: you'll see it when you believe it.

Tools for Transformation:
More, Less, Stop

In our frenetically busy lives, we all smack up against the same obstacle: time. The twenty-four-hour clock is a brutal and unforgiving foe. It's easy to fill the hours, feeling busy and anxious, only to look back at a stunningly puny amount of productivity. Having the discipline to pursue your calling and the most worthy efforts along the way will allow you to have the biggest impact. With unlimited access to information and frictionless global markets for goods, services, and talent, you need to make each minute count in order to remain competitive. Sounds easier said than done? Let's explore a simple yet effective approach to making the most of the clock. I want you to make three lists:

1. *More.* What do you need more of in your life? Where are your efforts spent that deliver the highest value? More time in strategy meetings? Crafting the brand? Coaching a colleague? Reading to your kids? Make a list of the top seven things that you want to prioritize and do more of. These are the areas that will lead to your biggest goals, drive the most progress, and contribute at your highest capacity.

2. *Less.* What do you need less of? Less time updating your Facebook status, gossiping at the watercooler, or regretting a decision? You may feel busy by triple-checking a report or holding yet another mind-numbing meeting, but these low-return time investments can rob you of the ability to focus on what matters most. What are seven items that should be reduced to make room for higher value activities?

3. *Stop.* We all have to-do lists, but how many of us have a stop-doing list? This list should include the most notorious and unproductive activities that should be eliminated completely. Each of us knows what to include for our own lists. For some it may be eating junk food. Some may need to cut out negative self-talk. For others, they need to stop impulsively checking e-mail while driving (author's note: guilty as charged). These habits are tempting, to be sure, but they deplete value and lure you away from your calling. Make sure to include the seven worst offenders you need to guard against and then exterminate them as if they were fire ants.

Try following your lists for thirty days: three lists, seven items for each list. While the first week may be a bit rough as you break old patterns, you'll be delighted with the results by the end of week 2: more time, higher impact, focused creativity, deeper connections, increased discipline.

Conclusion

A ship is safe in harbor, but that's not what ships are for.
—WILLIAM G. T. SHEDD

It's your choice. Regardless of the circumstances that have led you to this point in your life, you have a decision to make. Proactive reinvention is a route that leads to success in all areas of life if you firmly commit to embracing it. You are the only one who can make that choice. Too often, we feel that life happens to us, as if we are simply a passenger along for the ride. This is your time to slide over into the driver's seat and speed toward the enormous opportunities that lie ahead. Despite the obstacles, both real and perceived, that may be holding you back, it's time to shed your barriers in the same way a snake sheds its skin.

The decision is yours: disrupt or be disrupted.

While the times may be challenging, we're living in a world of endless possibility. You get to write the script of your own screenplay, paint your own masterpiece. Take personal responsibility for the outcomes you desire and then proceed with passion and conviction. Now is the time to choose:

New ideas over old ones
Abundance over scarcity
Fresh thinking over conventional wisdom

Innovation over stagnation
Growth over protection
Exploration over fear
Your dream over someone else's

The tools and frameworks we've explored throughout this book have armed you for a successful journey. You have all the approaches, tactics, and strategies you need to transform your organization and yourself. Now it's up to you to make a deep commitment to change—to craft a beautiful vision and then unleash your creativity and resolve in order to bring it to life. Letting go of the past in favor of what can be takes courage, and I applaud you for exploring the possibilities. As this book concludes, your journey begins. While the ride may have a few bumps along the way, the destination of fulfillment and success will be well worth the effort.

Your full potential awaits. Retool. Reimagine. Rework. Rebuild. Recreate. Reestablish. Relaunch. Rekindle. Renew. Rejoice.

Reinvent.

NOTES

Chapter 1

1. Han, Jiwon. "Historical Review of Samsung's Innovations and Further Steps." Master's thesis, MIT, 2011.
2. Grobart, Sam. "How Samsung Became the World's No. 1 Smartphone Maker." *Businessweek*, March 28, 2013.
3. Han, "Historical Review."
4. "Rupert Murdoch." *BrainyQuote*. N.d. http://www.brainyquote.com/quotes/authors /r/rupert_murdoch.html.
5. "Reinvent." *Merriam-Webster*. N.d. http://www.merriam-webster.com/dictionary /reinvent.
6. "Reinvent." *Oxford Dictionaries*. *Oxford Dictionaries*. N.d. http://www .oxforddictionaries.com/us/definition/american_english/reinvent.
7. Jennings, Jason. *The Reinventors: How Extraordinary Companies Pursue Radical Continuous Change*. New York: Portfolio/Penguin, 2012.
8. Schultz, E. J. "Why Kmart Lost the Attention of Discount Shoppers." *Advertising Age*, March 19, 2012.
9. Kary, Tiffany. "Borders Files Bankruptcy, Is Closing Up to 275 Stores." *Bloomberg .com*, February 16, 2011. http://www.bloomberg.com/news/2011–02–16/borders -book-chain-files-for-bankruptcy-protection-with-1–29-billion-debt.html.
10. Clarke, Michael. "Post-Mortem of a Book Empire—Borders, and the Mismanagement of the Future." *Scholarly Kitchen*, July 28, 2011.
11. Hamilton, Anita. "Business and Money." *Time*, November 11, 2008.
12. Ibid.
13. Anderson, Derek. "From the Garage to 200 Employees in 3 Years: How Nest Thermostats Were Born." *techcrunch.com*, May 11, 2013, http://techcrunch.com/2013/05/11 /from-the-garage-to-200-employees-in-3-years-how-nest-thermostats-were-born/.
14. Duncan, Geoff. "Nest Labs: We're Sold out of Thermostats." *Digital Trends*. November 3, 2011.
15. "About Whirlpool." Whirlpool Corporation. http://www.whirlpoolcorp.com/about /history.aspx.

16. "Whirlpool Online Annual Report 2012." 2013. http://www.whirlpoolcorp.com /2012annual/WHR_2012AR.pdf.

17. Nelson, Rebecca. "Jewelry Designer Jessica Mindich: Fighting Gun Violence with Bracelets." *Time*, January 29, 2013.

18. Nocera, Joe. "Notes from a Gun Buyback." *New York Times*, February 15, 2013.

19. Gull, Nicole. "Fighting Crime with Jewelry." *Inc. Magazine*, May 7, 2012.

20. "Jack Welch." *Goodreads*, November 7, 2013. http://www.goodreads.com/author /quotes/3770.Jack_Welch.

21. "Timeline of Detroit." Detroit Historical Society. http://detroithistorical.org/learn /timeline-detroit, accessed August 24, 2013.

22. Ibid.

23. "Detroit History." *About Detroit*. www.detroitmi.gov, accessed August 24, 2013.

24. Timeline of Detroit.

25. Bomey, Nathan, and Gallagher, John. "How Detroit Went Broke: The Answers May Surprise You—and Don't Blame Coleman Young." *Detroit Free Press*, September 15, 2013.

26. Myler, Kofi. "Detroit's Population from 1840 to 2012 Shows High Points, Decades of Decline." *Detroit Free Press*, July 23, 2013.

27. Bomey and Gallagher, "How Detroit Went Broke."

28. Timm, Jane C. "Urban Farming Takes Hold in Blighted Motor City." MSNBC, September 10, 2013.

Chapter 2

1. Carr, Austin. "Nike: The No. 1 Most Innovative Company of 2013." *Fast Company*, February 11, 2013.

2. Ibid.

3. Ibid.

4. "Bill Gates." *BrainyQuote*. November 9, 2013. http://www.brainyquote.com/quotes /authors/b/bill_gates.html.

5. Falcione, Olivia, and Henderson, Laura. "The Dove Campaign for Real Beauty." *Public Relations Problems and Cases*, March 1, 2009. http://psucomm473.blogspot .com/2009/03/dove-campaign-for-real-beauty.html.

6. *Berkshire Hathaway Annual Report*. N.p.: Berkshire Hathaway, 2012.

7. Livy, Julian. "History of Berkshire Hathaway." Warren Buffett Secrets, January 21, 2013. http://www.buffettsecrets.com/berkshire-hathaway.htm.

8. "Feds Approve $140M Woodward Light Rail Project." *CBS Detroit*, April 22, 2013. http://detroit.cbslocal.com/2013/04/22/feds-approve-woodward-light-rail-project/.

9. "Detroiters Work: The Lighter, Quicker, Cheaper Regeneration of a Great American City." *By Project for Public Spaces*, November 10, 2013. https://www.pps.org/blog /detroiters-work-the-lighter-quicker-cheaper-regeneration-of-a-great-american-city/.

10. Ibid.

11. "Donations to Restore Arts, Sports Programs in Detroit Schools," *CBS Detroit*, September 27, 2013. http://detroit.cbslocal.com/2013/09/27/donations-to-restore -arts-sports-programs-in-detroit-schools/.

12. "Chrysler Corporation, ARISE Detroit!, and Detroit Public Schools Announce Community Service Partnerships for Neighborhoods Day." Detroit Public Schools, July 23, 2013. http://detroitk12.org/content/2013/07/23/chrysler-corporation-arise -detroit-and-detroit-public-schools-announce-community-service-partnerships-for -neighborhoods-day/.

Chapter 3

1. Deutsch, Claudia H. "Deep in Debt Since 1988, Polaroid Files for Bankruptcy." *New York Times*, October 13, 2001.

2. Constine, Josh, and Cutler, Kim-Mai. "Facebook Buys Instagram for $1 Billion, Turns Budding Rival into Its Standalone Photo App." *TechCrunch*, April 9, 2012. http://techcrunch.com/2012/04/09/facebook-to-acquire-instagram-for-1-billion/.

3. Rifkin, Glenn. "Losing Focus." *Boston Magazine*, January 2002.

4. Klomp, Luuk, and Van Leeuwen, George. "Linking Innovation and Firm Performance: A New Approach." *International Journal of the Economics of Business* 8(2001): 343–364.

5. Snuba. "Aloha Surf Guide." N.d. http://www.alohasurfguide.com/snuba/.

6. Linkner, Josh. *Disciplined Dreaming: A Proven System to Drive Breakthrough Creativity*. San Francisco: Jossey-Bass, 2011.

7. Bate, Roger. "The Deadly World of Fake Medicine." *CNNHealth, CNN Online*, July 17, 2012. http://www.cnn.com/2012/07/17/health/living-well/falsified-medicine-bate/.

8. Federer, J. Lester. "07_Sproxil." *Fast Company*, February 11, 2013.

9. Henry, Jim. "Engineering a Comeback." *SUCCESS*. N.d. http://www.success.com /article/engineering-a-comeback.

10. Taylor III, Alex. "Fixing Up Ford." *CNNMoney*, May 12, 2009. http://money.cnn .com/2009/05/11/news/companies/mulally_ford.fortune/.

11. Henry, "Engineering a Comeback." *SUCCESS*. November 15, 2013, http://www .success.com/article/engineering-a-comeback.

12. Strumpf, Dan, and Johnson, Kimberly S. "GM Files for Bankruptcy." *Huffington Post*. June 1, 2009.

13. Ford Motor Company. "Ford Now Has Industry's Highest Customer Satisfaction with Quality, New Survey Shows." *PR Newswire*, April 19, 2010.

14. Sarasohn-Kahn, Jane. "An Rx for Improving Health Care: Lessons from Target." *Health Populi*. December 10, 2010.

15. Campbell-Dollaghan, Kelsey. "An Ingenious Minefield Sweeper Rolls like Tumble-weed in the Wind." *Fast Company*, October 30, 2012. http://www.fastcodesign .com/1671115/an-ingenious-minefield-sweeper-rolls-like-tumbleweed-in-the-wind.

16. "Henry Ford Leaves Edison to Start Automobile Company." *This Day in History: August 18, 1899*. http://www.history.com/this-day-in-history/henry-ford-leaves-edison-to-start-automobile-company.

17. Ibid.

18. "The Innovator and Ford Motor Company." Henry Ford Museum. http://www.hfmgv.org/exhibits/hf/The_Innovator_and_Ford_Motor_Company.asp.

19. "Henry Ford's $5-a-Day Revolution." Ford Motor Company. http://corporate.ford.com/news-center/press-releases-detail/677–5-dollar-a-day, accessed July 11, 2013.

20. Worstall, Tim. "The Story of Henry Ford's $5 a Day Wages: It's Not What You Think." *Forbes*, March 4, 2012.

21. "The Innovator and Ford Motor Company."

22. Ibid.

23. "Tiffany's Increasingly Higher Price Points Improve Takeover Appeal." *Seeking Alpha*, June 3, 2013.

Chapter 4

1. Abrashoff, D. Michael. *It's Your Ship: Management Techniques from the Best Damn Ship in the Navy*. New York: Warner, 2002.

2. Bird, John. "How to Turn $4000 into Millions." *Inside Retail Asia*, March 19, 2013.

3. Hammer, Michael. "Deep Change: How Operational Innovation Can Transform Your Company." *Harvard Business Review*, April 2004.

4. "The Story of Motown Records." *Classic Motown*. 2012. http://classic.motown.com/history/.

5. Van Petten, Vanessa. *You're Grounded: How to Stop Fighting and Make the Teenage Years Easier*. Lincoln, NE: iUniverse, 2007.

6. "UPS Annual Report." December 31, 2012. http://www.investors.ups.com/phoenix.zhtml?c=62900&p=irol-reportsannual.

7. "We Shrink the Globe: UPS Annual Report 2012." UPS, November 15, 2013. http://media.corporate-ir.net/media_files/irol/62/62900/UPS_AR_Final_mobile/AR/index.html.

8. "Art." *Oxford Dictionaries*. N.d. http://www.oxforddictionaries.com/us/definition/american_english/art?q=ART.

9. Zimmerman, Dwight Jon. "Automobile Factories Switched to War Production as America Entered World War II." *Defense Media Network*, February 10, 2012.

10. Ibid.

11. Ibid.

12. Wilson, Marion F. *The Story of Willow Run*. Ann Arbor: University of Michigan Press, 1956.

13. Ibid.

14. Samilton, Tracy. "Museum Tries to Save the Plant Where Rosie Riveted." *NPR.org*, August 4, 2013. http://www.npr.org/2013/08/04/208762134/museum-tries-to-save-the-plant-where-rosie-riveted.

Chapter 5

1. Burns, Megan. "The Customer Experience Index, 2012." *Forrester Research*, January 23,2012. http://www.forrester.com/The+Customer+Experience+Index+2012/fulltext /-/E-RES59377.

2. Barnes, Brooks. "Theme Park Income Spurs Profits at Disney." *New York Times*, February 7, 2012.

3. Chai, Carmen. "Children's Cancer Wing Transforms into Superhero Ward Offering 'Superformula' Chemotherapy." *Global News*, June 7, 2013.

4. Ibid.

5. "2011–2012 Annual Report—Finance." *Henry Ford Health System*. N.d. http://www .henryford.com/body.cfm?id=57806.

6. Sacks, Danielle. "How Jenna Lyons Transformed J.Crew into a Cult Brand." *Fast Company*, April 15, 2013.

7. Morris, Tricia. *Tricia's Customer Service Success Blog*, January 23, 2012, http://www .forrester.com/The+Customer+Experience+Index+2012/fulltext/-/E-RES59377. Burns, Megan. "The Customer Experience Index, 2012." *Forrester Research*, January 23, 2012.

8. "The Cost of Poor Customer Service: The Economic Impact of the Customer Experience and Engagement in 16 Key Economies." *Marketingdeservicios.com*, November 2009. http://www.marketingdeservicios.com/wp-content/uploads/Genesys_Global _Survey09_screen.pdf.

9. Taylor, Bill. "A Geek's Guide to Great Service." *HBR Blog Network*, August 7, 2008. http://blogs.hbr.org/2008/08/a-geeks-guide-to-great-service/.

10. "Interview: Robert Stephens Founded the Geek Squad and Took It from Bootstrapped Inception to over $1 Billion in (Estimated) Revenues (Just Watch This Interview. Trust Me. It's Good.)." *LeadPages Blog Free Landing Page Templates*, November 15, 2013. https://blog.leadpages.net/robert-stephens-geek-squad-best-buy/.

11. "Pleasant Rowland." *Wikipedia*, August 22, 2013.

12. "2011 Customer Experience Impact Report: Getting to the Heart of the Consumer and Brand Relationship." *Right Now*, September 26, 2013. http://www.oracle.com /us/products/applications/cust-exp-impact-report-epss-1560493.pdf.

13. "America's Best and Worst Airports." *Travel and Leisure*, April 2012.

14. "Multichannel Customer Experience Report." *Econsultancy.com*, November 2011. http:// http://econsultancy.com/reports/multichannel-customer-experience-report.

15. Myler, Kofi. "Detroit's Population from 1840 to 2012 Shows High Points, Decades of Decline." *Detroit Free Press*, July 23, 2013.

16. Staes, J. A. "Comparing Detroit to Other Cities? Look at the Map!" *Detroit Unspun*. August 12, 2010.

Chapter 6

1. "Downtown Detroit Occupancy Rate Is Now over 99 Percent." *Deadline Detroit*, July 3, 2013.

2. Story, Louise. "Anywhere the Eye Can See, It's Now Likely to See an Ad." *New York Times*, January 15, 2007.

3. Elsen, Tracy, and Gonzalez, Mariana. "Environmental Entrepreneurs: Mexico's YoReciclo Recycles for a Profit." *World Resources Institute*, May 18, 2011. http://www.wri.org /blog/environmental-entrepreneurs-mexico%E2%80%99s-yoreciclo-recycles-profit.

4. "Luis Duarte, Fellow 2011." *Unreasonable Institute*. N.d. http://unreasonableinstitute .org/profile/lduarte/.

5. Jordan, Miriam. "The Big War over a Small Fruit." *Wall Street Journal*, July 13, 2012.

6. "Stewart and Lynda Resnick." *Forbes Magazine*, September 2013.

7. Peterson, Hayley. "The Sheer Yoga Pants That Lululemon Recalled Are Back in Stores and Selling for $92." *Business Insider*, November 12, 2013.

8. "Nick Friedman: How I Started College Hunks Hauling Junk." *Entrepreneur*, November 16, 2010.

9. "Firebrands." *Dictionary.com unabridged*, November 15, 2013.

10. "The Detroit Riots of 1967: Events." *The Detroit Riots of 1967: Events*. N.d. http://www .67riots.rutgers.edu/d_index.htm.

11. Ibid.

12. "Michigan Legal Milestones: 36. Milliken v. Bradley." *Michigan Legal Milestones: 36. Milliken v. Bradley*. State Bar of Michigan, September 16, 2011. http://www.michbar .org/programs/milestone/milestones_Milliken-v-Bradley.cfm.

Chapter 7

1. McGray, Douglas. "House of Second Chances." *Fast Company*, April 16, 2012.

2. Collins, J., and Porras, J. *Built to Last*. New York: HarperCollins, 1994.

3. Jennings, Jason. *The Reinventors: How Extraordinary Companies Pursue Radical Continuous Change*. New York: Portfolio/Penguin, 2012.

4. Shen, Aviva. "New York Sushi Restaurant Eliminates Tipping Because It Pays Waiters a Salary with Benefits." *ThinkProgress RSS*, June 11, 2013. http://thinkprogress .org/economy/2013/06/11/2134891/new-york-sushi-restaurant-eliminates-tipping -because-they-pay-waiters-a-salary-with-benefits.

5. McKay, Carol. "Survey: Consumers Support Improved Conditions for Restaurant Workers." *National Consumers League*, January 16, 2013. http://www.nclnet.org /newsroom/press-releases/734-survey-consumers-support-improved-conditions-for -restaurant-workers.

6. Sutton, Ryan. "NYC's Sushi Yasuda Eliminates Tipping" Gratuities No Long Accepted (Updated)." *The Price Hike*. N.d. http://thepricehike.com/post/52308734397 /nycs-sushi-yasuda-eliminates-tipping-gratuities-no.

7. Washenko, Anna. "Five Radical New Approaches to Corporate Culture." *Sprout Insights*, June 21, 2012. http://sproutsocial.com/insights/innovative-corporate-culture/.

8. Guenzi, Paulo. "How Ritual Delivers Performance." *HBR Blog Network*, February 25, 2013. http://blogs.hbr.org/2013/02/how-ritual-delivers-performanc/.

9. Reiss, Robert. "How Ritz-Carlton Stays at the Top." *Forbes Magazine*. October 30, 2009.

10. Sharma, Robin S. *The Leader Who Had No Title: A Modern Fable on Real Success in Business and in Life*. New York: Free Press 2010.

11. "Detroit Mayor Swearing-In Ceremony." *C-Span Video Library*, January 4, 2002.

12. "Michigan: Detroit Mayor's Expenses." *New York Times*, May 4, 2005.

13. "$150 Million Lawsuit over Rumored Mansion Party." Online, *WDIV-TV*, December 12, 2007. http://www.clickondetroit.com/news/14884764/detail.html.

14. Ashenfelter, David, Swickard, Joe, and Gorchow, Zachary. "Kilpatrick and Beatty Surrender. *Detroit Free Press*, March 24, 2008.

15. "Kilpatrick Headed to Prison." *ClickonDetroit.com*, May 25, 2010. http://abclocal .go.com/wtvd/story?section=news/state&id=7460511.

16. "Kwame Kilpatrick and Bobby Ferguson Arrive at Federal Prison in Milan After Guilty Convictions." *WXY*, March 9, 2013. http://www.wxyz.com/dpp/news/region/detroit /kwame-kilpatrick-and-bobby-ferguson-remanded-to-detention-facility-immediately.

Chapter 8

1. Linderman, Matt. "Learning from Harley-Davidson's Comeback." *Signal vs. Noise*. 37 Signals, October 29, 2008.

2. Gross, Daniel. *Forbes Greatest Business Stories of All Time*. New York: Wiley, 1997. See "The Turnaround at Harley-Davidson" (298–313).

3. Ibid.

4. Denove, Chris, and Power IV, James D. *Satisfaction: How Every Great Company Listens to the Voice of the Customer*. New York: Portfolio, 2007.

5. Gargiulo, Susanne. "Women-Only Hotel Floors Tap Boom in Female Business Travel." *CNN*, March 20, 2012. http://edition.cnn.com/2012/03/07/business /women-hotels-business-travelers/.

6. Ibid.

7. Ibid.

8. "About Us." *Curves*. N.d. http://www.curves.com/about-curves.

9. Wagner, Vivian. "Roaring Reinvention: How a Grandmother Started a Motorcycle Shop." *Entrepreneur*. April 28, 2011.

10. "Information about Lady Jane's Haircuts for Men." *Lady Jane's Haircuts for Men*. N.d. http://www.ladyjanehaircuts.com/company.html.

11. Ibid.

12. "#1 Community for STD Dating and Support." *STD, HPV, HIV AIDS, Herpes Dating & Support Site @ Positive Singles*. Positive Singles. N.d. http://www.positivesingles.com/.

13. "Gallery of Innovation." Detroit Historical Society. N.d. http://detroithistorical.org /detroit-historical-museum/exhibitions/signature-exhibitions/gallery-innovation.

14. Rao, Leena. "Eying an IPO in the Next Year, LegalZoom Raises $66M from Kleiner Perkins and IVP." *TechCrunch*. July 24, 2011.

15. Welch, Liz. "The Way I Work: John Paul DeJoria, John Paul Mitchell Systems." *Inc. Magazine*, June 2013.

16. "IKEA." *Forbes Magazine*, September 26, 2013.

17. Coren, Michael. "How Valuable Is Your Roof? Put It Up for Solar Auction." *Fast Company*, June 7, 2012.

18. Stock, Kyle. "The Secret of SodaStream's Success." *Businessweek*, July 31, 2013.

19. Cohen, Deborah L. "Makeup Startup Thinks Inside the Box." Thomson Reuters, November 17, 2010.

20. *What Is Birchbox?* Birchbox. N.d. http://www.birchbox.com/about/birchbox.

21. "Hand-Selected Clothing for Men." *Trunk Club*, 26 Sept. 2013.

22. MacDonald, Christine, and Wilkinson, Mike. "Half of Detroit Property Owners Don't Pay Taxes." *Detroit News*, February 21, 2013.

23. Davey, Monica. "Bankruptcy Lawyer Is Named to Manage an Ailing Detroit." *New York Times*, March 14, 2013.

24. Davey, Monica, and Walsh, Mary Williams. "Billions in Debt, Detroit Tumbles into Insolvency." *New York Times*, July 18, 2013.

Chapter 9

1. Josh Linkner, interview with Carlo Sweeney, November 26, 2013.

2. Ortved, John. "Sophia Amoruso Expands Nasty Gal." *Wall Street Journal*, August 22, 2013.

3. Ibid.

4. Covey, Stephen. *The Seven Habits of Highly Successful People*. New York: Free Press, 1989.

5. "Postmortem." *Merriam-Webster*. N.d. http://www.merriam-webster.com/dictionary/postmortem.

6. "See What Great Teachers Need for Their Students." *DonorsChoose.org*. N.d. http://www.donorschoose.org/.

7. Memon Yaqub, Reshma. "Company to Watch: Joor." *Inc. Magazine*, April 30, 2013.

8. Goudreau, Jenna. "Actress Jessica Alba Leverages Fame for Entrepreneurial Success." *Forbes*, May 18, 2012. Gavigan, Christopher. *Healthy Child Healthy World*. New York: Penguin, 2009.

9. "Jessica Alba Net Worth." *Celebrity Networth*. N.d. http://www.celebritynetworth.com/richest-celebrities/actors/jessica-alba-net-worth/.

10. "Ruth Fertel." *Wikimedia*. September 17, 2013, http://en.wikipedia.org/wiki/Ruth_Fertel.

11. "AutoNation." *Wikimedia*, September 21, 2013. http://en.wikipedia.org/wiki/AutoNation.

12. "H. Wayne Huizenga." *Forbes*. N.d.

13. Freedman, David H. "Innovative Rebel: High-Tech Camera Maker Jim Jannard." *Inc. Magazine*, April 30, 2013.

14. Grossmann, John. "Whiskey Rebellion: A Serial Entrepreneur Fast-Forwards the Bourbon Aging Process." *Inc. Magazine,* June 2013.

15. JK Rowling. "JK Rowling: The Fringe Benefits of Failure." *TED*. June 2008. http://www.ted.com/talks/jk_rowling_the_fringe_benefits_of_failure.html.

16. "Best Selling Copyright Book." *Guinness World Records*. N.d. http://www.guinnessworldrecords.com/world-records/3000/best-selling-copyright-book.

17. "Franchise Index." *Movie Franchises and Brands Index. Box Office Mojo*. N.d. http://www.boxofficemojo.com/franchises/.

18. "J.K. Rowling." *Forbes*. N.d.

19. "Whole Foods Co-CEO: Detroit Exceeding Expectations: Video." *Bloomberg.com*, August 1, 2013.

Chapter 10

1. Agassi, Andre. *Open: An Autobiography*. New York: Knopf, 2009.

2. Haidt, Jonathan. *The Happiness Hypothesis: Finding Modern Truth in Ancient Wisdom*. New York: Basic Books, 2006.

3. Linkner, Josh. *Disciplined Dreaming: A Proven System to Drive Breakthrough Creativity*. San Francisco: Jossey-Bass, 2011.

4. Headlee, Celeste. "Detroit Has Worst High-School Graduation Rate." *NPR*, 29 June 29, 2007.

5. Duckworth, Angela L., Peterson, Christopher, Matthews, Michael D., and Kelly, Dennis R. "Grit: Perseverance and Passion for Long-Term Goals." *Journal of Personality and Social Psychology* 92 (2007): 1087–1101.

ACKNOWLEDGMENTS

A work of this nature is never an individual effort. While I have the privilege of being listed as author, many other people contributed in profound ways. Without their commitment, help, and support, this effort would not be possible.

Thank you to Leah Moss, whose research, editing, and support immensely contributed to this book's success. Special thanks to my incredible editor, Karen Murphy; my literary agent, Esmond Harmsworth; and my business partner and friend, Jordan Broad, for your enormous contribution in bringing this work to life. Thank you to Nick Morgan for both his contribution to this book and his continued mentorship and support. Thanks to Lorna Gentry for her thoughtful polish, and to Angela Baggetta for her promotional wizardry.

A big thank you to Dan Gilbert, Brian Hermelin, Jake Cohen, Ted Serbinski, Gabe Karp, Jared Stasik, Sharon Shebib, Jim Xiao, Brentt Baltimore, and Eleanor Meegoda, my partners and colleagues at Detroit Venture Partners, for their support and commitment to the rebirth of Detroit. Thanks to Jay Farner, Bill Emerson, Matt Cullen, Jim Ketai, Ross Sanders, and all the many others who are focused on bringing our city back to life. Also, thank you to all the incredible entrepreneurs who are so passionate about reshaping Detroit's future.

Without the love and support of my family, I could have never completed this project. Thank you to my amazing and creative kids, Noah and Chloe Linkner. A big thanks to Renita Linkner, Sarah and Nick Zagar, Ethan and Tara Linkner, Ryan and Carla Deisenroth,

Constantin and Marcelle Kouchary, Michael Farris, Joe Wert, Mickey Farris (of blessed memory), and all my crazy cousins—and, of course, our two-pound dog with a two-hundred-pound heart, daVinci Linkner.

Thanks to David Farbman, Craig Erlich, Paul Glomski, Bob Marsh, Greg Schwartz, and Jeff Davidson, my closest friends who have helped shape this work and me.

And finally, I wish to honor the loving memory of my mom, Monica Farris Linkner, and my father, Robert Linkner. They both contributed greatly to the ideas and views I share in this book. I deeply miss them.

ABOUT THE AUTHOR

Josh Linkner is the *New York Times* bestselling author of *Disciplined Dreaming: A Proven System to Drive Breakthrough Creativity*. He is the CEO and managing partner of Detroit Venture Partners, playing a key role in the well-publicized turnaround of his hometown, Detroit, Michigan.

He is also the founder and former CEO of ePrize, the largest interactive promotion agency in the world, which provides digital marketing services for seventy-four of the top one hundred brands. Prior to ePrize, he was the founder and CEO of three other successful technology companies. He has been honored as the Ernst & Young Entrepreneur of the Year (2003) and is a President Barack Obama Champion of Change award recipient (2011). Linkner is a regular columnist for *Forbes*, the *Detroit Free Press*, and *Inc. Magazine*. His work on innovation and urban revitalization has been featured in the *Wall Street Journal, Fast Company, CNN*, and the *New York Times*. He is also a Berklee-trained jazz guitarist and has performed in thousands of venues throughout the world.

For more information, visit joshlinkner.com.

INDEX